P9-DTN-760

PAUL RUDOLPH
and
LOUIS KAHN:

A Bibliography

by

CHARLES R. SMITH

The Scarecrow Press, Inc.
Metuchen, N.J., & London
1987

Frontispiece: Yale Art and Architecture Building by Paul
Rudolph on the left with the Yale Art Gallery
by Louis Kahn in the center

Library of Congress Cataloging-in-Publication Data

Smith, Charles R. (Charles Richard), 1938–
   Paul Rudolph and Louis Kahn.

   Includes indexes.
   1. Architecture, Modern--20th century--United States
--Bibliography. 2. Rudolph, Paul, 1918–   --
Bibliography. 3. Kahn, Louis I., 1901–1974--Bibliography.
I. Title.
Z5941.5.S63 1987 [NA712]   016.72'092'2   87-12781
ISBN 0-8108-2003-X

For my wife, Louise,
my Father,
and in memory of my Mother

ACKNOWLEDGMENTS

Many thanks to my family, friends and co-workers for the encouragement and support during the past several years. Special thanks go to a student, Mary Ellen, who helped with the beginning bibliography at Syracuse; to June McLaren for the first typed copy from index cards; and to Emmette Jackson, who took my poor camera work and turned it into beautiful photographs.

CONTENTS

LIST OF ILLUSTRATIONS

INTRODUCTION

This work had its beginnings while I was at Syracuse University in 1968. A faculty member in the Department of Architecture asked if I would compile a short bibliography on Paul Rudolph. After doing a quick search of Art Index, I soon found that I wanted to continue and make a more complete listing of citations to works by Mr. Rudolph. Over the years the number of 3 X 5 index cards got a little out of control until I gained access to a word processor. My work continued until a publication was a possibility. In 1976, Eric Moon of Scarecrow Press suggested that I include another architect in order that a book-length work might result. To me, Louis Kahn was an obvious choice. Paul Rudolph and Louis Kahn seem to share some common ground. Many times their designs are reflected in the same usage of materials and can, at times, be found in close proximity to each other. Their designs have similarities and at the same time they are so different. Both Rudolph and Kahn have distinguished themselves as important American architects through their individual approaches to architecture and the ways each has handled the materials used in their designs.

It is always hard to finish a bibliography and this one is no exception. There are several citations on both Kahn and Rudolph which I was unable to obtain; these for the most part have been left out of this work. Because of the importance of these two architects, new writings appear constantly about them or their works. I have tried to be as comprehensive as possible, looking at all indexes and bibliographies available to me and checking indexes of books in many libraries. Within this bibliography one will find citations dating from the early careers of these architects and going through part of 1986. There is a monumental work at the press now that is not included in this work and that all who do any

work on Louis Kahn will need to consult. I am speaking of
the seven-volume work The Louis I. Kahn Archive being published by Garland Publishing Inc. during 1986 and 1987.

PART I

PAUL M. RUDOLPH

BIBLIOGRAPHIC CHRONOLOGY OF WORKS

DENMAN RESIDENCE

Siesta Kay, Florida. 1946. In association with Ralph Twitchell.

"Chronological list of works by Paul Rudolph, 1946-1974."
il., plan. Architecture and Urbanism 49 (January 1975):
149.
"Denman residence." il., plan. Architecture and Urbanism
80 (July 1977): 20.
"Round-robin critique, four houses." il., plan. Progressive
Architecture 31 (August 1950): 65-69.
"Work in progress: beach house." il., plan. Architectural
Forum 86 (April 1947): 92-93.

ALEXANDER S. HARKAVY RESIDENCE

Sarasota, Florida. 1946. In association with Ralph Twitchell.

"Small house in Southeast." il., plan, sec., port. Architectural Forum 87 (September 1947): 85-89.

TASTEE FREEZE

Florida. Project, 1946.

"Chronological list of works by Paul Rudolph, 1946-1974."
il. Architecture and Urbanism 49 (January 1975): 149.

ROBERTA FINNEY GUEST COTTAGE

Siesta Key, Florida. Project, 1947.

"Chronological list of works by Paul Rudolph, 1946-1974."
il., plan. Architecture and Urbanism 49 (January 1975):
149.
"Finney guest cottage." il., plan. Architecture and Urbanism 80 (July 1977): 21-23.
"Maison de vacances en Floride." il., plan, sec., elev.
Architecture D'Aujourd'hui 20 (July 1950): 4 pages be-
tween 66 and 67.
"Plateau, inlet, and house for Florida vacations." il., plan,
sec., elev. Interiors 109 (January 1950): 104-109.
Quantrill, Malcolm. "Is this geometry really environment?"
il. Royal Institute of British Architects. Journal 82
(October 1975): 5.
Rudolph, Paul. The Architecture of Paul Rudolph. Introduc-
tion by Sibyl Moholy-Nagy. New York: Praeger, 1970.
il., plan. pp. 32-33.
_____. Paul Rudolph, Dessins D'Architecture. Fribourg:
Office du Livre, 1974. il. pp. 18-19.
"Rudolph." il. Architects' Journal 160 (4 September 1974):
526.

MILLER RESIDENCE AND GUEST HOUSE

Casey Key, Florida. 1947. In association with Ralph Twitchell.

"Boat house." il., plans, elev. Arts and Architecture 65
(August 1948): 34-35.
"Chronological list of works by Paul Rudolph, 1946-1974."
il. Architecture and Urbanism 49 (January 1975): 149.
"Maisons en Floride." il., plan. Architecture D'Aujourd'hui
20 (July 1950): 60-63.

RESIDENCE

Sarasota, Florida. 1947. In association with Ralph Twitchell.

"House in Florida." il., plan, elev. Arts and Architecture
65 (November 1948): 32-34.

RESIDENCE

Sarasota, Florida. 1947. In association with Ralph Twitchell.

"House in Florida." il., plan, sec. Architectural Forum 89
(July 1948): 97-103.
"House: Sarasota, Florida." il., plan. Progressive Archi-
tecture 30 (June 1949): 69.

REVERE QUALITY HOUSE

Siesta Key, Florida. 1948. In association with Ralph Twitchell.

"Chronological list of works by Ralph Rudolph, 1946-1974."
il. Architecture and Urbanism 49 (January 1975): 149.
"Concrete home in Florida is one of eight prototype houses
designed to solve regional building problems." il., plan,
sec. Architectural Forum 89 (October 1948): 101-105.
"Four 1948 houses." il., plan. House and Garden 96 (August
1949): 76-77, 81-82.
"House in Florida." il., plan, sec. Architectural Review 105
(June 1949): 287-290.
"Lamolithic steel forms." il., sec. Architectural Forum 89
(October 1948): 109-111.
"Maisons en Floride." il., plan, diag. Architecture D'Aujourd-
'hui 20 (July 1950): 64-66.
"Progressive architecture for housing--1952." il., plan.
Progressive Architecture 33 (January 1952): 63.
"Revere Quality House." il. Architecture and Urbanism 80
(July 1977): 24-25.
Rudolph, Paul. "Revere house grouping." il. Architectural
Forum 89 (December 1948): 28.
Schroeder, Francis de N. "Year's work." il. Interiors 109
(August 1949): 90.
"Twelve architect suggestions for the merchant builder." il.
Architectural Forum 94 (January 1951): 112, 122-123.

FOUR BEACH HOUSES

Lamolithic Industries, Sarasota, Florida. 1948. In association
with Ralph Twitchell.

"Four concrete beach houses provide hallmarks of luxury on
a small scale." il., plan, sec. Architectural Forum 89
(October 1948): 106-111.

W. R. HEALY GUEST HOUSE

(Cocoon House). Siesta Key, Florida. 1948-1949. In association with Ralph Twitchell.

Boyd, Robin. The Puzzle of Architecture. London: Cam-
bridge, 1965. il. pp. 109-111.
"Chronological list of works by Paul Rudolph, 1946-1974."
il., plan. Architecture and Urbanism 49 (January 1975):
150.
"Cocoon house." il., plan. Architectural Forum 94 (June
1951): 156-159.
"Cocoon house." il. Kenchiku Bunka 22 (March 1967): 68-
69.
"Debut works of architects." il., plan. Kokusai Kentiku 33
(October 1966): 11-51.
"Healy guest house." il., plan. Architecture and Urbanism
80 (July 1977): 26-28.
Hitchcock, Henry Russell, ed. Built in USA: Post-War Architecture. New York: Simon and Schuster, 1952. il.,
plan. pp. 112-113.
Jacobus, John. Twentieth Century Architecture; the Middle
Years, 1940-1965. New York: Praeger, 1966. il. pp.
49, 51.
Kemper, Alfred M. Presentation Drawings by American Ar-
chitects. New York: Wiley, 1977. il. p. 263.
Koike, Shinji. World's Contemporary Houses. (Japanese
text, English captions). Tokyo: Shokokusha, 1954. il.,
plans, sec. pp. 106-111.
McCallum, Ian. Architecture Use. New York: Reinhold,
1959. il., plan. pp. 197-198.
Olgyay, Aladar and Victor Olgyay. Solar Control and Shading
Devices. Princeton: Princeton University, 1957. il.
p. 119.
"Paul Rudolph." il. Architecture D'Aujourd'hui 28 (September
1957): 88.
Pile, John. Drawings of Architectural Interiors. New York:
Whitney Library of Design, 1967. il. p. 154.
"Postwar houses of quality and significance." il. House and
Home 3 (February 1953): 123.
Rudolph, Paul. The Architecture of Paul Rudolph. Intro-
duction by Sibyl Moholy-Nagy. New York: Praeger,
1970. il., plan. pp. 34-35.
"Rudolph and the roof." il. House and Home 3 (June 1953):
141-142.

"Sagging ceiling on Siesta Key." il., plan, elev. Interiors
110 (January 1951): 94-101.

MAYNARD E. RUSSELL RESIDENCE

Sarasota, Florida. 1948. In association with Ralph Twitchell.

"Children in the plan." il., plan. House and Garden 96
(December 1949): 144-149.
"Chronological list of works by Paul Rudolph, 1946-1974." il.
Architecture and Urbanism 49 (January 1975): 150.
"For joyous living and five children." il. (pt. col.), plan,
sec. Architectural Record 107 (January 1950): cover,
76-83.
"Maisons en Floride." il., plan, diag. Architecture
D'Aujour'hui 20 (July 1950): 58-59.

ARTHUR CHEATHAM RESIDENCE

Lakeland, Florida. 1949. In association with Ralph Twitchell.

"Chronological list of works by Paul Rudolph, 1946-1974."
il. Architecture and Urbanism 49 (January 1975): 150.
"Swimming pool." il., plan. Progressive Architecture 33 (February 1952): 80-82.

DEEDS RESIDENCE

Siesta Key, Florida. 1949. In association with Ralph Twitchell.

"Chronological list of works by Paul Rudolph, 1946-1974." il.
Architecture and Urbanism 49 (January 1975): 150.
"Tailor-made houses." il., plan. Architectural Forum 92
(April 1950): 167-171.
"Twelve architect suggestions for the merchant builder." il.,
plan. Architectural Forum 94 (January 1951): 112, 122.

GOOD DESIGN EXHIBITION

Merchandise Mart, Chicago, IL. Museum of Modern Art, New
York, NY. 1951.

"Chronological list of works by Paul Rudolph, 1946-1974."
    il., plan. Architecture and Urbanism 49 (January 1975):
    150.
"Display techniques." il., plan. Progressive Architecture
    33 (October 1952): 110-111.
"Good design exhibition; installation by Paul Rudolph." il.
    Arts and Architecture 69 (May 1952): 16-19.
"Good design 1952: Rudolph's installation gets raves." il.
    Architectural Record 111 (March 1952): 26.
Gueft, Olga. "Good design in chiaroscuro; Paul Rudolph
    designs the Mart's third exhibition." il., plan, diags.
    Interiors 111 (March 1952): 130-137, 186-190.
"New York version." il. Interiors 112 (November 1952):
    130-131.

C. RICHARD LEAVENSGOOD RESIDENCE

St. Petersburg, Florida. 1951. In association with Ralph
    Twitchell.

"Chronological list of works by Paul Rudolph, 1946-1974." il.
    Architecture and Urbanism 49 (January 1975): 150.
"Leavengood residence." il. Architecture and Urbanism 80
    (July 1977): 29.
Olgyay, Aladar and Victor Olgyay. Solar Control and Shading
    Devices. Princeton: Princeton University, 1957. il.
    p. 118.
"One-story house on the second floor." il., plan. Architect-
    ural Forum 95 (October 1951): 186-189.
Rudolph, Paul. Paul Rudolph, Dessins D'Architecture. Fri-
    bourg: Office du Livre, 1974. il. pp. 24-25.

GUEST HOUSE

Naples, Florida. 1951. In association with Ralph Twitchell.

Fiske, Jane. "In defense of hosts: a friendly design con-
    spiracy." il., plan. Interiors 112 (September 1952): 80-85.

LEWIS H. HASKINS RESIDENCE

Sarasota, Florida. 1951. In association with Ralph Twitchell.

"This house has an easy retirement plan." il., plan. House and Garden 102 (August 1952): 44-47.

MARION W. COWARD RESIDENCE

Siesta Key, Florida. 1951. In association with Ralph Twitchell.

"Chronological list of works by Paul Rudolph, 1946-1974." il. Architecture and Urbanism 49 (January 1975): 151.
"Pavilion living on the Gulf of Mexico." il., plan. House and Garden 103 (June 1953): 76-77, 154-155.

BURNETTE RESIDENCE

Sarasota, Florida. 1951. In association with Ralph Twitchell.

"Burnette residence." il. Architecture and Urbanism 80 (July 1977): 30-31.
"Chronological list of works by Paul Rudolph, 1946-1974." il. Architecture and Urbanism 49 (January 1975): 151.

KATE WHEELAN COTTAGE

Siesta Key, Florida. 1951. In association with Ralph Twitchell.

"Chronological list of works by Paul Rudolph, 1946-1974." il. Architecture and Urbanism 49 (January 1975): 151.
Ford, Katherine Morrow. Quality Budget Houses: A Treasury of 100 Architect-Designed Houses from $5,000 to $20,000. Reinhold, 1954. plan, sec. pp. 138-139.
"Guest houses with plastic roofs." il., plan, sec. Progressive Architecture 33 (July 1952): 103-105.
Morand, Francois C. Small Homes in the New Tradition. New York: Sterling, 1959. il., plan, sec. pp. 34-37.
"Three new directions: Paul Rudolph, Philip Johnson, Buckminster Fuller." il., plan, sec., diag. Perspecta 1 (Summer 1952): 18-25.

APARTMENT HOUSE

Sarasota/Brandenton, Florida. Project, 1951.

"Current work of Paul Rudolf." il. Architectural Record
121 (February 1957): 175.
Rudolph, Paul. Paul Rudolph, Dessins D'Architecture. Fribourg: Office du Livre, 1974. il., plan. pp. 26-27.

EUGENE KNOTT RESIDENCE

Yankeetown, Florida. 1952.

"Chronological list of works by Paul Rudolph, 1946-1974."
il., plan. Architecture and Urbanism 49 (January 1975):
151.
"House in Florida." il., plan. Arts and Architecture 74 (June
1957): 14-15.
Kemper, Alfred M. Presentation Drawings by American Ar-
chitects. New York: Wiley, 1977. il. p. 195.
"Knott residence." il., plan. Architecture and Urbanism 80
(July 1977): 33-35.
"Quatre habitations en Floride, U.S.A." il., plan. Archi-
tecture D'Aujourd'hui 26 (November 1955): 33.
Rudolph, Paul. The Architecture of Paul Rudolph. Introduction by Sibyl Moholy-Nagy. New York: Praeger, 1970.
il., plan. pp. 40-41.
_____. Paul Rudolph, Dessins D'Architecture. Fribourg:
Office du Livre, 1974. il., plan. pp. 28-29.
"Rudolph and the roof." il., sec. House and Home 3 (June
1953): 140-141.
Tentori, Franceso. "Due edifici per l'universita." il. Casa-
bella 234 (December 1959): 12.
"Three new directions: Paul Rudolph, Philip Johnson, Buckminster Fuller." il., plan. Perspecta 1 (Summer 1952):
18-22.

DAVID COHEN RESIDENCE

Siesta Key, Florida. 1952.

"Chronological list of works by Paul Rudolph, 1946-1974."
il., sec. Architecture and Urbanism 49 (January 1975):
152.
"Cohen residence." il., sec. Architecture and Urbanism 80
(July 1977): 36-37.

"First design award: house, Siesta Key, Florida." il., plan,
    sec., elev. Progressive Architecture 36 (January 1955):
    65-67.
"House by Paul Rudolph." il., plan, sec., elev. Arts and
    Architecture 71 (September 1954): 14-15.
"Open plan, prefab units cut Florida costs." il. (pt.col.),
    plan. Architectural Record 119 (Mid-May 1956): 175-179.
"P/A design awards." plan, sec. Interiors 114 (March 1955):
    16.
"Paul Rudolph." il. Architecture D'Aujourd'hui 28 (September
    1957): 88.
"Quatre habitations en Floride, U.S.A." il., plan, sec.,
    elev. Architecture D'Aujourd'hui 26 (November 1955):
    34-35.
Rudolph, Paul. Paul Rudolph, Dessins D'Architecture. Fri-
    bourg: Office du Livre, 1974. il., plan, sec. pp. 30-31.

SANDERLING BEACH CLUB

Siesta Key, Florida. 1952-1953.

"Chronological list of works by Paul Rudolph, 1946-1974."
    il. Architecture and Urbanism 49 (January 1975): 151.
"Current work of Paul Rudolph." il. Architectural Record
    121 (February 1957): 174.
"Genetrix: personal contributions to American architecture."
    il. Architectural Review 121 (May 1957): 379.
"Paul Rudolph." il. Architecture D'Aujourd'hui 24 (December
    1953): 110-111.
Rudolph, Paul. The Architecture of Paul Rudolph. Intro-
    duction by Sibyl Moholy-Nagy. New York: Praeger, 1970.
    il. pp. 38-39.
"Sanderling beach club." plans, sec., elev. Architectural
    Record 114 (October 1953): 150-155.
"Sanderling beach club." il. Architecture and Urbanism 80
    (July 1977): 139.

W. W. WALKER GUEST RESIDENCE

Sanibel Island, Florida. 1952-1953.

"Chronological list of works by Paul Rudolph, 1946-1974." il.,

plan. Architecture and Urbanism 49 (January 1975): 151.
"Design/techniques 1953." il., plan. Progressive Architecture
    34 (January 1953): 72.
Ford, Katherine Morrow. Quality Budget Houses; A Treasury
    of 100 Architect-Designed Houses from $5,000 to $20,000.
    New York: Reinhold, 1954. il., plan. pp. 34-35.
"Genetrix; personal contributions to American architecture."
    il. Architectural Review 121 (May 1957): 380.
Gillies, Mary Davis. "Open to all outdoors." il., plan.
    McCall's 81 (July 1954): 36-37.
Kemper, Alfred M. Presentation Drawings By American Ar-
    chitects. New York: Wiley, 1977. il. p. 241.
Morand, Francois C. Small Homes in the New Tradition. New
    York: Sterling, 1959. il., plan, sec. pp. 44-47.
Olgyay, Aladar and Victoy Olgyay. Solar Control and Shading
    Devices. Princeton: Princeton University, 1957. il.,
    plan. pp. 120-121.
Rudolph, Paul. The Architecture of Paul Rudolph. Intro-
    duction by Sibyl Moholy-Nagy. New York: Praeger, 1970.
    il., plan. pp. 42-43.
_____. Paul Rudolph, Dessins D'Architecture. Fribourg:
    Office du Livre, 1974. il. pp. 20-21.
"Walker guest house." il., plan. Architecture and Urbanism
    80 (July 1977): 32.

ALBERT SIEGRIST RESIDENCE

Venice, Florida. 1953. In association with Ralph Twitchell.

"Chronological list of works by Paul Rudolph, 1946-1974."
    il., plan. Architecture and Urbanism 49 (January 1975):
    152.
Hitchcock, Henry Russell, ed. Built In USA: Post-War Ar-
    chitecture. New York: Simon and Schuster, 1952. il.,
    plan. pp. 110-111.
"Maisons en Floride." il., plan, elev. Architecture
    D'Aujourd'hui 20 (July 1950): 55-57.
"Postwar houses of quality and significance." il. House and
    Home 3 (February 1953): 126.
"Quality house." il., plan, sec., diag. House and Home 3
    (April 1953): 96-101.
"Siegrist residence." il., plan. Architecture and Urbanism
    80 (July 1977): 38.
"Twelve architect suggestions for the merchant builder." il.
    Architectural Forum 94 (January 1951): 112, 123.

SEWELL C. BIGGS RESIDENCE

Delray Beach, Florida. 1953.

"Biggs residence." il. Architecture and Urbanism 80 (July
    1977): 39.
"Chronological list of works by Paul Rudolph, 1946-1975."
    il. Architecture and Urbanism 49 (January 1975): 152.
"Custom-house winners of the 1959 Homes for Better Living
    Awards." il., plan. House and Home 15 (June 1959):
    124-125.

SIGMA ALPHA EPSILON FRATERNITY HOUSE

Miami University, Miami, Florida. 1953.

"Formal building for formal rituals: a fraternity house for
    Miami University." il., plan, diag. Architectural Forum
    99 (August 1953): 117-119.
"Maison d'etudiants pour l'Universite de Miami, Floride." il.,
    plan. Architecture D'Aujourd'hui 24 (December 1953):
    112-113.

FLOATING ISLAND

Leesburg, Florida. Project, 1953.

"Baroque formality in a Florida tourist attraction." il., plan.
    Interiors 113 (January 1954): 74-79.
"P/A annual design survey for 1954; recreation." il., plan.
    Progressive Architecture 35 (January 1954): 117.

BASIC HOUSE

Variations. Project, 1953.

"Variations on a basic house." il., plan. Arts and Architec-
    ture 74 (September 1957): 18-19.

UNITED STATES EMBASSY

Amman, Jordan. Project, 1954.

"Chronological list of works by Paul Rudolph, 1946-1974."
    il. Architecture and Urbanism 49 (January 1975): 152.
Collins, Peter. "Whither Paul Rudolph?" elev., port.
    Progressive Architecture 42 (August 1961): 130-131.
"Current work of Paul Rudolph." il., plan, sec., elev.
    Architectural Record 121 (February 1957): 161-165.
"New U.S. Embassy in Amman." il. Architecture and Urban-
    ism 80 (July 1977): 140-141.
"Paul Rudolph." il., plans, sec. Architecture D'Aujourd'hui
    28 (September 1957): 90-91.
"Second group of American embassy buildings." il. Archi-
    tectural Record 119 (June 1956): 164-165.
Tentori, Franceso. "Due edifici per l'universita." il. Casa-
    bella 234 (December 1959): 12.
"USA abroad." il. Architectural Forum 107 (December 1957):
    122.

ALBERT BOSTWICK RESIDENCE

Palm Beach, Florida. Project, 1954.

"Chronological list of works by Paul Rudolph, 1946-1974."
    il., plan. Architecture and Urbanism 49 (January 1975):
    152.
Rudolph, Paul. Paul Rudolph, Dessins D'Architecture. Fri-
    bourg: Office du Livre, 1974. il., plan, sec. pp. 32-35.

INGRAM HOOK GUEST COTTAGE

Siesta Key, Florida. 1954.

"Chronological list of works by Paul Rudolph, 1946-1974." il.
    Architecture and Urbanism 49 (January 1975): 152.
"Good design knows no date." il., plan. House and Garden
    102 (October 1952): 164-169.
"Hook guest cottage." il. Architecture and Urbanism 80
    (July 1977): 42-43.
Koike, Shinji. World's Contemporary Houses. (text in Japan-
    eese with English captions). Tokyo: Shokokusha, 1974.
    il., plan, sec. pp. 86-89.
"Maisons au bord de l'eau." il., plan, sec., diag. Archi-
    tecture D'Aujourd'hui 24 (October 1953): 64-67.

Rudolph, Paul. The Architecture of Paul Rudolph. Introduction by Sibyl Moholy-Nagy. New York: Praeger,
1970. il. pp. 36-37.
"Rudolph and the roof." il., plan, sec. House and Home
3 (June 1953): 140-145.

WILSON RESIDENCE

Sarasota, Florida. 1954.

"Chronological list of works by Paul Rudolph, 1946-1974."
il. Architecture and Urbanism 49 (January 1975): 153.
"Paper prefab is strong, well insulated and cheap." il., plan,
sec. House and Home 7 (January 1955): 144-147.

J. V. TAYLOR RESIDENCE

Venice, Florida. 1954.

"Chronological list of works by Paul Rudolph, 1946-1974."
il. Architecture and Urbanism 49 (January 1975): 153.
"8 houses designed and built with budget in mind." il., plan.
Architectural Record 124 (November 1958): 187-189.
"Patio house for a small lot." il., plan, sec. House and Home
13 (February 1958): 112-115.
"Taylor residence." il. Architecture and Urbanism 80 (July
1977): 41.

PHILIP HISS RESIDENCE

(Umbrella House). Lido Shores, Florida. 1954.

Cantacuzino, Sherban. Modern Houses of the World. New
York: Dutton, 1964. il., plan. pp. 62-65.
"Chronological list of works by Paul Rudolph, 1946-1974." il.,
plan. Architecture and Urbanism 49 (January 1975): 153.
"Genetrix; personal contributions to American architecture."
il., port. Architectural Review 121 (May 1957): 378-379.
"Hiss residence." il. plan. Architecture and Urbanism 80
(July 1977): 40.
"House for Florida." il., elev. Arts and Architecture 70
(October 1953): 20-21.

"How to build cool houses for the hot and humid American
    summer." il. (pt.col.), plan. House and Home 6 (July
    1954): 101-105.
McCallum, Ian. Architecture USA. New York: Reinhold,
    1959. il. pp. 199-200.
Olgyay, Aladar and Victor Olgyay. Solar Control and Shading
    Devices. Princeton: Princeton, 1957. il., plan. pp.
    196-197.
"Quatre habitations en Floride, U.S.A." il., plan, elev.
    Architecture D'Aujourd'hui 26 (November 1955): 30-31.
Rudolph, Paul. The Architecture of Paul Rudolph. Intro-
    duction by Sibyl Moholy-Nagy. New York: Praeger, 1970.
    il., plan. pp. 44-45.

MARY COOPER JEWETT ARTS CENTER

Wellesley College, Wellesley, Massachusetts. 1955-1958. In
    association with Anderson, Beckwith, Haible.

"Bright new arrival." il., port. Time 75 (1 February 1960):
    60-63.
"Chronological list of works by Paul Rudolph, 1946-1974." il.,
    plan. Architecture and Urbanism 49 (January 1975): 153.
Collins, Peter. "Whiter Paul Rudolph?" il., port. Progres-
    sive Architecture 42 (August 1961): 130-133.
Cook, John Wesley and Heinrich Klotz. Conversations With
    Architects. New York: Praeger, 1973. il. p. 94.
Drexler, Arthur. Transformations in Modern Architecture.
    New York: Museum of Modern Art, 1979. il. p. 158.
"Fitting the future into the past; Mary Cooper Jewett Arts
    Center, Wellesley College." il., plan, sec. Architectural
    Forum 105 (December 1956): 100-106.
"Genetrix; personal contributions to American architecture."
    il. Architectural Review 121 (May 1957): 379.
Goody, Joan E. New Architecture in Boston. Cambridge:
    M.I.T., 1965. il., plan. pp. 86-87.
Hammett, Ralph Warner. Architecture in the United States:
    A Survey of Architectural Styles Since 1776. New York:
    Wiley, 1976. p. 297.
Jacobus, John. Twentieth Century Architecture: The Middle
    Years, 1940-1965. New York: Praeger, 1966. il. pp.
    150, 152.
"Jewett Arts Center." il., plan. Architecture and Urbanism
    80 (July 1977): 220-223.

Johnson, Philip. "Three architects." il. Art in America
    48 (Spring 1960): 70-73.
Jones, Cranston. Architecture Today and Tomorrow. New
    York: McGraw-Hill, 1961. col. il. pp. 173, 176-177.
"Kunstzentrum der Universitat Wellesley, Mass./USA." il.,
    plan. Deutsche Bauzeitung 66 (December 1961): 936-939.
McCallum, Ian. Architecture USA. New York: Reinhold,
    1959. il., plan, elev. pp. 201-203.
Maki, Fumihiko. "American architecture," in Contemporary
    Architecture of the World, 1961. Tokyo: Shokokusha,
    1961. il., elev. pp. 322-323, 346.
"Marriage of heaven and hell: art, music, and drama center
    at Wellesley." il. Interiors 121 (February 1962): 12.
"Mary Cooper Jewett Arts Center at Wellesley." il., plan.
    Architectural Record 121 (February 1957): 166-169.
Millon, Henry A. "Rudolph at the cross-roads." il. Archi-
    tectural Design 30 (December 1960): 497-499.
"New architecture in an old setting." il. (pt.col.), plan,
    sec., diag. Architectural Record 126 (July 1959): 175-
    186.
"Not neo-Tiffany: Jewett Arts Center." il., plan. Archi-
    tectural Review 127 (February 1960): 78.
"Paul Rudolph." il., plan, sec. Architecture D'Aujourd'hui
    28 (September 1957): 92-95.
Peter, John. Design With Glass. (Materials in Modern Ar-
    chitecture Series, 1). New York: Reinhold, 1964. il.
    pp. 24-27.
Rudolph, Paul. The Architecture of Paul Rudolph. Introduc-
    tion by Sibyl Moholy-Nagy. New York: Praeger, 1970.
    il., plan, sec., elev. pp. 50-55.
    _____. Paul Rudolph, Dessings D'Architecture. Fribourg:
    Office du Livre, 1974. il., plan, elev. pp. 90-93.
    _____. Paul Rudolph. Introduction and notes by Rupert
    Spade. New York: Simon and Schuster, 1971. il. (pt.
    col.), plan, sec. plates 18-25, p. 124.
"Rudolph buildings at Yale and Wellesley open." il. Progres-
    sive Architecture 40 (July 1959): 87.
"Scuola d'arte a Wellesley." il., plan. Edilizia Moderna 68
    (December 1959): 1-8.
"Scuola d'arte Mary Cooper Jewett al Wellesley College, Welles-
    ley, 1959." il., plan, sec., elev. Casabella 234 (Decem-
    ber 1959): 18-25.
"Selearchitettura: Il futuro nel passato." il., plan. Archi-
    tettura 2 (April 1957): 880-881.

Stern, Robert A. M. New Directions in American Architecture.
    New York: Braziller, 1969. il. pp. 31-32.
    _____. New Directions in American Architecture, revised
    ed. New York: Braziller, 1977. il. pp. 31-32.
"Travaux récents de trios agences Américaines." il., plan,
    map, sec., diag. Architecture D'Aujourd'hui 30 (Septem-
    ber 1959): 33-40.
"Wellesley's alternative to collegiate Gothic." il., plan. Ar-
    chitectural Forum 111 (July 1959): 88-95, with criticism
    by James Marston Fitch, pp. 94-95.

SARASOTA-BRADENTON AIRPORT

Sarasota, Florida. Project, 1955.

"Current work of Paul Rudolph." il., plan, elev. Architect-
    ural Record 121 (February 1957): 170-171.
"Paul Rudolph." il., plan, sec., diags. Architecture
    D'Aujourd'hui 28 (September 1957): 88-89.
Rudolph, Paul. Paul Rudolph, Dessins D'Architecture. Fri-
    bourg: Office du Livre, 1974. il. pp. 178-179.

FAMILY OF MAN EXHIBIT

Installation. 1955.

"Family of man, exhibition installation at Museum of Modern
    Art, by Paul Rudolph." il., plan, diags. Interiors 114
    (April 1955): 114-117.

R. J. BURGESS RESIDENCE

Burgess Island, Florida. 1955.

"Chronological list of works by Paul Rudolph, 1946-1974." il.
    Architecture and Urbanism 49 (January 1975): 153.

BOTANICAL GARDENS

Project, 1956.

"Botanical garden, Tile Council of America prize." Beaux Arts
Institute of Design Bulletin 32 (June 1956): 3-4.

MODEL HOME

Women's Home Companion, St. Louis, Missouri. 1956.

"57 houses for a better '57." il. (pt. col.), plan, sec. House
and Home 10 (October 1956): 206-207.

MODEL HOUSE REPRESENTING THE SOUTHEAST

Homestyle Center, Grand Rapids, Michigan. 1956.

"Genetrix: personal contributions to American architecture."
il. Architectural Review 121 (May 1957): 380.

FRANK APPLEBEE RESIDENCE

Auburn, Alabama. 1956.

"Applebee residence." il. Architecture and Urbanism 80 (July
1977): 44.
"Cantilevers create multi-level interest; house for F. Applebee,
Auburn, Alabama." il., plan, sec. Architectural Record
119 (Mid-May 1956): 200-201.
"Chronological list of works by Paul Rudolph, 1946-1974." il.
Architecture and Urbanism 49 (January 1975): 153.
"House by Paul Rudolph." il., plan, elev., diag. Arts and
Architecture 72 (May 1955): 24-25.

BRAMLETT EQUIPMENT COMPANY

Office Building, Miami, Florida. 1956.

"Chronological list of works by Paul Rudolph, 1946-1974." il.
Architecture and Urbanism 49 (January 1975): 154.
"Current work of Paul Rudolf." il., plans, elev. Architect-
ural Record 121 (February 1957): 172-173.
"Paul Rudolph." il. Architecture D'Aujourd'hui 28 (Septem-
ber 1957): 88.

DAVIDSON RESIDENCE

Bradenton, Florida. 1956.

"Chronological list of works by Paul Rudolph, 1946-1974." il.
    Architecture and Urbanism 49 (January 1975): 154.
"Davidson residence." il. Architecture and Urbanism 80
    (July 1977): 45.
"Vaulted ceiling, four porches in the south." il., plan.
    Architectural Record 120 (November 1956): 177-181.

LAMBIE BEACH DEVELOPMENT

Siesta Key, Florida. 1956.

"Chronological list of works by Paul Rudolph, 1946-1974." il.
    Architecture and Urbanism 49 (January 1975): 154.

STAND FOR DOUGHNUTS

Tampa, Florida. Project, 1956.

"Current work of Paul Rudolph." il. Architectural Record
    121 (February 1957): 174.
"Paul Rudolph." il. Architecture D'Aujourd'hui 28 (Septem-
    ber 1957): 88.

BARNET YANOFSKY RESIDENCE

Newton, Massachusetts. 1956.

"Chronological list of works by Paul Rudolph, 1946-1974." il.
    Architecture and Urbanism 49 (January 1975): 154.
"Six new houses by Paul Rudolph." il., plan, sec. Archi-
    tectural Record 132 (November 1962): 136-138.
"Yanofsky residence." il. Architecture and Urbanism 80
    (July 1977): 46-47.

ST. BONIFACE EPISCOPAL CHURCH

Sarasota, Florida. Project, 1957.

"Chronological list of works by Paul Rudolph, 1946-1974." il.
   Architecture and Urbanism 49 (January 1975):   154.
Collins, Peter.   "Whither Paul Rudolph?" il., port.   Pro-
   gressive Architecture 42 (August 1961):   130-131.
"Current work of Paul Rudolph." il., plan, elev.   Architectu-
   ral Record 121 (February 1957):   174-175.
"Paul Rudolph." il.   Architecture D'Aujourd'hui 28 (Septem-
   ber 1957):   89.

MARTIN HARKAVY RESIDENCE

Lido Shores, Florida.   1957.

"Castles in the air." il.   Living for Young Homemakers 14
   (October 1961):   108-109.
"Chronological list of works by Paul Rudolph, 1946-1974." il.
   Architecture and Urbanism 49 (January 1975):   155.
"Custom house winners of the 1959 Homes for Better Living
   Awards." il., plan.   House and Home 15 (June 1959):
   126.
"Harkavy residence." il.   Architecture and Urbanism 80 (July
   1977):   50.
Tentori, Francesco.   "Due edifici per l'universita." il.
   Casabella 234 (December 1959):   12.

THEODORE BURKHARDT RESIDENCE

Casey Key, Florida.   1957.

"Burkhardt residence." il.   Architecture and Urbanism 80
   (July 1977):   48-49.
"Chronological list of works by Paul Rudolph, 1946-1974."
   il.   Architecture and Urbanism 49 (January 1975):   155.
"Tranquillity at home." col. il.   House and Garden 123 (Jan-
   uary 1963):   62-63.

RIVERVIEW JUNIOR-SENIOR HIGH SCHOOL

Sarasota, Florida.   1957-1958.

Boyarsky, Alvin.   "Paul Rudolph retrospective exhibition."

il. Royal Institute of British Architects. Journal 71
     (December 1964):   524-525.
"Chronological list of works by Paul Rudolph, 1946-1974."
     il., plan. Architecture and Urbanism 49 (January 1975):
     154.
McQuade, Walter. "School board that dared." il., plan.
     Architectural Forum 110 (February 1959):   78-81.
Rudolph, Paul. The Architecture of Paul Rudolph. Intro-
     duction by Sibyl Moholy-Nagy. New York: Praeger,
     1970. il., plan. pp. 58-61.
_____. Paul Rudolph. Introduction and notes by Rupert
     Spade. New York: Simon and Schuster, 1971. il. (pt.
     col.), plan, sec. plates 4-7, p. 123.
"Schools." il., plan, sec. Architectural Record 125 (Febru-
     ary 1959):   203-204, 217-219.
"Steel frame in the pines." il., plan, sec. Architectural
     Forum 110 (April 1959):   112-117.
"Travaux récents de trois agences Américaines." il., plan,
     sec. Architecture D'Aujourd'hui 30 (September 1959):
     30-34.
Waugh, Edward. The South Builds: New Architecture in the
     Old South. Chapel Hill: University of North Carolina,
     1960. il., plan. pp. 51-53.

Fig. 1:   Greeley Memorial Laboratory at the Yale University
          Forestry School

GREELEY MEMORIAL LABORATORY

Yale University Forestry School, 370 Prospect Street, New
Haven, Connecticut.   1957-1959.

"Chronological list of works by Paul Rudolph, 1946-1974."
    il., plan.   Architecture and Urbanism 49 (January 1975):
    155.
"Concrete orchard: Yale's architectural renaissance is fur-
    thered by a laboratory for forestry research by Paul
    Rudolph." il., plan, diag. Architectural Forum 111
    (October 1959):   138-141.
"Electrical distribution: forestry laboratory at Yale." il.,
    plan. Progressive Architecture 41 (February 1960):   172-
    173.
"Exploded landscape." il. Perspecta 7 (1961):   83-84.
"Greeley Memorial Laboratory." il., elev. Architecture and
    Urbanism 80 (July 1977):   224-225.
Johnson, Philip. "Three architects." il. Art in America
    48 (Spring 1960):   70-73.
Jones, Cranston, Architecture Today and Tomorrow. New
    York: McGraw-Hill, 1961. il. p. 177.
Maki, Fumihiko. "American architecture." Contemporary
    Architecture of the World, 1961. Tokyo: Shokokusha,
    1961. il. p. 331.
Metz, Don. New Architecture in New Haven. Cambridge:
    M.I.T., 1966. il., plan. pp. 28-29.
_____ . New Architecture in New Haven. Revised ed.
    Cambridge: M.I.T., 1973. il., plan. pp. 54-55.
Millon, Henry A. "Rudolph at the cross-roads." il. Archi-
    tectural Design 30 (December 1960):   497-499.
Rudolph, Paul. The Architecture of Paul Rudolph. Intro-
    duction by Sibyl Moholy-Nagy. New York: Praeger,
    1970. il. pp. 56-57.
_____ . Paul Rudolph. Introduction and notes by Rupert
    Spade. New York: Simon and Schuster, 1971. il., diag.
    plates 14-17, pp. 123-124.
_____ . Paul Rudolph, Dessins D'Architecture. Fribourg:
    Office du Livre, 1974. il. pp. 94-97.
Tentori, Francesco. "Greeley Memorial Laboratory per la
    facolta d'agraria di Yale, New Haven, Conn., 1959." il.,
    plan, sec., diag. Casabella 234 (December 1959):   13-17.

BLUE CROSS-BLUE SHIELD BUILDING

133 Federal Street, Boston, Massachusetts. 1957-1960. In
association with Anderson, Beckwith and Haible.

Architectural Record. Office Buildings. New York: McGraw-
   Hill, 1961. il., plan, sec. Reprinted from Architectural
   Record. pp. 75-79.
"Boston bucks a trend: Blue Cross office building." il.,
   plans. Architectural Forum 113 (December 1960): 64-69.
"Chronological list of works by Paul Rudolph, 1946-1974." il.,
   plan. Architecture and Urbanism 49 (January 1975):
   155.
Goody, Joan E. New Architecture in Boston. Cambridge:
   M.I.T., 1965. il., plan. pp. 68-69.
"Inside out office buildings: Blue Cross-Blue Shield head-
   quarters office building." il., plans, sec., elev. Archi-
   tectural Record 128 (December 1960): 111-116.
Lovorud, Robert, Leon Setti and John Shenofield. Thesis.
   The Blue Cross-Blue Shield Building; A Case Study in
   Architectural Practice. Cambridge: Harvard University,
   Department of Architecture, 1960. il., plans, maps. sec.
   unp.
Lyndon, Donlyn. The City Observed. Boston--A Guide to
   the Architecture of the Hub. New York: Random House,
   1982. il. pp. 259-260.
Millon, Henry A. "Rudolph at the cross-roads." il. Archi-
   tectural Design 30 (December 1960): 497-498, 500.
"Office headquarters building." il., plan. Architecture and
   Urbanism 80 (July 1977): 142-143.
"Pattern with a purpose." il., plan, sec. Architectural Forum
   109 (August 1958): 110-113.
"Quietly contemporary: new look on Boston's Federal Street."
   il. Interiors 121 (April 1962): 118-119.
Rudolph, Paul. Paul Rudolph. Introduction and notes by
   Rupert Spade. New York: Simon and Schuster, 1971.
   il., plan, sec. plates 26-30, p. 124.
Scully, Vincent. American Architecture and Urbanism. New
   York: Praeger, 1969. il. pp. 204-205.

GEORGE McCANDLISH RESIDENCE

1 Mount Pleasant Street, Cambridge, Massachusetts. 1958.

"Chronological list of works by Paul Rudolph, 1946-1974."
  il. Architecture and Urbanism 49 (January 1975): 156.
Evans, Edith Braywell. "What's right with architecture." il.,
  plan. Architectural Record 127 (Mid-May 1960): 66-75.
Goody, Joan E. New Architecture in Boston. Cambridge:
  M.I.T., 1965. il., plan, pp. 20-21.
"How to turn an empty shell into a wonderful house." il.
  (pt. col.), plan. House and Garden 111 (April 1960):
  130-133.
"En ombygget garage." il., plan. Arkitektur 5 (February
  1961): A6-A14.

INTERDENOMINATIONAL CHAPEL AND MASTER PLAN

Tuskegee Institute, Tuskegee, Alabama. 1958-1969. In association with Fry and Welch.

Abercrombie, Stanley. "Two-way relationship of drawings and
  design." il. American Institute of Architects. Journal
  71 (September 1982): 68-69.
"Architektur heute." il., plan. Deutsche Bauzeitung 66 (February 1961): 83.
"Chiesa per il Tuskegee Institute, Alabama." il., plan, sec.
  Architettura 15 (March 1970): 740-743.
"Chronological list of works by Paul Rudolph, 1946-1974."
  il., plan. Architecture and Urbanism 49 (January 1975):
  156.
Collins, Peter. "Whither Paul Rudolph?" il., port. Progres-
  sive Architecture 42 (August 1961): 130-133.
"Concrete sanctuary." il., plan, sec. Arts and Architecture
  77 (December 1960): 22-23.
"Drawings and sketches of Paul Rudolph." col. sec. Archi-
  tecture and Urbanism 49 (January 1975): 144.
Gordon, Barclay F., ed. Interior Spaces Designed by Archi-
  tects. New York: McGraw-Hill, 1974. il. (pt. col.),
  plan, sec. pp. 74-77.
Gowans, Alan. Images of American Living. Philadelphia:
  Lippincott, 1964. il. pp. 452-453.
"Interdenominational chapel." il. (pt. col.), plan, sec., elev.
  Architecture and Urbanism 80 (July 1977): 132, 149-151.
Kemper, Alfred M. Drawings by American Architects. New
  York: Wiley, 1973. il. p. 481.
_____. Presentation Drawings by American Architects.
  New York: Wiley, 1977. il. p. 110.

Kennedy, Roger G. American Churches. New York: Stewart, Tabori and Chang, 1982. col. il., pp. 54-55.
Millon, Henry A. "Rudolph at the cross-roads." il., plan, sec. Architectural Design 30 (December 1960): 497-498, 501-502.
Pile, John. Drawings of Architectural Interiors. New York: Whitney Library of Design, 1967. il. p. 157.
Rudolph, Paul. The Architecture of Paul Rudolph. Introduction by Sibyl Moholy-Nagy. New York: Praeger, 1970. il. (pt. col.), plan, sec., elev. pp. 86-93.
_____. Paul Rudolph, Dessins D'Architecture. Fribourg: Office du Livre, 1974. il., plan. pp. 108-111.
_____. Interdenominational Chapel, Tuskegee Institute, Tuskegee, Alabama 1960-1969. Boston, Massachusetts, 1962-1971. Tokyo: A.D.A., 1973. (Global Architecture 20). il. (pt. col.), plans. pp. 2-4, 8-21, 42-43.
"Sanctuary of sculptured concrete." il., plan. Architectural Forum 113 (September 1960): 102-105.
Schmertz, M. F. "Chapel for Tuskegee." il. (pt. col.), plan, sec., diag. Architectural Record 146 (November 1969): 117-126.
Smith, G. E. Kidder. A Pictorial History of Architecture in America. New York: American Heritage, 1976. il. pp. 390-391.
Veronesi, G. "Paul Rudolph." il., plan, diag. Zodiac 8 (1961): 148-161.

SARASOTA SENIOR HIGH SCHOOL

Sarasota, Florida. 1958-1959.

"Chronological list of works by Paul Rudolph, 1946-1974." il., plan. Architecture and Urbanism 49 (January 1975): 155.
Collins, Peter. "Whither Paul Rudolph?" il., port. Progressive Architecture 42 (August 1961): 130-133.
Cook, John Wesley. Conversations With Architects. New York: Praeger, 1973. il. pp. 94-95.
"Ecole secondaire, Sarasota." il., plan, sec., diag. Architecture D'Aujourd'hui 31 (September 1960): 78-81.
"Escuela en Sarasota, Florida." il., plan, sec. Revista Informes de la Construction 140 (May 1962).
"Hohere schule in Sarasota, Florida." il., plan, diag. Baukunst und Werkform 15 (September 1962): 508-512.

"Hohere schule Riverview in Sarasota, Florida." il., plan,
    sec. Deutsche Bauzeitschrift (October 1964): 264-267.
Jacobus, John. Twentieth Century Architecture: The Middle
    Years, 1940-1965. New York: Praeger, 1966. il. p.
    186.
Jones, Cranston. Architecture Today and Tomorrow. New
    York: McGraw-Hill, 1961. col. il. pp. 173, 177-178.
McQuade, Walter. "Exploded landscape." il. Perspecta 7
    (1961): 83-84.
Maki, Fumihiko. "American architecture," in Contemporary
    Architecture of the World, 1961. Tokyo: Shokokusha,
    1961. il., plan. pp. 343-345.
Millon, Henry A. "Rudolph at the cross-roads." il., sec.
    Architectural Design 30 (December 1960): 497-498.
Molitor, Joseph W. Architectural Photography. New York:
    Wiley, 1976. il. p. 86.
Nevins, Deborah. The Architect's Eye. New York: Pantheon,
    1979. il. pp. 154-155.
"1962 AIA honor awards." il., plan. American Institute of
    Architects. Journal 37 (May 1962): 58-59.
Pile, John, comp. Drawings of Architectural Interiors. New
    York: Whitney Library of Design, 1967. il. p. 155.
"Return to Florida." il., sec. Architectural Review 126
    (August 1959): 129-130.
Roth, Ucli. "Amerikanische architektur heute." il., port.
    DU 24 (June 1964): 26, 45.
Rudolph, Paul. The Architecture of Paul Rudolph. Intro-
    duction by Sibyl Moholy-Nagy. New York: Praeger, 1970.
    il., plan, diag. pp. 62-67.
_____. Paul Rudolph. Introduction and notes by Rupert
    Spade. New York: Simon and Schuster, 1971. il. (pt.
    col.), plan. plates 8-13, p. 123.
_____. Paul Rudolph, Dessins D'Architecture. Fribourg:
    Office du Livre, 1974. il. pp. 96-97.
"Rudolph's sun-shaded school ends first semester." il. Pro-
    gressive Architecture 41 (May 1960): 75.
"Sarasota high school." il., plan, sec., diag. Architectural
    Record 125 (March 1959): 189-194.
"Sarasota high school, Florida." il. Arkitektur 3 (October
    1959): 266, 268-270.
"School designed to control Florida climate." il., plan. Archi-
    tectural Record 127 (March 1960): 198-202.
"School in the sun." il., plan, sec., diag. Architectural
    Forum 112 (May 1960): 94-101.

Tentori, Francesco. "Due edifici per l'universita." il. Casa-
    bella 234 (December 1959): 12.
"Travaux recents de trois agences Americaines." il., plan,
    sec. Architecture D'Aujourd'hui 30 (September 1959):
    41-44.
"Una scuola a Sarasota." il., plan, diag. Domus 371 (Oc-
    tober 1960): 1-4.
Veronesi, Giulia. "Paul Rudolph." il., plan, sec., diag.
    Zodiac 8 (1961): 150-152.

FREDERICK A. DEERING RESIDENCE

Casey Key, Florida. 1958-1959.

"Cabana in concrete." il. (pt. col.), plan, sec. Architectural
    Forum 110 (May 1959): 122-127.
"Chronological list of works by Paul Rudolph, 1946-1974."
    il. Architecture and Urbanism 49 (January 1975): 158.
"Custom house winners of the 1959 Homes for Better Living
    Awards." il., plan. House and Home 15 (June 1959):
    120-121.
"Deering residence." il. Architecture and Urbanism 80 (July
    1977): 58-59.
"Fashions in living." il. Vogue 135 (January 1960): 151-152.
"Five levels give a dramatic sequence of spaces; residence,
    Casey Key, Florida." il., plan, sec. Architectural Record
    125 (Mid-May 1959): 76-79.
"From concrete block: a serene house of rare beauty." il.
    (pt. col.), plan, diag. House and Garden 118 (July 1960):
    68-73.
"House on the keys." il., plans. American Institute of Ar-
    chitects. Journal 33 (January 1960): 70-71.
Johnson, Philip. "Three architects." il. Art in America 48
    (Spring 1960): 70-73.
McQuade, Walter, "Exploded landscape." il. Perspecta 7
    (1961): 83-84.
Rudolph, Paul. The Architecture of Paul Rudolph. Intro-
    duction by Sibyl Moholy-Nagy. New York: Praeger,
    1970. il. (pt. col.), plans, sec. pp. 46-49.
Tentori, Franceso. "Due edifici per l'universita." il. Casa-
    bella 234 (December 1959): 12.

Fig. 2:   The Art and Architecture Building at Yale University

Fig. 3:   Detail of the Yale Art and Architecture Building

ART AND ARCHITECTURE BUILDING

Yale University, 170 York Street, New Haven, Connecticut.
   1958-1964.

"A&A: Yale school of art and architecture."   il. (pt. col.),
   plans, sec., diags.   Progressive Architecture 45 (February
   1964):   108-129.   Replies J. D. Lowenfish: R. H. Mutrux
   45 (July 1964):   179-180.
"Art and architecture building."   il., plan, elev.   Architecture
   and Urbanism 80 (July 1977):   234-239.

"Art and Architecture Building at Yale." il., plans. Architettura 10 (June 1964): 110-111.

"Art and Architecture Building, Yale Universitat in New
Haven." il., plan, sec., elev. Deutsche Bauzeitung 69
(September 1964): 688-696.

"Art and Architecture Building. Yale University, New Haven,
Conn." il., plans. Werk 51 (October 1964): sup 224-
225.

Berkeley, Ellen Perry. "Architecture on the campus: Yale;
a building as a teacher." il. Architectural Forum 127
(July-August 1967): 47-53.

Bissinger, Frederick L. "Ground breaking for new arts
building Saturday." il. Yale Daily News 83 (7 December
1961): 1.

Blake, Peter. Form Follows Fiasco: Why Modern Architecture
Hasn't Worked. Boston: Little Brown, 1977. il., sec.
pp. 16-18.

Boyd, Robin. The Puzzle of Architecture. London: Cambridge University, 1965. il., plans, sec. pp. 50, 150-
151.

Brolin, Brent C. The Failure of Modern Architecture. New
York: Van Nostrand Reinhold, 1976. il. pp. 28-29, 78.

"Chronological list of works by Paul Rudolph, 1946-1974."
il., plan. Architecture and Urbanism 49 (January 1975): 155.

Cook, John Wesley. Conversations With Architects. New
York: Praeger, 1973. il., plan, sec. pp. 91-100.

"Design jelled or Yale art and architectural school." il.
Progressive Architecture 43 (January 1962): 62.

Dober, Richard P. Campus Planning. New York: Reinhold,
1963. plan, map, sec. pp. 82-83.

Drexler, Arthur. Transformations in Modern Architecture.
New York: Museum of Modern Art, 1979. il. p. 18.

Fowler, John. "Art and architecture building, Yale, U.S.A."
il., plan. Architectural Design 34 (April 1964): 160-161,
178-180.

"Gebaude der kunst-und architekturabteilung, Universitat Yale,
New Haven." il., plan. Bauen und Wohnen 18 (November
1964): 435-441.

Goldberger, Paul. "Yale art building--decade of crises."
il. New York Times (30 April 1974): I, 48: 1.

Heinle, Erwin and Max Bacher. Building in Visual Concrete.
London: Technical Press, 1971. il., diags. pp. 102-103.

Hitchcock, Henry Russel. "Connecticut, U.S.A. in 1963."
il., plan, sec. Zodiac 13 (1964): 4-25.

Hofmann, Werner. Modern Architecture in Color. New York:
	Viking, 1970. col. il., plans. pp. 416-419.
Huxtable, Ada Louise. "Building you love to hate." il.
	New York Times (12 December 1971): II, 29: 4.
	_____. "Winner at Yale: the new art and architecture
	building lives up to great expectations." il. New York
	Times (10 November 1963): II, 19: 7.
"Institute of arts and architecture, Yale University, New
	Haven." il., plan, sec., port. Lotus (1964-1965): 192-
	197.
"Ivyless halls of Yale." col. port. Holiday 37 (May 1965):
	80-81.
Jacobs, David. "The Rudolph style: unpredictable." il.,
	port. New York Times Magazine (26 March 1967): 47.
Jacobus, John. Twentieth Century Architecture: The Middle
	Years, 1940-1965. New York: Praeger, 1966. il., plan.
	pp. 186-189.
Jencks, Charles. Modern Movements in Architecture. Garden
	City, N.Y.: Anchor, 1973. il. pp. 190-192.
Joedicke, Jurgen. Architecture Since 1945; Sources and
	Directions. New York: Praeger, 1969. il. pp. 129, 146.
Kemper, Alfred M. Drawings by American Architects. New
	York: Wiley, 1973. il. pp. 482-483.
	_____. Presentation Drawings by American Architects.
	New York: Wiley, 1977. il. pp. 195, 218.
Ligo, Larry L. The Concept of Function in Twentieth-Century
	Architectural Criticism. Ann Arbor, Mich.: UMI Research
	Press, 1984. il., plan, sec. pp. 47, 54, 85, 94, 168-171.
Magnago Lampugnani, Vittorio. Architecture of the 20th Cen-
	tury in Drawings. New York: Rizzoli, 1982. sec. p. 100.
Metz, Don. New Architecture in New Haven. Cambridge:
	M.I.T., 1966. il., plan. pp. 12-13.
	_____. New Architecture in New Haven. Revised ed.
	Cambridge: M.I.T., 1973. il., plan. pp. 6-7.
"New architecture at Yale." col. il., port. Time 82 (15
	November 1963): 84-85.
"1964 AIA honor awards: school of art and architecture, Yale
	University: Temple Street parking garage, New Haven."
	il., plans, sec. American Institute of Architects. Journal
	42 (July 1964): 26-27.
Pevsner, Nikolaus. "Address given at the opening of the Yale
	School of Art and Architecture, 1963," in Studies in Art,
	Architecture and Design. New York: Walker, 1968, v. 2.
	il. pp. 260-265.

_____. "At the inauguration of the new Art and Architecture Building of Yale University." il. Society of Architectural Historians. Journal 26 (March 1967): 4-7.

Pile, John. Drawings of Architectural Interiors. New York: Whitney Library of Design, 1967. sec. p. 159.

Pommer, Richard. "Art and architecture building at Yale, once again." il., plan. Burlington Magazine 114 (December 1972): 853-861.

"Recherches." il., plan, sec. Architecture D'Aujourd'hui 115 (June-July 1964): 62-65.

Reese, Ilse M. and James T. Burns. "Opposites: expressionism and formalism at Yale." Progressive Architecture 45 (February 1964): 128-129.

Roth, Leland M. A Concise History of American Architecture. New York: Harper & Row, 1979. il. pp. 303-304.

Rowan, Jan C. "New school of art and architecture." col. il. Progressive Architecture 45 (February 1964): 106-107.

Rudolph, Paul. The Architecture of Paul Rudolph. Introduction by Sibyl Moholy-Nagy. New York: Praeger, 1970. il., plan, sec., elev. pp. 120-137.

_____. Paul Rudolph, Dessins D'Architecture. Fribourg: Office du Livre, 1974. il., plan, sec., elev. pp. 98-103.

_____. Paul Rudolph. Introduction and notes by Rupert Spade. New York: Simon and Schuster, 1971. il. (pt. col.), plan, sec. plates 40-46, p. 125.

_____. "Yale's school of art and architecture; the architect." port. Architectural Forum 120 (February 1964): 84-89.

"Rudolph." il., plan, sec. Perspecta 7 (1961): 51-63.

"School for the arts at Yale." il., plans. Architectural Record 135 (February 1964): 111-120.

Scully, Vincent. American Architecture and Urbanism. New York: Praeger, 1969. il., sec. pp. 202-203.

_____. "Art and architecture building, Yale University." il., plans, sec., elev. Architectural Review 135 (May 1964): 324-332.

Sharp, Dennis. A Visual History of Twentieth-Century Architecture. Greenwich, Conn.: New York Graphic Society, 1972. il. pp. 252-253.

Smith, C. Ray. Supermannerism: New Attitudes in Post-Modern Architecture. New York: Dutton, 1977. plan. pp. 108-111.

Smith, G. E. Kidder. The Architecture of the United States, v. 1. Garden City, N.Y.: Anchor, 1981. il. p. 42.

"SOM, Rudolph, and Johnson at Yale." il. Architectural Forum
    119 (November 1963): 30-31.
Stern, Robert A. M. New Directions in American Architecture.
    New York: Braziller, 1969. il. pp. 33-34.
_____. New Directions in American Architecture. Revised
    ed. New York: Braziller, 1977. il. pp. 33-34.
"Ten buildings that point the future." col. il. Fortune 70
    (October 1964): 134-136.
Von Eckardt, Wolf. A Place to Live. New York: Delacorte,
    1967. pp. 55-58, 141, 148, 150.
Whiffen, Marcus. American Architecture, 1607-1976. Cam-
    bridge: M.I.T., 1981. il., plan. pp. 391-393.
"Yale: a building as a teacher." il., plan. Architectural
    Forum 127 (July 1967): 47-53.
"Yale Art and Architecture Building." il., plans. Arts
    and Architecture 81 (February 1964): 26-29.
"Yale to break ground for $4,000,000 art building." il. New
    York Times (7 December 1961) 50: 3.
"Yale's new art and architecture building." il., diag. Archi-
    tectural Record 131 (January 1962): 16-17.
"Yale's new school of art and architecture." il. Architectural
    Forum 113 (August 1960): 41.
"Yale's new school of art and architecture." il., plans.
    Architectural Record 131 (April 1962): 133-138.
"Yale's school of art and architecture." il. (pt. col.), plans,
    port., sec. Architectural Forum 120 (February 1964):
    cover, 62-89.
Zimring, Craig M. "A primer of postoccupacy evaluation:
    a set of six case histories." il. American Institute of
    Architects. Journal 70 (November 1981): 58.

LAKE REGION YACHT AND COUNTRY CLUB

Winter Haven, Florida. 1959. In association with Gene Leedy.

Veronesi, Giulia G. "Paul Rudolph." il. Zodiac 8 (1961):
    148-149.
"Yacht and country club." il., plan, sec. Progressive
    Architecture 43 (July 1962): 124-127.

R. AMBLER LIGGETT RESIDENCE

Tampa, Florida. 1959.

"Chronological list of works by Paul Rudolph, 1946-1974."
    il. Architecture and Urbanism 49 (January 1975): 156.
"Contemporary in the grand manner: house in Tampa." il.,
    plan. Architectural Record 131 (Mid-May 1962): 63-65.

Fig. 4:   Temple Street Parking Garage for the City of New
           Haven, Connecticut

TEMPLE STREET PARKING GARAGE

Between Church and Temple Streets at George Street, New
    Haven, Connecticut. 1959-1963.

Abercrombie, Stanley. "Two-way relationship of drawings and
    design." il. American Institute of Architects. Journal
    71 (September 1982): 68-69.
Blair, Samuel R. Thesis, unpub. The Temple Street Garage,
    New Haven, Connecticut. Cambridge: Harvard Univer-
    sity, Department of Architecture, 1962. il., maps, diags.
"Chronological list of works by Paul Rudolph, 1946-1974."
    il., sec. Architecture and Urbanism 49 (January 1975):
    156.
"City's newest landmark nearing completion." il. New Haven
    Register (23 Septembe 1962): 16.
Collins, Peter. "Whither Paul Rudolph?" il., port. Pro-
    gressive Architecture 42 (August 1961): 130-133.
Cook, John Wesley. Conversations with Architects. New
    York: Praeger, 1973. il. pp. 117-119.

"Four current projects by Rudolph." il., sec., elev., diag.
Architectural Record 129 (March 1961): 152-154.
"Garage at New Haven, Etats-Unis." il., plan, sec., diag.
Architecture D'Aujourd'hui 34 (October 1963): 34-37.
Goble, Emerson. "Horrors: a handsome garage." Architect-
ural Record 133 (February 1963): 9.
Gruen, Victor. The Heart of Our Cities: The Urban Crisis:
Diagnosis and Cure. New York: Simon and Schuster,
1964. il. pp. 153-155.
Heinle, Erwin. Building in Visual Concrete. London: Tech-
nical, 1971. il. p. 79.
Jacobs, David. "Rudolph style: unpredictable." il. New
York Times Magazine (26 March 1967): 49.
Klose, Dietrich. Metropolitan Parking Structures: A Survey
of Architectural Problems and Solutions. New York:
Praeger, 1965. il., plan, sec., elev. pp. 42-43, 136-139.
_____. Multi-Storey Car Parks and Garages. London:
Architectural Press, 1965. il., plan, sec., elev. pp. 42-
43, 136-139.
Kulski, Julian Eugene. Architecture in a Revolutionary Era.
Nashville, Tenn.: Aurora, 1971. il. pp. 162-163, 168-
169.
Metz, Don. New Architecture in New Haven. Cambridge:
M.I.T., 1966. il. pp. 62-63.
_____. New Architecture in New Haven, revised ed.
Cambridge: M.I.T., 1973. il. 14-15.
Millon, Henry A. "Rudolph at the cross-roads." il., sec.
Architectural Design 30 (December 1960): 497-498, 504.
"1964 AIA honor awards." il., plan, sec. American Institute
of Architects. Journal 42 (July 1964): 31.
"Parking garage for 1,500 cars." il., sec. Architecture and
Urbanism 80 (July 1977): 144-147.
"Paul Rudolph designs a place to park in downtown New
Haven." il., plan, sec., diag. Architectural Record
133 (February 1963): 145-150.
"Paul Rudolph garage at New Haven." il., diag. Architettura
9 (July 1963): 184-185.
"Paul Rudolph: young mover, changing the look of American
architecture." il., port. Vogue 141 (15 January 1963):
84-91, 106.
Roth, Ueli. "Amerikanische architektur heute." il., port.
Du 24 (June 1964): 27, 45.
Rudolph, Paul. The Architecture of Paul Rudolph. Intro-
duction by Sibyl Moholy-Nagy. New York: Praeger,
1970. il., sec., diags. pp. 114-119.

_____. Paul Rudolph. Introduction and notes by Rupert
   Spade. New York: Simon and Schuster, 1971. il., diag.
   plates 35-39, p. 125.
_____. Paul Rudolph, Dessins D'Architecture. Fribourg:
   Office du Livre, 1974. il., sec. pp. 104-107.
"Rudolph's Roman road." il., sec. Architectural Forum 118
   (February 1963): 104-109.
Scully, Vincent Joseph. American Architecture and Urbanism.
   New York: Praeger, 1969. il. p. 204.
"Sensually structured parking garage by Rudolph." il., elev.
   Progressive Architecture 41 (September 1960): 51.
Sharp, Dennis. A Visual History of Twentieth-Century Ar-
   chitecture. Greenwich, Conn.: New York Graphic So-
   ciety, 1972. il. p. 258.
Spring, Bernard P. and Donald Canty. "Concrete." il.
   Architectural Forum 117 (September 1962): cover, 78-81,
   88-89.
Stern, Robert A. M. New Directions in American Architecture.
   New York: Braziller, 1969. il. pp. 31-33.
_____. New Directions in American Architecture. Revised
   ed. New York: Braziller, 1977. il. pp. 31-33.
Veronesi, Giulia. "Paul Rudolph." il., sec., elev. Zodica
   8 (1961): 153.

MARRIED STUDENTS HOUSING

Yale University, 292-311 Mansfield Street, New Haven, Connecticut. 1960-1961.

"Alloggi per gli studenti di Yale." il., plans, sec. Architettura 8 (December 1962): 540.
"Alloggi per studenti sposati a Yale: Motel a Waverly e casa
   in Florida." il., plans, sec. Architecttura 7 (July 1961):
   187-189.
Banham, Reyner. The New Brutalism. London: Architectural
   Press, 1966. il. pp. 130, 164-165.
Burchard, Marshall. "New urban pattern: married students
   apartments at Yale." il., plan. Architectural Forum
   116 (March 1962): 98-101.
"Chronological list of works by Paul Rudolph, 1946-1974."
   il., plan. Architecture and Urbanism 49 (January 1975):
   156.
Drew, Philip. Third Generation: The Changing Meaning of
   Architecture. New York: Praeger, 1972. il. pp. 40-41.

Fig. 5: Married Students Housing at Yale University

"Four current projects by Rudolph." il., plan, sec. Archi-
tectural Record 129 (March 1961): 142-146.
"Habitat Universitaire à Yale, New Haven, Etats Unis." il.,
plan, diag. Architecture D'Aujourd'hui 33 (October 1962):
73-75.
Jacobus, John. Twentieth Century Architecture: The Middle
Years, 1940-65. New York: Praeger, 1966. il. pp.
173, 175.
Joedicke, Jurgen. Architecture Since 1945; Sources and
Directions. New York: Praeger, 1969. il. p. 129.
Maki, Fumikiko. "American architecture," in Contemporary
Architecture of the World, 1961. Tokyo: Shokokusha,
1961. il. pp. 326-327.
"Married students housing." il., plan. Architecture and
Urbanism 80 (July 1977): 88-91.
Metz, Don. New Architecture in New Haven. Cambridge:
M.I.T., 1966. il., plan. pp. 26-27.
Millon, Henry A. "Rudolph at the cross-roads." il., plan.
Architectural Design 30 (December 1960): 497-498, 503.
"Projects récents de Paul Rudolph." il., plan, sec. Archi-
tecture D'Aujourd'hui 33 (February 1962): 84-93.
Reese, Ilse Meissner. "Thoughts on urban housing." il.
Progressive Architecture 42 (October 1961): 144.
"Rudolph." il., plan. Perspecta 7 (1961): 52.
Rudolph, Paul. The Architecture of Paul Rudolph. Intro-
duction by Sibyl Moholy-Nagy. New York: Praeger,
1970. il., plan, elev. pp. 184-187.
_____. Paul Rudolph, Dessins D'Architecture. Fribourg:
Office du Livre, 1974. il., plan. pp. 50-55.
_____. Paul Rudolph. Introduction and notes by Rupert
Spade. New York: Simon and Schuster, 1971. il. (pt.
col.), plan, sec. plates 31-34, pp. 124-125.
Smith, G. E. Kidder. The Architecture of the United States.
Garden City, N.Y.: Anchor, 1981, v. 1. il. pp. 39-40.
Stern, Robert A. M. New Directions in American Architecture.
New York: Braziller, 1969. il. pp. 36-37.
_____. New Directions in American Architecture. Revised
ed. New York: Braziller, 1977. il. pp. 36-37.
"University to improve inadequate housing for married stu-
dents." il. Yale Daily News 82 (10 November 1960): 1.
Veronesi, Guilia. "Paul Rudolph." il., plan, sec. Zodiac
8 (1961): 157-159.
"Village for married students." il. Progressive Architecture
41 (December 1960): 60.

O'BRIEN'S MOTOR INN

Waverly, New York. Project, 1960.

"Alloggi per studenti sponsati a Yale: motel a Waverly e casa
    in Florida." il., plan., sec. Architettura 7 (July 1961):
    187-189.
"Chronological list of works by Paul Rudolph, 1946-1974."
    il., plan. Architecture and Urbanism 49 (January 1975):
    157.
"Four current projects by Rudolph." il., plans, sec., diags.
    Architectural Record 129 (March 1961):   147-151.
"Motor inn." il., plan. Architecture and Urbanism 80 (July
    1977):   152-153.
"Projects de Paul Rudolph." il., plan, sec. L'Architecture
    D'Aujourd'hui 33 (February 1962):   84-93.
Rudolph, Paul. The Architecture of Paul Rudolph. Intro-
    duction by Sibyl Moholy-Nagy. New York: Praeger,
    1970. il., plan. pp. 188-189.
_____. Paul Rudolph, Dessins D'Architecture. Fribourg:
    Office du Livre, 1974. il., sec. pp. 112-113.
Veronesi, G. "Paul Rudolph." il., plan. Zodiac 8 (1961):
    154-155.

ENDO LABORATORIES

Stewart Avenue at Endo Boulevard, Garden City, New York.
    1960-1964. In association with Walter Kidde.

Andrews, Wayne. Architecture in New York: A Photographic
    History. New York: Atheneum, 1969. il. pp. 172-173.
"Building in the news." il. Architectural Forum 119 (Septem-
    ber 1963):   16.
"Chateau Endo, pharmaceutical laboratories at Garden City."
    il. Architectural Review 137 (February 1965):   96.
"Chronological list of works by Paul Rudolph, 1946-1974."
    il., plan. Architecture and Urbanism 49 (January 1975):
    157.
Dixon, John M. "Fortress for pharmaceuticals." il., plans,
    sec. Progressive Architecture 45 (November 1964):   168-
    175.
"Endicott laboratories (Endo) in Garden City, Long Island."
    il., plan. Werk 52 (February 1965):   76-80.

"Endo Laboratories." Architecture Francaise 297-298 (1967):
    88-89.
"Endo Laboratories pharmaceutical building." il. (pt. col.),
    plan. Architecture and Urbanism 80 (July 1977): 132-133,
    154-157.
Hofmann, Werner. Modern Architecture in Color. New York:
    Viking, 1970. col. il., plans. pp. 480-483.
Huxtable, Ada Louise. "Design of Garden City plant stirs
    extreme reactions." il. New York Times (20 September
    1964): 8; 1: 2, 14: 1.
"I Labortori Endo a Garden City New York: il materiale come
    componente essenziale nella architettura di Paul Rudolph."
    il., plan. L'Industria Italiama del Cemento 37 (February
    1967): 73-88.
"Laboratori farmaceuti Endo a Garden City, New York." il.,
    plans, sec. Architettura 10 (April 1965): 816-817.
Lundy, Victor. "In pursuit of diversity." col. il. Time 86
    (2 July 1965): 56-58.
McQuade, Walter. "Structure and design: a pharmaceutical
    castle for the Long Island plain." il., plan, port.
    Fortune 70 (November 1964): 205-206.
"Pharmazeutische fabrik (Endo laboratories) Garden City,
    New York." il., plans. Deutsche Bauzeitung 5 (May
    1966): 355-359.
Rudolph, Paul. The Architecture of Paul Rudolph. Intro-
    duction by Sibyl Moholy-Nagy. New York: Praeger,
    1970. il., plans. pp. 142-151.
_____. Paul Rudolph. Introduction and notes by Rupert
    Spade. New York: Simon and Schuster, 1971. il. (pt.
    col.), plan. plates 47-53, p. 126.
_____. Paul Rudolph, Dessins D'Architecture. Fribourg:
    Office du Livre, 1974. il., plan. pp. 114-115.
"Sculptural forms for pharmaceutical research." il. (pt. col.),
    plan, sec. Architectural Record 151 (June 1972): 95-100.
"Sculptured factory in suburbia Endo laboratories headquarters
    in Garden City, New York." il., plan. Interiors 124
    (April 1965): 118-122.
Stern, Robert A. M. New Directions in American Architecture.
    New York: Braziller, 1969. il. p. 34.
_____. New Directions in American Architecture. Revised
    ed. New York: Braziller, 1977. il. p. 34.
"Work of Paul Rudolph." il. Building 210 (11 March 1966):
    87-89.

ARTHUR W. MILAM RESIDENCE

Jacksonville Beach, Florida. 1960.

"Alloggi per studenti sposati a Yale: motel a Waverly e casa
    in Florida." il., plan, sec. Architettura 7 (July 1961):
    186-189.
"Architectural changes forecast new adventures in living."
    col. il. House and Garden 122 (October 1962): 156-157.
"Casa at Jacksonville." il., plan. Architettura 8 (January
    1963): 622.
"Chronological list of works by Paul Rudolph, 1946-1974."
    il., plan. Architecture and Urbanism 49 (January 1975):
    157.
"Four current projects by Rudolph." il., plan, sec. Archi-
    tectural Record 129 (March 1961): 139-141.
"Habitation a Jacksonville, Fla." il., plan, sec. Architecture
    D'Aujourd'hui 33 (September 1962): 36-37.
Kemper, Alfred M. Presentation Drawings by American Ar-
    chitects. New York: Wiley, 1977. il. p. 153.
"Milam residence." il., plan, sec. Architecture and Urbanism
    80 (July 1977): 52-55.
Millon, Henry A. "Rudolph at the cross-roads." il., plan,
    sec. Architectural Design 30 (December 1960): 497-498,
    504.
Molitor, Joseph W. Architectural Photography. New York:
    Wiley, 1976. il. p. 122.
"Paul Rudolph: young mover, changing the look of American
    architecture." il., port. Vogue 141 (15 January 1963):
    84-91, 106.
"Progetto di casa." il., plan, sec. Architettura 12 (June
    1966): 103.
"Rudolph." il., plan, sec. Perspecta 7 (1961): 64.
Rudolph, Paul. The Architecture of Paul Rudolph. Introduc-
    tion by Sibyl Moholy-Nagy. New York: Prawger, 1970.
    il., plans, sec. pp. 68-71.
_____. Paul Rudolph, Dessins D'Architecture. Fribourg:
    Office du Livre, 1974. il. p. 38.
"Sculptured house of concrete block." il. (pt. col.), plan,
    sec. Architectural Record 133 (Mid-May 1963): 70-73.
"Six new houses by Paul Rudolph." il., plan, sec. Archi-
    tectural Record 132 (November 1962): 126-128.
Smith, Herbert L., ed. 25 Years of Record Houses. New
    York: McGraw-Hill, 1981. il., plan, sec. pp. 40-43.

"3 houses with daring new shapes." il. (pt. col.), plan,
    sec. House and Home 25 (April 1964): 136-137.
Veranisi, Giulia. "Paul Rudolph." il., plan, sec. Zodiac
    8 (1961): 156.

R. H. DAISLEY RESIDENCE

Inlet Cay, Florida. 1960.

"Chronological list of works by Paul Rudolph, 1946-1974."
    il. Architecture and Urbanism 49 (January 1975): 157.
"Daisley residence." il. Architecture and Urbanism 80 (July
    1977): 56-57.
"Six new houses by Paul Rudolph." il., plan, sec. Archi-
    tectural Record 132 (November 1962): 129-131.

THEME CENTER FOR 1964/65 NEW YORK WORLD'S FAIR

Portland Cement Company, Flushing, New York. Project,
    1960.

"Chronological list of works by Paul Rudolph, 1946-1974."
    il., sec. Architecture and Urbanism 49 (January 1975):
    157.
"Moon-viewing platform shows concrete." il., sec. Progressive
    Architecture 42 (July 1961): 45.
Rudolph, Paul. Paul Rudolph, Dessins D'Architecture.
    Fribourg: Office du Livre, 1974. il., sec. pp. 116-119.
"Rudolph designs for the New York fair." il. Architectural
    Record 130 (July 1961): 12.

THEATRE

Ford Foundation, New York, New York. Project, 1960. In
    association with Ralph Alswang.

American Federation of arts. The Ideal Theater: Eight Con-
    cepts. New York: The American Feeration of Arts,
    1962. il., plans, sec. pp. 13-26.
Athanasopulos, Christos G. Contemporary Theater Evolution
    and Design. New York: Wiley-Interscience, 1983. il.,
    plan, sec. pp. 297-300.

"Centre administratif d'état de Massachusetts a Boston; Hotel
de Ville, Syracuse, N.Y.; projet pour un théâtre à
Boston." il., plan, diags. Architecture D'Aujourd'hui
35 (September 1965): 32-35.
"Chronological list of works by Paul Rudolph, 1946-1974."
il. Architecture and Urbanism 49 (January 1975): 157.
Clurman, Harold. "Eight ideal theaters." il., plan, sec.
Industrial Design 9 (April 1962): 46-47.
"Film and action theater." il. Architecture and Urbanism
80 (July 1977): 159.
"Ideal theatre Ford Foundation program." Progressive Archi-
tecture 42 (December 1961): 51.
Miller, Richard A. "Eight concepts for the ideal theater."
il., plan, sec. Architectural Forum 116 (January 1962):
115.
"Recherches Américaines pour un théâtre idéal." il., plan,
sec. Architecture D'Aujourd'hui 34 (February 1964): 39.
Rudolph, Paul. The Architecture of Paul Rudolph. Introduction by Sibyl Moholy-Nagy. New York: Praeger,
1970. il., plans, sec. pp. 84-85.
"Theatre project for the Ford Foundation." il., plans, sec.
Progressive Architecture 43 (February 1962): 110-111.

CIBA PHARMACEUTICAL COMPANY

Additional office facilities, Summit, New Jersey. Project, 1961.

"Chronological list of works by Paul Rudolph, 1946-1974."
il. Architecture and Urbanism 49 (January 1975): 158.

KAPPA SIGMA FRATERNITY HOUSE

Auburn University, Auburn, Alabama. 1961.

"Chronological list of works by Paul Rudolph, 1946-1974." il.
Architecture and Urbanism 49 (January 1975): 158.

N. LESLIE SILVAS RESIDENCE

Greenwich, Connecticut. 1961.

"Six new houses by Paul Rudolph." il., plan, sec. Architectural Record 132 (November 1962): 134-135.

JOHN W. WALLACE RESIDENCE

Athens, Alabama. 1961-1964.

"Chronological list of works by Paul Rudolph, 1946-1974."
    il., plan. Architecture and Urbanism 49 (January 1975):
    158.
"Daring house, emphatically contemporary." il. (pt. col.),
    plan. House and Garden 129 (April 1966): 186-193.
"Home in classic style." col. il., diag. Life 58 (26 February
    1965): 94-97.
Rudolph, Paul. The Architecture of Paul Rudolph. Intro-
    duction by Sibyl Moholy-Nagy. New York: Praeger,
    1970. il., plans. pp. 72-75.
"Six new houses by Paul Rudolph." il., plan, elev. Archi-
    tectural Record 132 (November 1962): 132-133.
Smith, Herbert L., ed. 25 Years of Record Houses. New
    York: McGraw-Hill, 1981. il., plan. pp. 152-155.
"Wallace residence." il. (pt. col.), plan. Architecture and
    Urbanism 80 (July 1977): 9-10, 60-61.

PAUL RUDOLPH RESIDENCE

New Haven, Connecticut. 1961.

"Chronological list of works by Paul Rudolph, 1946-1974." il.
    Architecture and Urbanism 49 (January 1975): 158.
"Paul Rudolph: projected extension of the architect's office,
    October, 1961/The architect's apartment." il., plan, sec.,
    elev. Perspecta 9/10 (1965): 249-264.
"Paul Rudolph, young mover, changing the look of American
    architecture." il., port. Vogue 141 (15 January 1963):
    84-91, 106.

IBM CORPORATION

Research and Manufacturing Facilities, East Fishkell, New
    York. 1962-1966.

"Chronological list of works by Paul Rudolph, 1946-1974."
    il., plan. Architecture and Urbanism 49 (January 1975):
    158.

Dixon, J. M. "IBM thinks twice." il. Architectural Forum
124 (March 1966): 32-33.
"Research, office and manufacturing facilities." il., plan.
Architecture and Urbanism 80 (July 1977): 162-165.
Rudolph, Paul. Paul Rudolph, Dessins D'Architecture. Fri-
bourg: Office du Livre, 1974. il. pp. 122-125.

RESIDENCE

Palm Beach, Florida. Project, 1962.

"Six new houses by Paul Rudolph." il., plan, sec. Architectural Record 132 (November 1962): 123-125.

CRAWFORD MANOR

North Frontage Road and Park Street, New Haven, Connecticut.
1962-1966.

"Alterwohnungen Crawford Manor in New Haven, USA." il.,
plan. Werk 54 (March 1967): 125-129.
"Balconies for the elderly." il. Architectural Forum 124
(March 1966): 57.
"Chronological list of works by Paul Rudolph, 1946-1974."
il., plan. Architecture and Urbanism 49 (January 1975):
159.
Cook, John Wesley. Conversations With Architects. New
York: Praeger, 1973. il. pp. 118-120.
"Crawford Manor housing for the elderly." il., plan. Archi-
tecture and Urbanism 80 (July 1977): 92-95.
"Crawford Manor public housing, New Haven, Connecticut."
il., plans, sec., diags. Progressive Architecture 48 (May
1967): 124-129.
"Edificie per anziani, New Haven." il., plans. Architettura
13 (July 1967): 184-185.
"Immeuble d'habitation a New Haven, Connecticut." il., plan.
Architecture D'Aujourd'hui 130 (February-March 1967):
38-39.
"Implied spaces." il., plan. Architectural Review 142 (September 1967): 172.
Macsai, John. Housing. 2nd ed. New York: John Wiley,
1982. il., plans, pp. 390-391.

Fig. 6: Crawford Manor near downtown New Haven, Con-
necticut

Metz, Don. New Architecture in New Haven. Cambridge:
    M.I.T., 1966. il., plan. pp. 70-71.
_____. New Architecture in New Haven. Revised ed.
    Cambridge: M.I.T., 1973. il., plan. pp. 8-9.
Middleton, Robin. "Disintegration." il., plan. Architectural
    Design 37 (May 1967): 203-204.
"Rudolf: balconate per anziani." il. Architettura 12 (July
    1966): 188.
Rudolph, Paul. The Architecture of Paul Rudolph. Intro-
    duction by Sibyl Moholy-Nagy. New York: Praeger,
    1970. il., plans. pp. 192-195.
_____. Paul Rudolph. Introduction and notes by Rupert
    Spade. New York: Simon and Schuster, 1971. il.,
    plans. plates 58-62, p. 126.
Scully, Vincent Joseph. American Architecture and Urbanism.
    New York: Praeger, 1969. il. pp. 204, 246-248.
Venturi, Robert. "Ugly and ordinary architecture or the
    decorated shed." il., plan. Architectural Forum 135 (No-
    vember 1971): 64-67.

HOTCHKISS SCHOOL

Lakeville, Connecticut. Project, 1962.

"Chronological list of works by Paul Rudolph, 1946-1974." il.
    Architecture and Urbanism 49 (January 1975): 159.

CHRISTIAN SCIENCE STUDENT CENTER

University of Illinois, Fourth Street and Gregory Drive, Ur-
    bana, Illinois. 1962-1967. In association with Smith,
    Seaton and Olach.

"Architecture strongly manipulated in space and scale: a
    Christian Science student center." il. (pt. col.), plans,
    diags. Architectural Record 141 (February 1967): 137-
    142.
"Christian Science organization building." il. (pt. col.),
    plan, sec. Architecture and Urbanism 80 (July 1977):
    130, 240-241.
"Chronological list of works by Paul Rudolph, 1946-1974."
    il., plan. Architecture and Urbanism 49 (January 1975):
    159.

"Implied spaces." il., plan. Architectural Review 142 (Sep-
tember 1967): 171.
Koeper, Frederick. Illinois Architecture From Territorial
Times to the Present. Chicago: University of Chicago,
1968. il. pp. 284-285.
Marlin, William. "Paul Rudolph: drawings." sec. Archi-
tectural Forum 138 (June 1973): 48-49.
"Paul Rudolph's elaborated spaces: six new projects." il.,
plans, sec., elev. Architectural Record 139 (June 1966):
146-147.
Religious Buildings by the editors of Architectural Record.
New York: McGraw-Hill, 1979. il., plan, sec. pp. 26-31.
Riley, Robert B. "Light and texture in a student center."
col. il. AIA Journal 68 (September 1979): 84-85.
Rudolph, Paul. The Architecture of Paul Rudolph. Intro-
duction by Sibyl Moholy-Nagy. New York: Praeger,
1970. il. (pt. col.), plans, sec. pp. 138-141.
_____. Paul Rudolph. Introduction and notes by Rupert
Spade. New York: Simon and Schuster, 1971. il. (pt.
col.), plan. plates 82-87, p. 127.
_____. Paul Rudolph, Dessins D'Architecture. Fribourg:
Office du Livre, 1974. sec. pp. 120-121.

BOSTON GOVERNMENT SERVICE CENTER

Cambridge and New Chardon Streets, Boston, Massachusetts.
1962-1971. In association with Desmond and Lord, H. A.
Dyer, Pedersen and Tilney.

"Another major project for Boston government service center."
il., plan. Progressive Architecture 45 (February 1964):
62-64.
Black, Carl Joh. "Vision of human space; Boston state serv-
ice center." il., plans, sec. Architectural Record 154
(July 1973): 105-116.
"Boston government center." il., diag. Architecture
D'Aujourd'hui 157 (August 1971): 88-91.
"Boston government service center." il., plan, sec. Archi-
tecture and Urbanism 80 (July 1977): 286-291.
Boston Society of Architects. Architecture Boston. Barre,
Mass.: Barre, 1976. il., map. pp. 4, 10, 12.
"Boston's monuments." il., plan. Architectural Review 142
(September 1967): 169-170.

"Boston's state government center approved." il. Architect-
    ural Record 135 (January 1964): 26.
"Centre administratif de l'état de Massachusetts à Boston."
    il., plan. Architecture D'Aujourd'hui 35 (September-
    November 1965): 32.
"Centro servizi publici a Boston." il., sec. Architettura
    17 (April 1972): 813-815.
"Chronological list of works by Paul Rudolph, 1946-1974."
    il., plan. Architecture and Urbanism 49 (January 1975):
    159.
Cook, John Wesley and Heinrich Klotz. Conversations With
    Architects. New York: Praeger, 1973. il. pp. 114-
    115.
"Coordinated architecture for government center." il., plan,
    sec. Architectural Record 135 (March 1964): 195-200.
Davern, Jeanne M., ed. Architecture 1970-1980: A Decade
    of Change. New York: McGraw-Hill, 1980. il. pp.
    100-101.
"Drawings and sketches of Paul Rudolph." col. il. Archi-
    tecture and Urbanism 49 (January 1975): 144.
Drexler, Arthur. Transformations in Modern Architecture.
    New York: Museum of Modern Art, 1979. il. pp. 26-27.
Goody, Joan E. New Architecture in Boston. Cambridge:
    M.I.T., 1965. il., plan. pp. 70-71.
Huxtable, Ada Louise. "Complex in Boston is radically de-
    signed." il. New York Times (7 November 1963): I,
    25: 2.
Jacobus, John. Twentieth Century Architecture: The Middle
    Years, 1940-1965. New York: Praeger, 1966. il. pp.
    194- 196.
Kemper, Alfred M. Drawings by American Architects. New
    York: Wiley, 1973. il., sec. p. 488.
Lyndon, Donlyn. The City Observed: Boston. A Guide to
    the Architecture of the Hub. New York: Random House,
    1982. il. pp. 84-85.
Middleton, Robin. "Disintegration." plan. Architectural
    Design 37 (May 1967): 203-204.
"Paul Rudolph: dal 1962 a oggi." il. Casabella 364 (Decem-
    ber 1973): 53.
"Paul Rudolph's elaborated spaces: six new projects." il.,
    plan. Architectural Record 139 (June 1966): 140-141.
"Das picknick des photographen: Boston government service
    center, Boston, Mass., U.S.A." il., plan, diag. Werk
    59 (January 1972): 40-44.

"Recherches." il., plan, sec., elev. Architecture D'Aujourd'hui
    115 (June-July 1964):   66-69.
"Drei regierungsgebaude in Boston, USA." il., plan. Deutsche
    Bauzeitung 103 (1 November 1969):   794-796.
"Regierungszentrum in Boston." il., plan, sec. Deutsche
    Bauzeitung 69 (August 1964):   587-588.
Rudolph, Paul. The Architecture of Paul Rudolph. Intro-
    duction by Sibyl Moholy-Nagy. New York: Praeger,
    1970. il., plans, sec. pp. 94-101.
_____. Interdenominational Chapel, Tuskegee Institute.
    Tuskegee, Alabama, 1960-69. Boston Government Service
    Center, Boston, Massachusetts, 1962-71. Tokyo: A.D.A.
    Edita, 1973. (Global Architecture 20). il. (pt. col.),
    plans, sec. pp. [5-7], 22-40, [44-47].
_____. Paul Rudolph, Dessins D'Architecture. Fribourg:
    Office du Livre, 1974. il., plan, sec. pp. 126-135.
Schmertz, M. F. "County government by Paul Rudolph."
    il. (pt. col.), plan, sec. Architectural Record 150 (Aug-
    ust 1971):   83-92.
Scully, Vincent. American Architecture and Urbanism. New
    York: Praeger, 1969. il. pp. 204, 206.
Smith, G. E. Kidder. The Architecture of the United States.
    Garden City, N.Y.:   Anchor, 1981, v. 1. il. pp. 257-
    258.
_____. A Pictorial History of Architecture in America.
    New York: American Heritage, 1976. il. pp. 103-105.
Stern, Robert A. M. New Directions in American Architecture.
    New York: Braziller, 1969. il. pp. 34-36.
_____. New Directions in American Architecture. Revised
    ed. New York: Braziller, 1977. il. pp. 34-36.

ORANGE COUNTY GOVERNMENT CENTER

Goshen, New York. 1963-1971. In association with Peter
    Barbone.

"Chronological list of works by Paul Rudolph, 1946-1974." il.,
    plan. Architecture and Urbanism 49 (January 1975):   159.
Davern, Jeanne M., ed. Architecture 1970-1980:   A Decade
    of Change. New York: McGraw-Hill, 1980. il., sec. pp.
    32-33.
Michigan, University. Law School. The American Courthouse,
    Planning and Design for the Judicial Process. Ann Arbor,

Mich.:   Institute of Continuing Education, 1973. il.,
  plan, sec. pp. 262-263.
Middleton, Robin. "Disintegration." plan. Architectural
  Design 37 (May 1967):   203-204.
"Orange Country office and courthouse building." il. (pt.
  col.), plan, sec. Architecture and Urbanism 80 (July
  1977):   133, 166-169.
"Paul Rudolph's elaborated spaces: six new projects." il.,
  plan, sec. Architectural Record 139 (June 1966):   135-
  139.
Schmertz, Mildred F. "County government center by Paul
  Rudolph." il. (pt. col.), plan, sec., diag. Architectural
  Record 150 (August 1971):   83-92.
Smith, G. E. Kidder. The Architecture of the United States.
  Garden City, N.Y.:   Anchor, 1981, v. 1. il. pp. 435-
  436.
"Spazi gomito a gomito." il., plan, sec. Architettura 17
  (December 1971):   540-542.
"Tribunal du comte d'orange a Goshen, N.Y." il., plan, sec.
  Architecture D'Aujourd'hui 128 (October-November 1966):
  6-7.

SOUTHEASTERN MASSACHUSETTS TECHNOLOGICAL INSTITUTE

North Dartmouth, Massachusetts. 1963-1972. In association
  with Desmond and Lord.

"Architecture gives campus unity of a single building." il.,
  sec., diag. College and University Business 42 (February
  1967):   72-75.
"Architecture that gives a campus a single building unity;
  will Rudolph's vision of the SMTI campus be fully recog-
  nized?" il. (pt. col.), plans, sec. Architectural Record
  140 (October 1966):   145-160. Reply with rejoinder by
  Jan Reiner 141 (February 1967):   48.
Chermayeff, Ivan. Observations on American Architecture.
  New York: Viking, 1972. il. (pt. col.). pp. 68, 70.
"Chronological list of works by Paul Rudolph, 1946-1974." il.,
  plan. Architecture and Urbanism 49 (January 1975):   159.
Cook, John Wesley. Conversations With Architects. New
  York: Praeger, 1973. plan. pp. 91-92.
"Institute de technology à North Dartmouth, Mass." il., plan,
  sec. Architecture D'Aujourd'hui 36 (October 1966):   2-5.

Jacob, Eva. New Architecture in New England. Lincoln,
    Mass.: De Cordova Museum, 1974. il. pp. 16-17, 96-97.
Jacobs, David. "Rudolph style: unpredictable." il. New
    York Times Magazine (26 March 1967): 46.
Molitor, Joseph W. Architectural Photography. New York:
    Wiley, 1976. il. pp. 88-89.
Rudolph, Paul. The Architecture of Paul Rudolph. Intro-
    duction by Sibyl Moholy-Nagy. New York: Praeger, 1970.
    il. (pt. col.), plans, secs., elev. pp. 152-165.
_____. Paul Rudolph. Introduction and notes by Rupert
    Spade. New York: Simon and Schuster, 1971. il. (pt.
    col.), plan, sec. plates 72-81, p. 127.
_____. Paul Rudolph, Dessins D'Architecture. Fribourg:
    Office du Livre, 1974. il., plan, sec., elev. pp. 162-
    169.
"Paul Rudolph with Desmond and Lord; Southeastern Massa-
    chusetts Technological Institute, North Dartmouth, Mass.
    completion; 1970." il., plans, sec. Global Architecture
    Document. Special Issue 1970-1980 (1980): 24-27.
Smith, G. E. Kidder. The Architecture of the United States.
    Garden City, N.Y.: Anchor, 1981, v. 1. il. pp. 298-
    300.
_____. A Pictorial History of Architecture in America.
    New York: American Heritage, 1976. il. pp. 114-115.
"Southeastern Massachusetts Technological Institute." il. (pt.
    col.), plan. Architecture and Urbanism 80 (July 1977):
    131, 242-247.
"Southeastern Massachusetts University." il. (pt. col.), plan.
    Architectural Record 157 (January 1975): 126-131.
Yamashita, Tsukasa. "Recent works of Paul Rudolph." il.
    (pt. col.), plan, map, sec. Architecture and Urbanism 49
    (January 1975): 37, 46-64, 144.

CHARLES A. DANA CREATIVE ARTS CENTER

Colgate University, Hamilton, New York. 1963-1966.

"Another art center by Rudolph unveiled." il., plans, sec.
    Progressive Architecture 45 (May 1964): 57.
"Campus porte cochere." il. Architectural Forum 124 (June
    1966): 64.
Charles A. Dana Creative Arts Center. Colgate University.
    Hamilton: Colgate University, n.d. il., plans. 10 p.

Chermayeff, Ivan. Observation of American Architecture.
    New York: Viking, 1972. il. (pt. col.), pp. 68-69.
"Chronological list of works by Paul Rudolph, 1946-1974."
    il., plan. Architecture and Urbanism 49 (January 1975):
    160.
"Colgate: creative arts center." il., plans, sec. Progressive
    Architecture 48 (February 1967): 114-121.
"Colgate: creativity can't be delegated." il., plans. Pro-
    gressive Architecture 46 (October 1965): 212.
"Colgate University, Hamilton, N.Y.: creative arts center."
    il., plan, sec. Architecture D'Aujourd'hui 39 (April 1968):
    26-27.
"Creative arts center." il., plan, sec. Architecture and
    Urbanism 80 (July 1977): 248-251.
"Implied spaces." il., plan. Architectural Review 142 (Sep-
    tember 1967): 171.
"Inside out." il. Time 87 (11 March 1966): 72.
Kemper, Alfred M. Drawings By American Architects. New
    York: Wiley, 1973. sec. p. 489.
"Preview: 73." il., plan, sec. Architectural and Engineering
    News 8 (December 1964): 65-67.
"Projet pour un theatre a Boston." il., plan, sec. Archi-
    tecture D'Aujourd'hui 35 (September-November 1965): 34.
Rudolph, Paul. The Architecture of Paul Rudolph. Intro-
    duction by Sibyl Moholy-Nagy. New York: Praeger,
    1970. il., plans, sec. pp. 166-173.
_____. Paul Rudolph. Introduction and notes by Rupert
    Spade. New York: Simon and Schuster, 1971. il., plan,
    sec. plates 63-71, pp. 126-127.
_____. Paul Rudolph, Dessins D'Architecture. Fribourg:
    Office du Livre, 1974. il., sec., elev. pp. 136-139.
"Rudolph designs for Colgate." il., plan, sec. Architecutral
    Record 135 (May 1964): 10.

APARTMENT BUILDING FOR BENEFICENT HOUSE

Weybosset Hill Housing, Providence, Rhode Island. 1963-1968.

"Chronological list of works by Paul Rudolph, 1946-1974." il.,
    plan. Architecture and Urbanism 49 (January 1975): 160.
Middleton, Robin. "Disintegration." il. Architectural Design
    37 (May 1967): 203-204.
"Paul Rudolf's elaborated spaces: six new projects." il.,
    plan. Architectural Record 139 (June 1966): 144-145.

Rudolph, Paul. The Architecture of Paul Rudolph. Introduction by Sibyl Moholy-Nagy. New York: Praeger,
1970. il. pp. 190-191.
_____. Paul Rudolph. Introduction and notes by Rupert
Spade. New York: Simon and Schuster, 1971. il. (pt.
col.), plan. plates 54-57, p. 126.

SYRACUSE CITY HALL

Syracuse, New York. Project, 1964. In association with
Ketcham-Miller-Arnold.

"Bowl-shaped civic plaza." il., sec. Architectural Forum 125
(November 1966): 84-85.
"Centre administratif d'etat de Massachusetts a Boston: Hotel
de ville, Syracuse, N.Y., etc." Architecture D'Aujourd'hui
35 (September 1965): 32-35.
"Chronological list of works by Paul Rudolph, 1946-1974."
il., plan. Architecture and Urbanism 49 (January 1975): 160.
"Hotel de ville de Syracuse, USA." il., plan, sec. Archi-
tecture D'Aujourd'hui 39 (December 1967): 30-31.
"Hotel de ville, Syracuse, N.Y." il., plan, sec. Archi-
tecture D'Aujourd'hui 35 (September-November 1965): 33.
Jacobs, David. "Rudolph style: unpredictable." il. New
York Times Magazine (26 March 1976): 47.
Kemper, Alfred M. Drawings By American Architects. New
York: Wiley, 1973. il. p. 487.
Rudolph, Paul. The Architecture of Paul Rudolph. Intro-
duction by Sibyl Moholy-Nagy. New York: Praeger,
1970. il., plan, sec., elev. pp. 108-113.
_____. Paul Rudolph, Dessins D'Architecture. Fribourg:
Office du Livre, 1974. il., plan, sec. pp. 142-155.
"Syracuse new city hall." il., plan. Architecture and Urban-
ism 80 (July 1977): 170-173.

JOHN W. CHORLEY ELEMENTARY SCHOOL

Middletown, New York. 1964-1969. In association with Peter
Barbonne.

"Chronological list of works by Paul Rudolph, 1946-1974."
il., plan. Architecture and Urbanism 49 (January 1975):
160.

Cook, John Wesley and Heinrich Klotz. Conversations With
  Architects. New York: Praeger, 1973. il. pp. 102-104.
"Ecole primaire à Middletown, N.Y." il., plan, sec. Archi-
  tecture D'Aujourd'hui 128 (October-November 1966): 8-9.
Gordon, Barclay F., ed. Interior Spaces Designed By Archi-
  tects. New York: McGraw-Hill, 1974. il., plan, sec.
  pp. 29-32.
"Implied spaces." il., sec. Architectural Review 142 (Septem-
  ber 1967): 171.
"John Chorley elementary school at Middletown, N.Y." il.,
  plan, sec. Architettura 15 (December 1969): 530-531.
"John W. Chorley elementary school." il., plan, sec. Archi-
  tecture and Urbanism 80 (July 1977): 252-255.
Middleton, Robin. "Disintegration." sec., elev. Architectural
  Design 37 (May 1967: 203-204.
"Paul Rudolph's elaborated spaces: six new projects." il.,
  plan, sec. Architectural Record 139 (June 1966): 148-
  150.
Rudolph, Paul. The Architecture of Paul Rudolph. Intro-
  duction by Sibyl Moholy-Nagy. New York: Praeger,
  1970. il., plan, sec. pp. 178-183.
_____. Paul Rudolph, Dessins D'Architecture. Fribourg:
  Office du Livre, 1974. sec. pp. 174-175.
"Rudolph." sec. Architects Journal 160 (4 September 1974):
  526-527.
"Site and program generate a new school shape." il. (pt.
  col.), plan, sec. Architectural Record 145 (May 1969):
  135-140.

INTERAMA PROJECT

Miami, Florida. Project, 1965.

"Chronological list of works by Paul Rudolph, 1946-1974."
  il., plan. Architecture and Urbanism 49 (January 1975):
  160.
"Interama." il., port. Progressive Architecture 48 (April
  1967): 55, 57.
"INTERAMA exposition hailed as full-scale experiment in urban
  design." il. Architectural Record 141 (March 1967): 40.
"International bazaar." il., plan. Architecture and Urbanism
  80 (July 1977): 174-175.
Rudolph, Paul. Paul Rudolph, Dessins D'Architecture.
  Fribourg: Office du Livre, 1974. il., sec. pp. 172-173.

CALLAHAN RESIDENCE

Birmingham, Alabama. 1965.

Abercrombie, Stanley. "Two-way relationship of drawings and design." il. American Institute of Architects. Journal 71 (September 1982): 68-69.
"Chronological list of works by Paul Rudolph, 1946-1974." il., plan. Architecture and Urbanism 49 (January 1975): 160.
Magnago Lampugnani, Vittorio. Architecture of the 20th Century in Drawings. New York: Rizzoli, 1982. il. p. 101.
Middleton, Robin. "Disintegration." il. Architectural Design 37 (May 1967): 203-204.
"Paul Rudolph's elaborated spaces: six new projects." il., plan, sec., elev. Architectural Record 139 (June 1966): 142-143.
"Projet pour une habitation." il., plan, sec. Architecture D'Aujourd'hui 35 (September-November 1965): 35.
Rudolph, Paul. The Architecture of Paul Rudolph. Introduction by Sibyl Moholy-Nagy. New York: Praeger, 1970. il., plans, sec. pp. 76-79.
_____. Paul Rudolph, Dessins D'Architecture. Fribourg: Office du Livre, 1974. il. pp. 36-37.

ART BUILDING

Manoa Campus of the University of Hawaii, Honolulu, Hawaii. Project, 1965.

"Chronological list of works by Paul Rudolph, 1946-1974." il., plan. Architecture and Urbanism 49 (January 1975): 161.
"New art building." il., plan, sec. Architecture and Urbanism 80 (July 1977): 256-259.
Rudolph, Paul. Paul Rudolph, Dessins D'Architecture. Fribourg: Office du Livre, 1974. il., sec. pp. 176-177.

EAST PAKISTAN AGRICULTURAL UNIVERSITY

Mymensingh, East Pakistan. Project, 1966.

"Chronological list of works by Paul Rudolph, 1946-1974."
   il., plan. Architecture and Urbanism 49 (January 1975):
   161.
Rudolph, Paul. The Architecture of Paul Rudolph. Introduction by Sibyl Moholy-Nagy. New York: Praeger,
   1970. il. p. 230.
_____. Paul Rudolph, Dessins D'Architecture. Fribourg:
   Office du Livre, 1974. il. pp. 178-179.

PAUL RUDOLPH'S OFFICE

58th Street, New York, New York. 1966.

"Chronological list of works by Paul Rudolph, 1946-1974."
   il. Architecture and Urbanism 49 (January 1975): 161.
"Paul Rudolph Office." il., sec. Architecture and Urbanism
   80 (July 1977): 178-179.
Rudolph, Paul. Paul Rudolph, Dessins D'Architecture.
   Fribourg: Office du Livre, 1974. il., sec. pp. 140-141.
"Rudolph's dare-devil office destroyed." il., plan, sec.,
   port. Progressive Architecture 50 (April 1969): 98-105.
Smith, C. Ray. Supermannerism: New Attitudes in Post-
   Modern Architecture. New York: Dutton, 1977. il.,
   sec. pp. 147-149.

RESORT COMMUNITY

Stafford Harbor, Virginia. Project, 1966.

"Chronological list of works by Paul Rudolph, 1946-1974."
   il. Architecture and Urbanism 49 (January 1977): 161.
Cook, John Wesley and Heinrich Klatz. Conversations With
   Architects. New York: Praeger, 1973. il. p. 91.
Jacobs, David. "The Rudolph style: unpredictable." il.
   New York Times Magazine (26 March 1967): 46-57.
Janke, Rolf. Architectural Models. New York: Architectural
   Book, 1978. il. p. 43.
Kemper, Alfred M. Drawings By American Architects. New
   York: Wiley, 1973. il. pp. 484-485.
Marlin, William. "Paul Rudolph: drawings." il. Architectural
   Forum 138 (June 1973): 48-49.
"Master plan for resort community." il. (pt. col.), plan.
   Architecture and Urbanism 80 (July 1977): 134, 300-305.

"New town that conserves the landscape." il., plan. Archi-
tectural Record 141 (April 1967):   151-158.
"Nouvelle ville de Stafford Harbor, Virginia." il., plan, map.
Architecture D'Aujourd'hui 132 (June-July 1967):   92-95.
Piene, Nan R. "Paul Rudolph designs a town." il., plan (pt.
col.). Art in America 55 (July-August 1967):   58-63.
"Portfolio: proposed trailer tower; Stafford Harbor, Va."
il., plan. Perspecta 11 (1967):   178-218.
"Rudolph." il. Architects Journal 160 (4 September 1974):
527.
_____. The Architecture of Paul Rudolph. Introduction
by Sibyl Moholy-Nagy. New York: Praeger, 1970. il.,
plan, sec. pp. 210-217.
_____. Paul Rudolph, Dessins D'Architecture. Fribourg:
Office du Livre, 1974. il., plan, elev. pp. 56-63.
Stern, Robert A. M. New Directions in American Architecture.
New York: Braziller, 1969. il. pp. 113-114.
"That's what a town is." il., plan, sec. Progressive Archi-
tecture 48 (April 1967):   188-191.
"Town planned on 5,000-acre site." il. New York Times (5
November 1967): VIII, 1: 2.

SID W. RICHARDSON PHYSICAL SCIENCES BUILDING

Texas Christian University, Fort Worth, Texas. 1966-1971.
In association with Preston M. Geren.

American Institute of Architects, Dallas Chapter. Dallasights:
An Anthology of Architecture and Open Spaces. Alan
R. Sumna, ed. Dallas: American Institute of Architects,
Dallas Chapter, 1978. il. pp. 171, 179.
"Chronological list of works by Paul Rudolph, 1946-1974."
il., plan. Architecture and Urbanism 49 (January 1975): 161.
"Eyes on Texas: Fort Worth." il. Interiors 131 (April 1972):
124-125.
Rudolph, Paul. Paul Rudolph, Dessins D'Architecture. Fri-
bourg: Office du Livre, 1974. sec., elev. pp. 180-181.
"Sid W. Richardson Physical Science Building, Texas Christian
University." il. (pt. col.), plan, sec., elev. (In Japan-
ese with English captions). Architecture and Urbanism 3
(June 1973):   21-28.
"Sid W. Richardson Physical Sciences Building." il. (pt. col.),
plan. Architecture and Urbanism 80 (July 1977):   131,
260-263.

Fig. 7: The Sid W. Richardson Physical Sciences Building on the campus of Texas Christian University

"Two projects by Paul Rudolph." il., plan, elev., sec. Architectural Record 151 (February 1972): 87-93.

MONTEITH COLLEGE CENTER

Wayne State University, Detroit, Michigan. Project, 1966.

"Chronological list of works by Paul Rudolph, 1946-1974."
il., plan. Architecture and Urbanism 49 (January 1975):
162.
"Monteith College Center." il., plan, sec., elev. Architecture
and Urbanism 80 (July 1977): 264-267.
Rudolph, Paul. The Architecture of Paul Rudolph. Introduction by Sibyl Moholy-Nagy. New York: Praeger, 1970.
il., sec. pp. 176-177.
_____. Paul Rudolph, Dessins D'Architecture. Fribourg:
Office du Livre, 1974. il. pp. 182-183.

ALEXANDER HIRSCH RESIDENCE

101 East 63rd Street, New York, New York. 1966-1967.

"Article on planned conversion by architect P. Rudolph of
run-down carriage house." il. New York Times (19
February 1967): VIII, 1: 7.
Chermayeff, Ivan. Observations on American Architecture.
New York: Viking, 1972. il. p. 89.
"Chronological list of works by Paul Rudolph, 1946-1974."
il., plan. Architecture and Urbanism 49 (January 1975):
162.
Futagawa, Yukio, ed. Global Interior: Houses in U.S.A., 1.
Tokyo: A.D.A. Edita, 1971. il., plan, sec. pp. 160-167.
Goldberger, Paul. The City Observed: New York. New
York: Random House, 1979. il. pp. 234-235.
"Hirsch residence." il., plan, sec. Architecture and Urbanism
80 (July 1977): 64-65.
Rudolph, Paul. The Architecture of Paul Rudolph. Introduc-
tion by Sibyl Moholy-Nagy. New York: Praeger, 1970.
il., plans, sec. pp. 80-83.
_____. Paul Rudolph, Dessins D'Architecture. Fribourg:
Office du Livre, 1974. plan, sec. pp. 40-41.
Smith, Herbert L. "Record houses of 1970." il. (pt. col.),
plan, sec., port. Architectural Record 147 (Mid-May 1970):

42-45.
_____, ed. 25 Years of Record Houses. New York:
McGraw-Hill, 1981. il. (pt. col.), plan, sec. pp. 26-29.
"Total townhouse." il. (pt. col.), plan, sec. House and
Garden 136 (November 1969): 122-127.

BROOKHOLLOW PLAZA

Dallas, Texas. 1966-1970. In association with Harwood I.
Smith and Partners.

American Institute of Architects, Dallas Chapter. Dallasights.
Dallas: American Institute of Architects, Dallas Chapter,
1978. il., map. pp. 33, 52.
"Brookhollow plaza office complex." il. (pt. col.), plan.
Architecture and Urbanism 80 (July 1977): 134, 180-183.
"Chronological list of works by Paul Rudolph, 1946-1974." il.,
plan. Architecture and Urbanism 49 (January 1975):
162.
Rudolph, Paul. The Architecture of Paul Rudolph. Intro-
duction by Sibyl Moholy-Nagy. New York: Praeger, 1970.
il., plan. pp. 224-225.
_____. Paul Rudolph, Dessins D'Architecture. Fribourg:
Office du Livre, 1974. il. pp. 184-185.
Schmertz, Mildred R., ed. Office Building Design. 2nd ed.
New York: McGraw-Hill, 1975. il., plan, sec., diag.
pp. 154-156.
Smith, G. E. Kidder. Architecture of the United States.
Garden City, N.Y.: Anchor, 1981, v. 1. il. p. 651.
Tomlinson, Doug. Dallas Architecture, 1936-1986. Austin:
Texas Monthly Press, 1985. il. pp. 114-115.
"Two projects by Paul Rudolph." il., plan, sec., diag. Ar-
chitectural Record 151 (February 1972): 94-96.

JOHN JAY PARK

New York, New York. Project, 1966.

"Chronological list of works by Paul Rudolph, 1946-1974." il.
Architecture and Urbanism 49 (January 1975): 162.
Rudolph, Paul. The Architecture of Paul Rudolph. Introduction by Sibyl Moholy-Nagy. New York: Praeger, 1970.
il. pp. 231.

Fig. 8: Office building at Brookhollow Plaza in Dallas, Texas

NORTHWEST NO. 1. URBAN RENEWAL AREA

Washington, D.C. 1966.

"Chronological list of works by Paul Rudolph, 1946-1974."
    il., plan. Architecture and Urbanism 49 (January 1975):
    162.
Stern, Robert A. M. New Directions in American Architecture.
    New York: Braziller, 1969. diag. pp. 37-38.
    _____. New Directions in American Architecture. Revised
    edition. New York: Braziller, 1977. il. pp. 37-38.
Wagner, Walter F. "House in the sky--with terrace--under
    221-D-3." il., plan, sec., elev. Architectural Record
    143 (June 1968): 160-163.

BETH EL SYNAGOGUE

Addition, New London, Connecticut. 1966-1971.

"Addition to Beth el Synagogue." il., sec. Architecture and
    Urbanism 80 (July 1977): 176-177.
"Chronological list of works by Paul Rudolph, 1946-1974."
    il., sec. Architecture and Urbanism 49 (January 1975):
    161.
Rudolph, Paul. Paul Rudolph, Dessins D'Architecture. Fri-
    bourg: Office du Livre, 1974. sec. pp. 186-187.

GRAPHIC ARTS CENTER

New York, New York. Project, 1967.

Banham, Reyner. Megastructure: Urban Futures of the Re-
    cent Past. London: Thames and Hudson, 1976. il. pp.
    12-13.
"Chronological list of works by Paul Rudolph, 1946-1974."
    il., plan. Architecture and Urbanism 49 (January 1975):
    163.
Cook, John Wesley. Conversations With Architects. New
    York: Praeger, 1973. il. pp. 108-112.
"Graphic Arts Center." il. (pt. col.), plan, sec., elev.
    Architecture and Urbanism 80 (July 1977): 15, 102-105.
"Hangende garten in New York." il., plan. Deutsche Bauzeit-
    ung 102 (April 1968): 229-234.

Herrera, Philip. "U.S. architecture: a progress report."
    il. Fortune 76 (1 September 1967): 126.
Janke, Rolf. Architectural Models. New York: Architectural
    Book Publishing, 1978. il. pp. 50-51.
"Paul Rudolph's Graphic Arts Center." il., plan. Architect-
    ural Record 143 (April 1968): 137-146.
"Progetto del graphic arts center a New York." il., plans.
    Architettura 14 (August 1968): 320-321.
Rudolph, Paul. The Architecture of Paul Rudolph. Intro-
    duction by Sibyl Moholy-Nagy. New York; Praeger, 1970.
    il., plans, sec. pp. 196-205.
    _____. Paul Rudolph, Dessins D'Architecture. Fribourg:
    Office du Livre, 1974. plan, sec., elev. pp. 66-69.
Scully, Vincent Joseph. American Architecture and Urbanism.
    New York: Praeger, 1969. il. pp. 146, 149.
Sky, Alison. Unbuilt America: Forgotten Architecture in the
    United States from Thomas Jefferson to the Space Age.
    New York: McGraw-Hill, 1976. il., sec. pp. 213-214.
Stern, Robert A. M. New Directions in American Architecture.
    New York: Braziller, 1969. il. pp. 38-40.
    _____. New Directions in American Architecture. Revised
    ed. New York: Braziller, 1977. il. pp. 38-41.

MARRIED STUDENT HOUSING

University of Virginia, Charlottesville, Virginia. Project,
    1967.

"Chronological list of works by Paul Rudolph, 1946-1974."
    il., plan. Architecture and Urbanism 49 (January 1975):
    163.
"Married student housing." il. sec. Architecture and Urban-
    ism 80 (July 1977): 106-107.
Rudolph, Paul. The Architecture of Paul Rudolph. Intro-
    duction by Sibyl Moholy-Nagy. New York: Praeger,
    1970. il., plan, sec. pp. 206-209.
    _____. Paul Rudolph, Dessins D'Architecture. Fribourg:
    Office du Livre, 1974. il., plan, sec., elev. pp. 70-73.
Stern, Robert A. M. New Directions in American Architecture.
    New York: Braziller, 1969. il. p. 36.
    _____. New Directions in American Architecture. Revised
    ed. New York: Braziller, 1977. il. p. 41.

LOWER MANHATTAN EXPRESSWAY

Project for Ford Fundation, New York, New York. Project,
  1967-1972.

Abercrombie, Stanley. "Two-way relationship of drawings
  and design." il. American Institute of Architects.
  Journal 71 (September 1982):   68-69.
"Chronological list of works by Paul Rudolph, 1946-1974."
  il. Architecture and Urbanism 49 (January 1975):   163.
"Franzen and Rudolph address evolving urban landscape."
  il. Interiors 136 (October 1976):   6.
Franzen, Ulrich and Paul Rudolph. The Evolving City: Urban
  Design Proposals. New York: Whitney Library of Design,
  1974. Text by Peter Wolf. il. (pt. col.), maps (pt. col.),
  sec. (pt. col.), diag. pp. 52-87.
Herrera, Philip. "U.S. architecture: a progress report."
  il. Fortune 76 (1 September 1967): 126.
"In the future, multi-layered cities." il. (pt. col.), sec.
  Domus 558 (May 1976): 19-23.
Marlin, William. "Paul Rudolph: drawings." sec. Architectural Forum 138 (June 1973): 50-51.
"Rudolph." sec. Architects Journal 160 (4 September 1974):
  527.
Rudolph, Paul. Paul Rudolph, Dessins D'Architecture. Fribourg: Office du Livre, 1974. il., sec. pp. 82-87.
"Study of the Lower Manhattan Expressway in the project
  'new forms of the evolving city.'" il. (pt. col.), plan,
  sec. Architecture and Urbanism 80 (July 1977): 136,
  306-311.
Yamashita, Tsukusa. "Recent works of Paul Rudolph." il.
  (pt. col.), map, sec., diag. Architecture and Urbanism
  49 (January 1975): 43, 121-132, 144-145.

FRANK PARCELLS RESIDENCE

3 Cameron Place, Grosse Pointe, Michigan. 1967-1971.

Andrews, Wayne. Architecture in Michigan. Detroit: Wayne
  State University, 1982. il. pp. 170-171.
"Chronological list of works by Paul Rudolph, 1946-1974." il.,
  plan. Architecture and Urbanism 49 (January 1975): 163.
Futagawa, Yukio, ed. Global Interior: Houses in U.S.A. 2

(6). Tokyo: A.D.A. Edita, 1974. il., plan, sec. pp.
104-109.
"Parcells residence." il., plan, sec. Architecture and Urban-
ism 80 (July 1977): 66-67.
"Paul Rudolph, Grosse Pointe, Michigan." il., plan. Global
Interior 6 (1974): 104-109.
Rudolph, Paul. Paul Rudolph, Dessins D'Architecture. Fri-
bourg: Office du Livre, 1974. sec., elev. p. 39.

ROBERT BROWN RESIDENCE

New York, New York. Project, 1967.

"Brown town house." il. Architecture and Urbanism 80 (July
1977): 68.
"Chronological list of works by Paul Rudolph, 1946-1974."
il. of sec. Architecture and Urbanism 49 (January 1975):
163.

NATHAN SHORE DENTAL OFFICES

New York, New York. Project, 1967.

"Chronological list of works by Paul Rudolph, 1946-1974."
plan. Architecture and Urbanism 49 (January 1975):
163.

TWO APARTMENT HOUSES

New York City Housing Authority, Bronx, New York. 1967.

"Chronological list of works by Paul Rudolph, 1946-1974."
il. Architecture and Urbanism 49 (January 1975): 164.
White, Norval. AIA Guide to New York City. Revised ed.
New York: Macmillan, 1978. il. p. 355.

FOX HILL DEVELOPMENT

DeMatteis Development Company, Staten Island, New York.
1967. In association with Jerrald, L. Karland.

"Chronological list of works by Paul Rudolph, 1946-1974."
    il., plan. <u>Architecture and Urbanism</u> 49 (January 1975):
    164.

PAUL RUDOLPH APARTMENT

New York, New York. 1967, 1977-1978.

"La casa di un architetto: the apartment of Paul Rudolph in
    New York." il. (pt. col.), plan. <u>Domus</u> 575 (October
    1977): 36-38.
Hoyt, Charles K. <u>Interior Spaces Designed by Architects</u>.
    2nd ed. New York: McGraw-Hill, 1981. il., plan, pp.
    16-17.
"Paul Rudolph, N.Y. Apartment, New York, N.Y., 1977-78."
    il. (pt. col.), plan. <u>Global Architecture Houses</u> 6 (1979):
    88-89.
"Paul Rudolph, Paul Rudolph apartment, New York City,
    U.S.A." il., plan. <u>Global Architecture Houses</u> 5 (1978):
    106-109.
Progner, Jean W. "Kinetic electric environment." il. <u>Pro-</u>
    <u>gressive Architecture</u> 49 (October 1968): 198-206.
"Record interiors of 1978." il. (pt. col.), plan. <u>Architectural</u>
    <u>Record</u> 163 (January 1978): cover, 77-79.
Smith, C. Ray. "Designers: floating platforms." il. (pt.
    col.). <u>Progressive Architecture</u> 48 (May 1967): 149-151.
"White-on-white, its optical surprises." col. il. <u>House Beau-</u>
    <u>tiful</u> 109 (September 1967): 148-149.

TRACEY TOWERS

DeMatteis Development Company, 20 and 40 West Mosholu Park-
    way, Bronx, New York. 1967-1974.

"Chronological list of works by Paul Rudolph, 1946-1974."
    il., plan. <u>Architecture and Urbanism</u> 49 (January 1975):
    162.
Cook, John Wesley. <u>Conversations With Architects</u>. New York:
    Praeger, 1973. il. pp. 119-121.
"Drawings and sketches of Paul Rudolph." col. il. <u>Archi-</u>
    <u>tecture and Urbanism</u> 49 (January 1975): 144.
Rudolph, Paul. <u>The Architecture of Paul Rudolph</u>. Intro-
    duction by Sibyl Moholy-Nagy. New York: Praeger, 1970.

il., plans. pp. 220-223.
"Tracey Towers; wider design vocabulary for high-rise housing." il., plans. Architectural Record 145 (January
1969): 100-101.

ORIENTAL MASONIC GARDENS

50 Wilmot Road, New Haven, Connecticut. 1968-1971.

"La Brique du 20e siècle." il., plan. Techniques et Archi-
tecture 33 (February 1971): 9.
"Chronological list of works by Paul Rudolph, 1946-1974."
il., plan. Architecture and Urbanism 49 (January 1975):
164.
Cook, John Wesley and Heinrich Klatz. Conversations With
Architects. New York: Praeger, 1973. il. p. 112.
Kendig, Frank. "Facelift for mobile homes?" il., plan, diag.
Design and Environment 3 (Spring 1972): 42-51, 62.
Mackay, David. Multiple Family Housing: From Aggregation
to Integration. New York: Architectural Book, 1977.
(Text in English and German). il., plans. pp. 98-101.
"Modular apartments in New Haven." il. Architectural Record
150 (October 1971): 41.
"Modular development." il. Architectural Forum 133 (Septem-
ber 1970): 7.
Metz, Don. New Architecture in New Haven. Revised ed.
Cambridge: M.I.T., 1973. il., plan. pp. 80-81.
"Oriental Masonic Gardens housing." il. (pt. col.), plan.
Architecture and Urbanism 80 (July 1977): 13, 110-113.
Reif, Rita. "Thanks to prefabs, out of the slums and into
their own co-ops." il. New York Times (11 February
1972), I, 18: 1.
Rudolph, Paul. The Architecture of Paul Rudolph. New York:
Praeger, 1970. il., plans, pp. 218-219.
_____. Paul Rudolph, Dessins D'Architecture. Fribourg:
Office du Livre, 1974. il., plan. pp. 74-75.
"Rudolph's Oriental Gardens headed for demolition." il. Pro-
gressive Architecture 62 (January 1981): 44.
Thompson, Elisabeth K. "Apartments." il., plan, map. Ar-
chitectural Record 148 (September 1970): 143, 148-149.
"Twentieth century bricks." il., plan. Architectural Forum
136 (June 1972): 48-51.
Whitehouse, Franklin. "Modular co-ops for New Haven." il.
New York Times (31 August 1969), VIII, 1: 1+.

"Wohnquartier in New Haven, Connecticut." il., plan. Baumeister 69 (May 1972): 532, 534.

SPORTS STADIUM

Damman, Saudi Arabia. Project, 1968.

"Chronological list of works by Paul Rudolph, 1946-1974."
il., plan. Architecture and Urbanism 49 (January 1975):
164.
"Fit for a king; a stadium for Saudi Arabia." il., plan, diag.
Progressive Architecture 51 (May 1970): 104-107.
Janke, Rolf. Architectural Models. New York: Architectural
Book, 1978. il. p. 58.
Rudolph, Paul. The Architecture of Paul Rudolph. Intro-
duction by Sibyl Moholy-Nagy. New York: Praeger, 1970.
il. pp. 234-236.
_____. Paul Rudolph, Dessins D'Architecture. Fribourg:
Office du Livre, 1974. plan, sec. pp. 188-189.
"Stadium." il., plan, sec. Architecture and Urbanism 80
(July 1977): 188-191.
"Stadium, Damman, Saudi Arabia." il., plan. Architectural
Design 41 (February 1971): 110.

MAGNOLIA MOBILE HOME UNITS

Vicksburg, Mississippi. 1968.

Scully, Vincent. American Architecture and Urbanism. New
York: Praeger, 1969. il. pp. 14-15.

GOVERNMENT CENTER

New Haven, Connecticut. 1968-1972.

Davern, Jeanne M., ed. Architecture 1970-1980: A Decade
of Change. New York: McGraw-Hill, 1980. il. pp.
232-233.
Rudolph, Paul. Paul Rudolph, Dessins D'Architecture. Fribourg: Office du Livre, 1974. il. pp. 170-171.

FORT LINCOLN HOUSING

Washington, D.C. Project, 1968.

"Building-block houses." col. port. Life 65 (18 October 1968): 98-102.
"Chronological list of works by Paul Rudolph, 1946-1974."
 il., plan. Architecture and Urbanism 49 (January 1975): 164.
"Fort Lincoln housing." il., plan. Architecture and Urbanism 80 (July 1977): 114-115.
Rudolph, Paul. The Architecture of Paul Rudolph. Introduction by Sibyl Moholy-Nagy. New York: Praeger, 1970. il., plans. pp. 226-229.
_____. Paul Rudolph, Dessins D'Architecture. Fribourg: Office du Livre, 1974. il. pp. 76-79.

HERBERT GREEN RESIDENCE

Cherry Ridge, Pennsylvania. 1968.

"Chronological list of works by Paul Rudolph, 1946-1974."
 il., plan. Architecture and Urbanism 49 (January 1975): 165.
"Green residence." il. (pt. col.), plan, sec. Architecture and Urbanism 80 (July 1977): 10, 69-71.
"Paul Rudolph, Cherry Ridge, Pennsylvania." il. (pt. col.), plan. Global Interior 6 (1974): 96-103.
Stephens, Suzanne. "Standing by the twentieth century brick." il. (pt. col.), plan, sec. Progressive Architecture 55 (October 1974): 78-83. Reply by Jack B. Douthitt, "Architecture or industrialization?" Progressive Architecture 56 (January 1975): 6, 12.
Yamashita, Tsukasa. "Recent works of Paul Rudolph." il. (pt. col.), plan, sec., diag. Architecture and Urbanism 49 (January 1975): 42, 105-113.

FIRST AND SECOND CHURCH

64 Marlborough Street, Boston, Massachusetts. 1968. 1972.

Boston Society of Architects. Architecture Boston. Barre,

Mass.: Barre, 1976. il. pp. 67-68.
"Chronological list of works by Paul Rudolph, 1946-1974."
    il., plan. Architecture and Urbanism 49 (January 1975):
    164.
"First and second church in Boston: rebirth in back bay."
    il. (pt. col.), plans, sec. Progressive Architecture 54
    (December 1973): 44-49.
Lyndon, Donlyn. The City Observed: Boston. A Guide to
    the Architecture of the Hub. New York: Random House,
    1982. il. pp. 125-126.
Murphy, James A. "Rebirth in back bay." il. (pt. col.),
    plan, sec. Progressive Architecture 54 (December 1973):
    44-49.
Yamashita, Tsukasa. "Recent works of Paul Rudolph." il.
    (pt. col.), plan, sec. Architecture and Urbanism 49
    (January 1975): 39, 77-82, 142.

HARRY RAICH RESIDENCE

Quogue, New York. Project, 1969.

"Chronological list of works by Paul Rudolph, 1946-1974."
    il. Architecture and Urbanism 49 (January 1975): 165.
"Raich residence." il. Architecture and Urbanism 80 (July
    1977): 72.
Rudolph, Paul. The Architecture of Paul Rudolph. Intro-
    duction by Sibyl Moholy-Nagy. New York: Praeger,
    1970. il. p. 231.

BURROUGHS WELLCOME COMPANY

Research Triangle Park, North Carolina. 1969-1972.

"Burroughs Wellcome & Co. building." il., plan, sec. Archi-
    tecture and Urbanism 80 (July 1977): 196-201.
"Burroughs Wellcome Co. building." il., plan, sec., port.
    Architecture and Urbanism 3 (April 1973): 23-30.
"Chronological list of works by Paul Rudolph, 1946-1974." il.,
    plan. Architecture and Urbanism 49 (January 1975): 165.
Davern, Jeanne M., ed. Architecture 1970-1980: A Decade of
    Change. New York: McGraw-Hill, 1980. il., sec. pp.
    60-62.

"Drawings and sketches of Paul Rudolph." col. il. Archi-
tecture and Urbanism 49 (January 1975): 142.
Gordon, Barclay F., ed. Interior Spaces Designed by Archi-
tects. New York: McGraw-Hill, 1974. il., plan, sec.
pp. 88-90.
Kemper, Alfred M. Drawings by American Architects. New
York: Wiley, 1973. il. p. 486.
Molitor, Joseph W. Architectural Photography. New York:
Wiley, 1976. il. (pt. col.). pp. 44, 53, 75.
Rudolph, Paul. The Architecture of Paul Rudolph. Intro-
duction by Sibyl Moholy-Nagy. New York: Praeger, 1970.
il. p. 233.
_____. Paul Rudolph, Dessins D'Architecture. Fribourg:
Office du Livre, 1974. il., plan, sec. pp. 190-193.
Schmertz, Mildred F., ed. Office Building Design. 2nd ed.
New York: McGraw-Hill, 1975. il., plan, sec. pp. 79-84.
_____. "Paul Rudolph: work in progress." il., plan,
sec. Architectural Record 148 (November 1970): 92-95.
Smith, G. E. Kidder. A Pictorial History of Architecture in
America. New York: American Heritage, 1976. il. pp.
412-415.
"Ventidue gradi e mezzo." il., plan, sec. Architettura 18
(December 1972): 524-525.

EARL W. BRYDGES LIBRARY

1425 Main Street, Niagara Falls, New York. 1969-1974.

"A building which opens its arms." il., plans. Domus 557
(April 1976): 25-27.
"Chronological list of works by Paul Rudolph, 1946-1974."
il., sec. Architecture and Urbanism 49 (January 1975):
165.
"Earl W. Brydges Library." il., plan, sec. Architecture
and Urbanism 80 (July 1977): 192-195.
"Progetto della biblioteca centrale alle Niagara Falls, New
York." il. Architettura 17 (November 1971): 461.
"Public library for the city of Niagara Falls." il. (pt. col.),
plans. Architectural Record 157 (June 1975): 96-100.
Roth, Leland M. A Concise History of American Architecture.
New York: Harper & Row, 1979. il. pp. 336-337.
Rudolph, Paul. The Architecture of Paul Rudolph. Intro-
duction by Sibyl Moholy-Nagy. New York: Praeger, 1970.
il., sec. p. 232.

_____. Paul Rudolph, Dessins D'Architecture. Fribourg:
    Office du Livre, 1974. il., sec. pp. 194-197.
Schmertz, Mildred F. "Paul Rudolph: work in progress."
    il., plan, sec. Architectural Record 148 (November 1970):
    89-91.
Smith, G. E. Kidder. The Architecture of the United States.
    Garden City, N.Y.: Anchor, 1981, v. 1. il. pp. 445-
    446.
_____. A Pictorial History of Architecture in America.
    New York: American Heritage, 1976. il. p. 250.
Yamashita, Tsukasa. "Recent works of Paul Rudolph." il.
    (pt. col.), plan, map, sec. Architecture and Urbanism
    49 (January 1975): 38, 65-76.

BUFFALO WATERFRONT AND SHORELINE APARTMENTS

New York State Urban Development Corp., Buffalo, New York.
    1969-1977.

Buffalo Architecture: A Guide. Cambridge: M.I.T., 1981.
    il. p. 60.
"Buffalo waterfront housing." il. (pt. col.), plans. Archi-
    tecture and Urbanism 80 (July 1977): 14, 116-123.
"Buffalo waterfront project." il. (pt. col.): plans. Archi-
    tectural Record 152 (September 1972): 146-149.
"Chronological list of works by Paul Rudolph, 1946-1974."
    il., plan. Architecture and Urbanism 49 (January 1975):
    165.
Davern, Jeanne M., ed. Architecture 1970-1980: A Decade
    of Change. New York: McGraw-Hill, 1980. il. pp. 16-
    17, 64-65.
Macsai, John. Housing. 2nd ed. New York: John Wiley,
    1982. il., plans. pp. 524-525.
Marlin, William. "Paul Rudolph: drawings." il. Architectural
    Forum 138 (June 1973): 51.
"New York's urban housing program displays its innovative
    plans." il., plan. House and Home 38 (November 1970):
    28.
Rudolph, Paul. Paul Rudolph, Dessins D'Architecture. Fri-
    bourg: Office du Livre, 1974. il. pp. 64-65.
Schmertz, Mildred F. "Paul Rudolph: work in progress."
    il., plan, map. Architectural Record 148 (November 1970):
    96-100.

Smith, G. E. Kidder. The Architecture of the United States,
    v.1. Garden City, N.Y.: Anchor, 1981. il. pp. 421-
    422.
Yamashita, Tsukasa. "Recent works of Paul Rudolph." il.
    (pt. col.), plan, map. Architecture and Urbanism 49
    (January 1975): 41, 87-101, 143.

RICHARD PISTELL RESIDENCE

Lyford Cay, Nassau, Bahamas. 1969.

"Chronological list of works by Paul Rudolph, 1946-1974."
    il., plan. Architecture and Urbanism 49 (January 1975):
    166.
"Pistell residence." il., plan, sec. Architecture and Urbanism
    80 (July 1977): 73-75.

NATURAL SCIENCE BUILDING

State University of New York, Purchase, New York. 1969.

"Academic village: state university college, Purchase, N.Y.;
    natural science building." plan. Architectural Forum
    133 (November 1970): 38.
Yamashita, Tsukasa. "Recent works of Paul Rudolph." col.
    il. Architecture and Urbanism 49 (January 1975): 44.

MAURICE DEANE RESIDENCE

Great Neck, New York. 1970.

"Chronological list of works by Paul Rudolph, 1946-1974."
    il., plan. Architecture and Urbanism 49 (January 1975):
    166.
"Deane residence." il. (pt. col.), plan, sec. Architecture
    and Urbanism 80 (July 1977): 11, 76-77.
Israel, Frank. "Architecture: Paul Rudolph." col. il.
    Architectural Digest 35 (June 1978): 90-99.
Marlin, William. "Paul Rudolph: drawings." sec., port.
    Architectural Forum 138 (June 1973): 52-53.
"Paul Rudolph; private residence, New York, U.S.A. 1970-74."

il. (pt. col.), plan. Global Architecture Houses 1 (1976): 78-85.
"Paul Rudolph's dramatic design for a site facing Long Island Sound." il., plan, sec. Architectural Record 159 (Mid-May 1976): 68-71.
Rudolph, Paul. Paul Rudolph, Dessins D'Architecture. Fribourg: Office du Livre, 1974. plan, sec., elev. pp. 42-43.
"Selearchitettura." il., plan, sec. Architettura 22 (November 1976): 392-393.

725 UNITS OF PUBLIC HOUSING

New York State Urban Development Corp., New York, New York. Project, 1970.

"Chronological list of works by Paul Rudolph, 1946-1974." il. Architecture and Urbanism 49 (January 1975): 166.

TEN APARTMENT TOWERS

DeMatteis Development Company, Kew Gardens, New York. Project, 1970.

"Chronological list of works by Paul Rudolph, 1946-1974." il. Architecture and Urbanism 49 (January 1975): 166.

ROCKFORD CIVIC CENTER

Rockford, Illinois. Project, 1970.

"Chronological list of works by Paul Rudolph, 1946-1974." il., plan. Architecture and Urbanism 49 (January 1975): 166.
"Drawings and sketches of Paul Rudolph." col. plan. Architecture and Urbanism 49 (January 1975): 143.
Janke, Rolf. Architectural Models. New York: Architectural Book, 1978. il. p. 113.
Marlin, William. "Paul Rudolph: drawings." il. Architectural Forum 138 (June 1973): 46-47.
"Non costruito; Rudolph unbuilt." il. (pt. col.), plan, sec. Domus 536 (July 1974): 15-16.

"Rockford Center." il., plan, sec. Architecture and Urbanism 80 (July 1977): 202-205.
Rudolph, Paul. Paul Rudolph, Dessins D'Architecture. Fribourg: Office du Livre, 1974. il. pp. 198-199.

SUFFOLK OFFICE PARK

Hauppauge, Long Island, New York. 1970.

"Architect P. Rudolph planning to build office complex in Hauppauge, LI, with underground garage." il. New York Times (31 January 1971): VIII, 1: 1.
"Chronological list of works by Paul Rudolph, 1946-1974." il., plan. Architecture and Urbanism 49 (January 1975): 166.
"Office complex, Haupauge, Long Island, N.Y." il. Architectural Record 149 (May 1971): 43.

SID R. BASS RESIDENCE

Fort Worth, Texas. 1970-1972.

American Institute of Architects, Dallas Chapter. Dallasights. Dallas: American Institute of Architects, Dallas Chapter, 1978. il., map. pp. 171-178.
"Bass residence." il., plan. Architecture and Urbanism 80 (July 1977): 78-79.
"Chronological list of works by Paul Rudolph, 1946-1974." il., plan. Architecture and Urbanism 49 (January 1975): 166.
"I Rudolph." il. Architect's Journal 160 (4 September 1974): 526.
Rudolph, Paul. Paul Rudolph, Dessins D'Architecture. Fribourg: Office du Livre, 1974. il., sec. pp. 44-47.

JOHN M. SHUEY RESIDENCE

Bloomfield Hills, Michigan. Project, 1970.

"Chronological list of works by Paul Rudolph, 1946-1974." il., plan. Architecture and Urbanism 49 (January 1975): 166.

Janke, Rolf. Architectural Models. New York: Architectural
     Book Publishing, 1978. il. p. 61.
"Non costruito: Rudolph unbuilt." il., plan. Domus 536
     (July 1974): 17.
"Shuey residence." il., plan. Architecture and Urbanism
     80 (July 1977): 81.

MAURITS EDERSHEIM RESIDENCE

New York, New York. 1970.

"Chronological list of works by Paul Rudolph, 1946-1974."
     il., plan. Architecture and Urbanism 49 (January 1975):
     166.
"Edersheim apartment." il. (pt. col.), plan. Architecture
     and Urbanism 80 (July 1977): 12, 80.
Futagawa, Yukio. "Rudolph Apartment." il. (pt. col.), plan.
     Global Interior 5 (1973): 132-139.

URBAN COMPLEX FOR FAKHRI BROTHERS

Beirut, Lebanon. Project, 1971. In association with Samir
     H. Khairallah.

"Chronological list of works by Paul Rudolph, 1946-1974."
     il., plan. Architecture and Urbanism 49 (January 1975):
     166.
Rudolph, Paul. Paul Rudolph, Dessins D'Architecture. Fri-
     bourg: Office du Livre, 1974. il., elev. pp. 80-81.
"Urban complex in Beirut." il., plan. Architecture and Ur-
     banism 80 (July 1977): 315.

BERT DWECK RESIDENCE

Deal, New Jersey. 1971.

"Chronological list of works by Paul Rudolph, 1946-1974."
     il. Architecture and Urbanism 49 (January 1975): 166.
"Dweck residence." il. Architecture and Urbanism 80 (July
     1977): 82.

INTERNATIONAL HEADQUARTERS

First National Church of Exquisite Panic, 251 West 13th Street,
New York, New York. 1971 alteration. Built in 1887 by
Richard Morris Hunt.

White, Norval. AIA Guide to New York City. Rev. ed. New
York: Macmillan, 1978. il. p. 90.

DOROTHEA ELMAM APARTMENT

New York, New York. 1971.

"Interni a New York." col. il. Domus 502 (September 1971):
31-33.
"Designed by Paul Rudolph, New York." col. il., plan.
Global Interior 5 (1973): 130-133.
Smith, C. Ray. "Rural pop at Aston Magna." col. il. In-
teriors 134 (October 1974): 114R-115R, 134R.

DAIEI HOUSE BUILDING

Nagoya, Japan. 1971. In association with Tsukasa Yamashita.

"Chronological list of works by Paul Rudolph, 1946-1974."
il., plan. Architecture and Urbanism 49 (January 1975):
166.
"Daiei building." il., plan, sec. Architecture and Urbanism
80 (July 1977): 206-213.
"Daiei building, Nagoya." il. (pt. col.), plan, sec. Japan
Architect 49 (February 1974): 73-82.
"Recent work of Paul Rudolph--Daiei House building." il.
(pt. col.), port. Architecture and Urbanism 3 (December
1973): 5-6.
Rudolph, Paul. Paul Rudolph, Dessins D'Architecture. Fribourg: Office du Livre, 1974. il., sec. pp. 200-202.
_____. "Spatial considerations in the Daiei building." il.,
plan, sec. (In Japanese and English). Architecture and
Urbanism 3 (December 1973): 7-22.
Yamashita, Tsukasa. "From conception to final plan." il.
(pt. col.), plan, sec. Architecture and Urbanism 3 (December 1973): 23-28.

_____. "Its position and its background." il., plan, sec.
Architecture and Urbanism 3 (December 1973): 29.

LOUIS MICHEELS RESIDENCE

Westport, Connecticut. 1972.

"Chronological list of works by Paul Rudolph, 1946-1974." il.,
    plan. Architecture and Urbanism 49 (January 1975): 168.
"Micheels residence." il. (pt. col.), plan. Architecture and
    Urbanism 80 (July 1977): 11, 83-85.
Morton, David. "Rudolph." il. (pt. col.), plan. Progressive
    Architecture 57 (August 1976): 54-57.
"Residence près de Long Island." il., plan. Architecture
    D'Aujourd'hui 188 (December 1976): xxxi.
"Paul Rudolph; private residence, Connecticut, U.S.A. 1972-
    74." il. (pt. col.), plan. Global Architecture Houses
    1 (1976): 86-91.
Yamashita, Tsukasa. "Recent works of Paul Rudolph." il.,
    plan, sec., diag. Architecture and Urbanism 49 (January
    1975): 114-120.

JOHN PILLSBURY RESIDENCE

Cannes, France. 1972.

"Drawings and sketches of Paul Rudolph." col. sec. Archi-
    tecture and Urbanism 49 (January 1975): 143.

OFFICE BUILDING

For En Trecanales Y Tavora, Madrid, Spain. 1972.

"Chronological list of works by Paul Rudolph, 1946-1974."
    il. Architecture and Urbanism 49 (January 1975): 168.
Yamashita, Tsukasa. "Recent works of Paul Rudolph." il.
    (pt. col.), elev. Architecture and Urbanism 49 (January
    1975): cover, 40, 83-86.

STATEN ISLAND COMMUNITY COLLEGE

Staten Island, New York. 1972.

"Chronological list of works by Paul Rudolph, 1946-1974."
    il., plan. Architecture and Urbanism 49 (January 1975):
    168.
"Drawings and sketches of Paul Rudolph." col. plan, sec.
    Architecture and Urbanism 49 (January 1975): 142-143.

EAST NORTHPORT JEWISH CENTER

East Northport, New York. Project, 1973.

"Chronological list of works by Paul Rudolph, 1946-1974."
    il. Architecture and Urbanism 49 (January 1975): 169.
"Jewish center." il. New York Times (8 July 1973) 82: 1.

HOUSING FOR TWO HUNDRED STUDENTS

Davidson College, Davidson, North Carolina. Project, 1973.

"Chronological list of works by Paul Rudolph, 1946-1974."
    il. Architecture and Urbanism 49 (January 1975): 169.

3500 DWELLING UNITS

Carol Housing Corporation, Miami, Florida. Project, 1973.

"Chronological list of works by Paul Rudolph, 1946-1974." il.
    Architecture and Urbanism 49 (January 1975): 168.
Yamashita, Tsukasa. "Recent works of Paul Rudolph." il.,
    map. Architecture and Urbanism 49 (January 1975): 102-
    104, 142.

JOANNA STEICHEN RESIDENCE

New York, New York. 1973-1974.

"Paul Rudolph; Joanna Steichen apartment, New York City,
    U.S.A. 1973-74." il. (pt. col.), plan, elev. Global Ar-
    chitecture Houses 5 (December 1978): 100-105.
Schmertz, Mildred F. "Remodeling a small New York City
    apartment." il., plan, sec. Architectural Record 158
    (August 1975): 74-75.

MODULAR HOUSING EXHIBITION

Project, 1973.

"Chronological list of works by Paul Rudolph, 1946-1974."
    il. Architecture and Urbanism 49 (January 1975): 168.

APARTMENT HOTEL

Pan-Lon Engineering and Construction Co., Jerusalem, Israel.
    Project, 1974.

"Chronological list of works by Paul Rudolph, 1946-1974."
    il. Architecture and Urbanism 49 (January 1975): 169.

HOUSING, MORGAN ANNEX

New York State Urban Development Corp., New York, New
    York. Project, 1974.

"Chronological list of works by Paul Rudolph, 1946-1974."
    il. Architecture and Urbanism 49 (January 1975): 169.

WILLIAM R. CANNON CHAPEL

Emory University, Atlanta, Georgia. 1975.

Anderson, Grace. "Rudolph's chapel forms a quiet quadrangle."
    col. il., plan, map. sec. Architectural Record 170 (July
    1982): 94-101.
"Manierismo Rudolphiano." il., plan, sec. Architettura 28
    (December 1982): 852-853.
"William R. Cannon Chapel, Emory University." il. (pt. col.),
    plan, map, sec., elev. Architecture and Urbanism 152
    (May 1983): 40-49.

ROBERT BERNHARD RESIDENCE

Addition. Greenwich, Connecticut. 1976-1978.

"Paul Rudolph." il (pt. col.), plan. Global Architecture
    Houses 6 (1979): 84-87.

CITY CENTER

Fort Worth, Texas.   1979-1983.   In association with 3D/International.

"Clustered columns play hide-and-seek." il. (pt. col.), plan, diags. Architectural Record 170 (July 1982):   124-127.
"Multi-use complex underway in downtown Fort Worth." il. Texas Architect 30 (May-June 1980):   19.
"Paul Rudolph, the City Center." il. (pt. col.), plan, sec., elev. Global Architecture Document 7 (August 1983): 90-99.
Schmertz, Mildred F. "From object to space: an interview with Paul Rudolph." col. il., plan, sec. Architectural Record 173 (June 1985):   156-161.

OXLEY RISE CONDOMINIUM HOUSING

For Hong Fok Investment Holding Col, Ltd., Singapore.   1981.

Charlottesville Tapes. New York: Rizzoli, 1985. il., port. pp. 84-91.
"Lo spazio e come l'acqua in movimento." il. Architettura 30 (April 1984):   281.

URBAN LANDSCAPE

Project, 1983.

Irace, Fulvio. "Storie di ordinaria follia/follies." il. Domus 644 (November 1983):   29.

EXHIBITIONS AND AWARDS

"Architects panel selects 16 best buildings for 1964." il.
Architectural Forum 121 (July 1964): 9.

"Architecture: 48 drawings by Paul Rudolph on view." il.
New York Times (24 February 1986): 15; 1.

"Awards." port. Architectural Forum 108 (June 1958): 33.

"Barrows and Rudolph share Elsie de Wolfe Awards." port.
Contract Interiors 137 (August 1977): 8.

"Current works of Roche, Rudolph and Johnson on view:
Museum of Modern Art, New York; exhibit." il. Progressive Architecture 51 (October 1970): 27.

"Custom house winners of the 1959 Homes for Better Living
Awards." il., plan. House and Home 15 (June 1959):
120-121, 124-126.

"Family of man, exhibition installation at Museum of Modern
Art, by Paul Rudolph." il., plan, diags. Interiors
(April 1955): 114-117.

"First design award house Siesta Key, Fla." il., plans, sec.
Progressive Architecture 36 (January 1955): 65-67.

Huxtable, Ada Louise. "Creations of 3 top architects shown."
il. New York Times (30 September 1970): I, 38; 1.

"I nuovi faraoni d'America." il. Casabella 358 (November
1971): 11.

"Johnson, Roche, Rudolph and Lapidus subjects of two exhi-
bitions." il. Architecture Record 148 (November 1970):
37.

"P/A design awards, house by R. Rudolph wins." il., plan,
sec. Interiors 114 (March 1955): 16.

"Paul Rudolph awarded Brunner Memorial Prize in Architecture." port. Architectural Forum 108 (June 1958):
33.

"P. Rudolph wins Arts and Letters Inst. prize." port. New
York Times (23 April 1958) 37: 7 and (22 May 1958) 31:
6.

"Paul Rudolph elected National Arts and Letters Institute member." New York Times (19 February 1971) 25: 1.

"Paul Rudolph professeur à Yale." Architecture D'Aujourd'hui
29 (April 1958): v.

"Record names five architects to new panel of editorial con-
sultants." port. Architecture Record 131 (May 1962):
12.

"Regionalism and the South: excerpts." American Institute
of Architects. Journal 23 (April 1955): 179-180.

"Regionalism in architecture." Perspecta 4 (1957): 12-19.

"Rudolph to leave Yale." port. Progressive Architecture 45
(October 1964): 93.

"Work in progress by three top architects at New York's
MOMA." il., port. Interiors 130 (November 1970): 61.

"Work in retrospect: work in progress--architecture by Philip
Johnson, Kevin Roche, Paul Rudolph at the Museum of
Modern Art." il. Architecture Forum 133 (November
1970): 63.

BIOGRAPHY, PHILOSOPHY, WRITINGS, CRITIQUES AND PORTRAITS

"Architect P. Rudolph resigns contract for new high school." New York Times (1 February 1967) 41:5.

Albrecht, Johann. "Conversation with Paul Rudolph: December 9, 1983." port. Reflections 2 (Fall 1984): 70-77.

Bourne, Russell. "Yale's Paul Rudolph." il., port. Architectural Forum 108 (April 1958): 128-129, 192.

"Bright new arrival." il., port. Time 75 (1 February 1960): 60-63.

Chapman, Priscilla. "But does it work?" Sunday Times Magazine (1 August 1965): 16-21.

Charlottesville Tapes. New York: Rizzoli, 1985. il., port. Presentation of one of his works and criticisms of works by others.

Collins, Peter. "Whither Paul Rudolph?" il., port. Progressive Architecture 42 (August 1961): 130-133.

Cook, John Wesley and Heinrich Klatz. Conversations With Architects. New York: Praeger, 1973. il., plan, port., sec. pp. 178-217.

Davern, Jeanne M. "Conversation with Paul Rudolph." col. il., port. Architectural Record 170 (March 1982): 90-97.
"Dr. Danes named dean, P. Rudolph architecture department chairman at Architecture and Design School." New York Times (12 June 1957) 29: 6.

"Genetrix: personal contributions to American architecture." il., port. Architectural Review 121 (May 1957): 378-380.

Hollander, Jord den. "Surprising symbolism and multiplicity
    of form in the latest American architecture." il. Architect
    (The Hague) 11 (February 1980):   36-42.

Jencks, Charles. Modern Movements in Architecture. Garden
    City, N.Y.: Anchor, 1973. pp. 189-190.

Jacobs, David. "Rudolph style: unpredictable." il., port.
    New York Times Magazine (26 March 1967):   46-57.

Jones, Cranston. "Views compared by leading architects."
    il. Architectural Forum 105 (September 1956):   146-149,
    168-176.

Litchfield, Electus D. "Florida conversion." Architectural
    Forum 88 (February 1948): 20.

McCallum, Ian. Architecture USA. New York: Reinhold,
    1959. il., port. pp. 197-203.

McQuade, Walter. "Architects: a chance for greatness."
    port. Fortune 73 (January 1966): 151, 157-158.

"Names to remember." port. Vogue 127 (1 May 1956): 116-
    117.

"Nineteen questions to Paul Rudolph." port. Architecture
    and Urbanism 5 (January 1975): 133-140.

"Paul Rudolph." il., port. Japan Architect 45 (July 1970):
    73.

"People." Interiors 117 (September 1957): 205.

"Personalities." port. Progressive Architecture 41 (August
    1960): 59.

Pevsner, Nikolaus. "At the inauguration of the new Art and
    Architecture Building of Yale University." il. Society of
    Architectural Historians. Journal 26 (March 1967): 4-7.

"Portrait." port. Architectural Forum 86 (April 1947): 47.

"Portrait." port. Architectural Forum 89 (October 1948): 44.

"Portrait." port. Architectural Forum 92 (April 1950): 78.

"Portrait." port. Architectural Record 122 (July 1957): 24.

"Portrait." port. Progressive Architecture 31 (August 1950):
51.

"Record houses 1956-1966: a decade of innovations." il.
Architectural Record 139 (February 1966): 125-136.

Reynolds Metals Company. An International Review of Aluminum
in Modern Architecture. Richmond, VA: Reynolds Metal
Co., 1960. il., port. pp. 96-97.

Rudolph, Paul. "Adolescent architecture." Architectural
Forum 109 (September 1958): 177.

_____. "An Architect speaks his mind." House and Garden
136 (November 1969): 26, 30, 32, 76.

_____. "The architectural education in U.S.A." port.
Zodiac 8 (1961): 162-165.

_____. "Architectural education in the United States."
port. Voice of America. Forum Lectures (Architecture
series 9). 1962. 5 p.

_____. "Architecture fitting and befitting." port. Archi-
tectural Forum 114 (June 1961): 89.

_____. "The changing face of New York." American In-
stitute of Architects. Journal 31 (April 1959): 38-39.

_____. "The changing philosophy of architecture." Ameri-
can Institute of Architects. Journal 22 (August 1954):
65-70 also in Architectural Forum 101 (July 1954): 120-
121.

_____. "Cio che l'architetto non puo d elegare." Archi-
tettura 10 (August 1964): 266-267.

_____. "Creative use of architectural material." il. Pro-
gressive Architecture 40 (April 1959): 92, 94.

_____. "From conception to sketch to rendering to building"

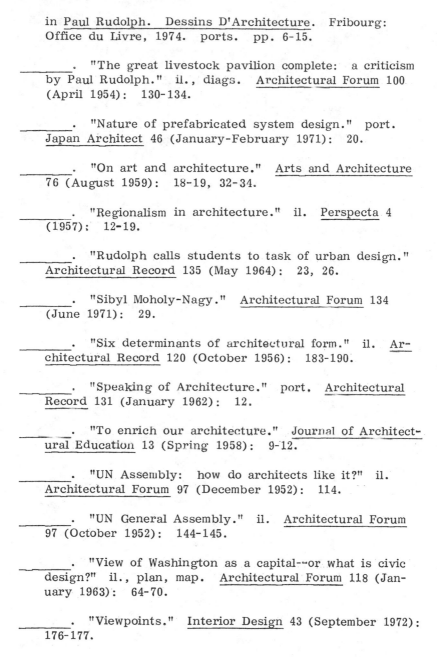

in Paul Rudolph.   Dessins D'Architecture.   Fribourg:
Office du Livre, 1974.   ports.   pp. 6-15.

_____.   "The great livestock pavilion complete: a criticism
by Paul Rudolph."   il., diags.   Architectural Forum 100
(April 1954):   130-134.

_____.   "Nature of prefabricated system design."   port.
Japan Architect 46 (January-February 1971):   20.

_____.   "On art and architecture."   Arts and Architecture
76 (August 1959):   18-19, 32-34.

_____.   "Regionalism in architecture."   il.   Perspecta 4
(1957):   12-19.

_____.   "Rudolph calls students to task of urban design."
Architectural Record 135 (May 1964):   23, 26.

_____.   "Sibyl Moholy-Nagy."   Architectural Forum 134
(June 1971):   29.

_____.   "Six determinants of architectural form."   il.   Ar-
chitectural Record 120 (October 1956):   183-190.

_____.   "Speaking of Architecture."   port.   Architectural
Record 131 (January 1962):   12.

_____.   "To enrich our architecture."   Journal of Architect-
ural Education 13 (Spring 1958):   9-12.

_____.   "UN Assembly: how do architects like it?"   il.
Architectural Forum 97 (December 1952):   114.

_____.   "UN General Assembly."   il.   Architectural Forum
97 (October 1952):   144-145.

_____.   "View of Washington as a capital--or what is civic
design?"   il., plan, map.   Architectural Forum 118 (January 1963):   64-70.

_____.   "Viewpoints."   Interior Design 43 (September 1972):
176-177.

_____. "Winners of the Misawa Homes International Pre-
    fabricated House Design Competition '70." il., plan, sec.
    Japan Architect 46 (January-February 1971): 143-152.

"22nd awards program." port. Progressive Architecture 56
    (January 1975): 41-65.

White, Norval. "Rudolph, Paul," in The Architecture Book.
    New York: Knopf, 1976. il. pp. 262-262.

"Yale gets new dean, new chairman, new rating." port.
    Architectural Forum 107 (July 1957): 6.

BOOK REVIEWS

Franzen, Ulrich, and Paul Rudolph. Evolving Cities: Urban
Design Proposals, with text by Peter Wolf. New York:
American Federation of Arts, 1974.

   Edwards, Dorothy A. "Evolving cities." American
   Institute of Planners. Journal 42 (July 1976):
   354-355.

Rudolph, Paul. The Architecture of Paul Rudolph, with introduction by Sibyl Moholy-Nagy. New York: Praeger,
1970.

   Bosch, Richard R. "Architecture of Paul Rudolph."
   Society of Architectural Historians. Journal 31
   (March 1972): 73.
   Gebhard, David. "Rudolph." Library Journal 95
   (August 1970): 2656.
   Jacobs, Jay. "Post functionalist." Art in America 58
   (November 1970): 63.
   Pica, Agnoldomenico. "Paul Rudolph." il. Domus
   493 (December 1970): 21.
   Schmertz, Mildred F. "Paul Rudolph in mid-career:
   an assessment." Architectural Record 148 (Septem-
   ber 1970): 141.

_____. Paul Rudolph: Dessins D'Architecture (Architect-
ural Drawings). New York: Architectural Book, 1981;
Tokyo: A.D.A. Edita, 1972.
   Abercrombie, Stanley. "Two-way relationship of drawings and design." il. American Institute of Architects. Journal 71 (September 1982): 68-69.
   Perrine, Richard H. "Paul Rudolph." Library Journal
   107 (15 April 1982): 803-804.

Quantrill, Malcolm. "Is this geometry really environ-
    ment?" il. Royal Institute of British Architects.
    Journal 82 (October 1975): 5.

BIOGRAPHICAL CHRONOLOGY

1918   Born October 23, Elkton, Kentucky
               Parents: Rev. Keener L. and Eurye (Stone)
                 Rudolph

1935-1940   Studied at Alabama Polytechnic Institute

1940   Bachelor Architecture, Alabama Polytechnic
                 Institute
               First Prize, Rorimer Competition, American
                 Institute of Decorators

1940-1943   Studied under Walter Gropius at Harvard
                 Graduate School of Design

1941-1942   Fellow in Architecture, Harvard University

1943-1946   Officer-in-Charge, Ship Construction, U.S.
                 Naval Reserve, Brooklyn Navy Yard

1946   Residence for Mr. and Mrs. Denman, Siesta
                 Key, FL
               Residence for Alexander S. Harkavy, Sarasota,
                 FL
               Tastee Freeze, Florida (Project)

1947   Master Architecture, Harvard University
               Guest Cottage for Mrs. Roberta Finney, Siesta
                 Key, FL (Project)
               Residence and Guest House for Mr. and Mrs.
                 Miller, Casey Key, FL
               Two residences, Sarasota, FL

1947-1951   Partner, architectural firm of (Ralph) Twitchell
                 and Rudolph, Sarasota, Florida

1948   Selected to design model house, Revere Copper
                 & Brass Company

Revere Quality House, Siesta Key, FL
Four beach houses for Lamolithic Industries,
    Sarasota, FL
Residence for Mr. and Mrs. Maynard E. Russell,
    Sarasota, FL

1948-1949   Wheelwright Traveling Fellowship in Architecture
    Travel in Europe and British Isles as advanced
        student of architecture, Harvard University
        Graduate School of Design
    Guest House for Mr. and Mrs. Healy, Siesta
        Key, FL (Cocoon House)

1949   Award of Merit, Best House of the Year, Ameri-
        can Institute of Architects
    Residence for Mr. and Mrs. Arthur Cheatham,
        Lakeland, FL
    Residence for Mr. and Mrs. Deeds, Siesta Key,
        FL

1950   Editor, special edition of Architecture
        D'Aujourd'hui entitled "The Spread of an
        Idea"

1951   Good Design Exhibition, Merchandise Mart,
        Chicago and Museum of Modern Art, New
        York
    Residence for Mr. and Mrs. C. Richard Leaven-
        good, St. Petersburg, FL
    Guest house, Naples, FL
    Residence for Mr. and Mrs. Lewis H. Haskins,
        Sarasota, FL
    Residence for Mrs. Marion W. Coward, Siesta
        Key, FL
    Residence for Mr. and Mrs. Burnette, Sarasota,
        FL
    Cottage for Mrs. Kate Wheelan, Siesta Key, FL
    Apartment House, Sarasota/Bradenton, FL
        (Project)

1951-1956   Visiting critic at Architectural Schools of Cor-
        nell, Tulane, Harvard and Princeton Uni-
        versities, University of California, University
        of Pennsylvania

1951-1958   Visiting lecturer at Architectural Schools of
Yale, Cornell, Toronto, Tulane, Harvard
and Princeton Universities, Smith and Clem-
son Colleges, Georgia Institute of Technology,
Institute of Design of Illinois Institute of
Technology, Alabama Polytechnic Institute,
University of Florida, University of Pennsyl-
vania, University of California

1952   Author, "Criticism of the United Nations
Buildings," Architectural Forum, October
Author, "New Directions," Perspecta, Summer
Residence for Mr. and Mrs. Eugene Knott,
Yankeetown, FL
Residence for Mr. and Mrs. David Cohen,
Siesta Key, FL

1952-1953   Sanderling Beach Club, Siesta Key, FL
Residence for Dr. and Mrs. W. W. Walker,
Sanibel Island, FL

1952-1958   Independent practice, Sarasota, FL and New
Haven, CT

1953   Author, "Notes on Row Housing," Pennsylvania
Triangle, January
Author, "Directions in Modern Architecture,"
Sarasota, Florida Review
Author, "Regionalism and the South," American
Institute of Architects Journal, April

Residence for Mr. and Mrs. Albert Siegrist,
Venice, FL
Residence for Mr. Sewell C. Biggs, Delray
Beach, FL
Sigma Alpha Epsilon Fraternity House, Miami
University, Miami, FL
Floating Island, Leesburg, FL (Project)
Basic House, variations (Project)

1954   Outstanding Young Architect Award, Sao Paulo
(Brazil) International Competition
Author, "Changing Philosophy of Architecture,"
Speech delivered before 1954 National

Convention of the American Institute of
Architects, The Florida Architect, July,
Architectural Forum, July
Author, "Evaluation of North Carolina Livestock
Judging Pavilion," Architectural Forum, April
U.S. Embassy in Amman, Jordan, U.S. Depart-
ment of State (Project)
Residence for Mr. and Mrs. Albert Bostwick,
Palm Beach, FL (Project)
Guest cottage for Mr. and Mrs. Ingram Hook,
Siesta Key, FL
Residence for Mrs. Wilson, Sarasota, FL
Residence for Mr. and Mrs. J. V. Taylor,
Venice, FL
Residence for Mr. and Mrs. Philip Hiss, Lido
Shores, FL (Umbrella House)

1955   Sarasota-Bradenton Airport, Sarasota, FL
                "Family of Man" Exhibit installation
                Residence for Mr. and Mrs. R. J. Burgess,
                Burgess Island, FL
                Experimental School, Plywood Association

1955-1958   Mary Cooper Jewett Arts Center, Wellesley
                College, Wellesley, MA

1956   Author, "On New School Design Research
                Team," Architectural Forum, September
                Botanical Gardens (Project)
                Four model houses for various regions in the
                United States, for Women's Home Companion
                Model house representing the Southeast, Home-
                style Center, Grand Rapids, MI
                Residence for Mr. and Mrs. Frank Applebee,
                Auburn, AL
                Office Building, Bramlett Equipment Company,
                Miami, FL
                Residence for Mr. and Mrs. Davidson, Braden-
                ton, FL
                Lambie Beach Development, Siesta Key, FL
                Stand for Doughnuts, Tampa, FL (Project)
                Architectural Design Consultant, Inter-American
                Center, Miami, FL
                Residence for Mr. and Mrs. Barnet Yanofsky,
                Newton, MA

1957   Author, "Genetrix: Personal Contributions to
                  American Architecture," Architectural Review,
                  May
                  Author, "Regionalism in Architecture," Per-
                  specta, Number 4
                  St. Boniface Episcopal Church, Sarasota, FL
                  (Project)
                  Residence for Mr. and Mrs. Martin Harkavy,
                  Lido Shores, FL
                  Residence for Mr. and Mrs. Theodore Burkhardt,
                  Casey Key, FL

1957-1958   Riverview Junior High School, Sarasota, FL

1957-1959   Greeley Memorial Laboratory, Yale University
                  Forestry School, New Haven, CT

1957-1960   Office Headquarters Building, Blue Cross-Blue
                  Shield, Boston, MA

1958   Arnold Brunner Prize in Architecture, American
                  Academy of Arts and Letters
                  Author, "The Six Determinants of Architectural
                  Form," Architectural Forum, December
                  Consultant Architect, Church Street Redevelop-
                  ment Project, New Haven, CT
                  Residence for Mr. and Mrs. George McCandlish,
                  Cambridge, MA
                  Master Plan, Tuskegee Institute, AL

1958-1959   Senior High School, Sarasota, FL
                  Residence for Mr. and Mrs. Frederick A. Deer-
                  ing, Casey Key, FL

1958-1964   Art and Architecture Building, Yale University,
                  New Haven, CT

1958-1965   Chairman, Department of Architecture, Yale
                  University, New Haven, CT

1959   Merit Awards, Homes for Better Living Awards,
                  American Institute of Architects in coopera-
                  tion with House & Home and McCall's
                  Author, "Changing Face of New York," American

Institute of Architects Journal, April
Author, "Creative Use of Architectural Material,"
Progressive Architecture, April
Author, "On Arts and Architecture," discussion
from the program "Yale Reports," Arts and
Architecture, August
May Memorial Unitarian Church, Syracuse, NY
Lake Region Yacht and Country Club, Winter
Haven, FL
Residence for Mr. and Mrs. Ambler Liggett,
Tampa, FL

1959-1963   Temple Street Parking Garage, City of New
Haven, New Haven, CT

1960   National Gold Medal Exhibition of the Building
Arts, Jewett Arts Center, Wellesley College,
MA
Member, Advisory Board, RCA Advanced
Designing and Styling Center
Residence for Mr. and Mrs. Sidney Friedberg,
Baltimore, MD
Administration Building, Tuskegee Institute,
Tuskegee, AL
O'Brien Motor Inn, Waverly, NY (Project)
Vacation house for Woman's Day
Pharmaceutical Laboratory-Office-Manufacturing
Building, Endo Laboratories, Long Island,
NY
Residence for Mr. and Mrs. Arthur W. Milam,
Jacksonville, FL
Residence for Mr. and Mrs. R. H. Daisley,
Inlet Cay, FL
Theme Center for 1964-1965 New York World's
Fair, Portland Cement Company (Project)
Cultural Center, Tuskegee Institute, Tuskegee,
AL
Theater, Film projection and live stage action
simultaneously, Ford Foundation (Project)
Pi Kappa Phi Fraternity House, University of
Florida, Gainesville, FL

1960-1961   Married Students Housing, Yale University,
New Haven, CT

1960-1969   Interdenominational Chapel, Tuskegee Institute,
             Tuskegee, AL

1961   Boston Arts Festival Architectural Award for
             Commercial Building Category, Blue Cross-
             Blue Shield Office Building
             Member, Citizens Advisory Committee for Federal
             Participation in the New York World's Fair
             Office Facilities Addition and Cafeteria, Ciba
             Pharmaceutical Company, Summit, NJ
             Kappa Sigma Fraternity House, Auburn Univer-
             sity, Auburn AL
             Manager's Office, Parking Authority, City of
             New Haven, New Haven, CT
             Residence for Mr. and Mrs. N. Leslie Silvas,
             Greenwich, CT
             Residence for Mr. and Mrs. John W. Wallace,
             Athens, AL
             Juvenile Detention Home, Addition, Bridgeport,
             CT
             Residence for Paul Rudolph, New Haven, CT

1962   Award of Merit for Sarasota High School, Ameri-
             can Institute of Architects Honor Awards
             Program
             Honorable Mention, Gold Medal Committee, Archi-
             tectural League of New York
             Master Plan and Library, Guilford Free Library
             Association, Guilford, CT
             Master Plan, Two Dormitories, Auditorium Build-
             ing, and Classroom Building, The Hotchkiss
             School, Lakeville, CT (Project)
             Mental Health Building, Boston Government
             Service Center, Boston, MA
             Health, Education and Welfare Building, Boston
             Government Service Center, Boston, MA
             Project for a residence, Palm Beach, FL

1962-1964   IBM Corporation, Research, Office and Manu-
             facturing Facilities, East Fishkill, NY
             Endo Laboratories, Long Island, NY (in associa-
             tion with Walter Kidde)

1962-1966   Crawford Manor Housing for the Elderly, New
             Haven Housing Authority, New Haven, CT

1962-1967   Christian Science Organization Building, Uni-
                 versity of Illinois, Urbana, IL

1963   Author, "A View of Washington as a Capital--
                 or What Is Civic Design?" Architectural
                 Forum, January
                 Author, "Architecture--The Patron and The
                 Public," Response Magazine, April
                 Author, "In Search of a Comprehensive Style,"
                 New Homes Guide, 25th Anniversary Issue
                 Coordinating Architect, Boston Government
                 Service Center, Boston, MA
                 Award of Excellence for House Design by Ar-
                 chitectural Record (Milam Residence)

1963-1966   Charles A. Dana Creative Arts Center, Colgate
                 University, Hamilton, NY

1963-1968   Apartment Building, Beneficent House, Weybos-
                 set Hill Housing, Providence, RI

1963-1971   Orange County Government Office and Court
                 House Building, Goshen, NY

1963-1972   Southeastern Massachusetts Technological In-
                 stitute, Master Plan and First Stage including
                 classrooms, auditorium, library, cafeteria,
                 and service building, North Dartmouth, MA

1964   First Honor Award for Art and Architecture
                 Building, American Institute of Architects
                 Award of Merit for Parking Garage, American
                 Institute of Architects
                 Annual Award for Endo Laboratories, Concrete
                 Industry Board
                 City Hall, Syracuse, NY

1964-1969   John W. Chorley Elementary School, Middletown,
                 NY

1965   Exhibit, "Architecture-USA," U.S. Department
                 of State for exhibition abroad
                 Citation, Outstanding Collaboration between
                 Architecture and the Allied Arts, Gold Medal

Exhibition, The Architectural League of New
York
Begins practice in New York, NY
International Bazaar, International Area of the
Interama Project, Miami, FL
Art Building, Manoa Campus of the University
of Hawaii, Honolulu, HI
Master Plan, Auditorium, Instruction, Dormi-
tories, Recreation Facilities, and Laboratories,
East Pakistan Agricultural University, My-
mensingh, East Pakistan
Residence for Callahan, Birmingham, AL

1966   Honorary Doctorate of Arts, Colgate University
Honor Award for Design Excellence, U.S. De-
partment of Housing and Urban Development
(Crawford Manor)
Office for Paul Rudolph, New York, NY
Resort Community, Master plan, town houses,
apartments, hotel, boatel and commercial
buildings, Stafford Harbor, VA (Project)
Sid W. Richardson Physical Sciences Building,
Texas Christian University, Fort Worth, TX
Monteith College Center, Wayne State University,
Detroit, MI
Townhouse for Mr. Alexander Hirsch, New York,
NY
Master plan and office buildings, Brookhollow
Corporation, Dallas, TX
John Jay Park, Department of Parks, New York,
NY (Project)
Master plan, apartment house, community center
and shopping center, Northwest #1 Urban
Renewal Area, Washington, DC
Penthouse for Mr. and Mrs. Joseph Caspi, New
York, NY
Beth El Synagogue, addition, New London, CT
Visual Arts Center, Manoa Campus, University
of Hawaii, Honolulu, HI

1967   Graphic Arts Center, New York, NY (Project)
Married Student Housing, University of Vir-
ginia, Charlottesville, VA
Lower Manhattan Expressway "New Forms of the

Evolving City," Ford Foundation, New York,
    NY (Project)
Residence for Dr. and Mrs. Frank Parcells,
    Grosse Pointe, MI
Townhouse for Mr. and Mrs. Robert Brown,
    New York, NY
Dental Offices for Dr. Nathan Shore, New York,
    NY (Project)
Three Parks and Playgrounds, Department of
    Parks, New York, NY
Apartment for Mrs. Henry J. Kaiser, New York,
    NY
Laboratory Building and Office Addition, Endo
    Laboratories, Garden City, NY
Two Apartment Houses, New York City Housing
    Authority, Bronx, NY
Fox Hill Development, DeMatteis Development
    Company, Staten Island, NY (Project)
Tracey Towers, DeMatteis Development Company,
    Bronx, NY

1968   Oriental Masonic Gardens, Housing utilizing
                    mobile housing units, New Haven Redevelop-
                    ment Agency, New Haven, CT
                Student Union, Southeastern Massachusetts
                    Technological Institute, North Dartmouth,
                    MA
                Stadium, Kingdom of Saudi Arabia, Dammam,
                    Saudi Arabia
                Housing utilizing mobile housing units, Magnolia
                    Homes, Vicksburg, MS
                Government Center, New Haven, CT
                Fort Lincoln housing, District of Columbia Re-
                    development Land Agency, Washington, DC
                Residence for Mr. Herbert Green, Cherry Ridge,
                    PA
                Study of the uses of Extruded Cement Asbestos,
                    United States Plywood, New York, NY
                First and Second Church in Boston, Boston,
                    MA

1969   Medal of Honor, American Institute of Architects,
                    New York Chapter
                Residence for Mr. and Mrs. Harry Raich,

Quogue, NY
Residence for Mr. and Mrs. Arne Lewis, Boston,
    MA
Burroughs Wellcome and Company, Inc., Re-
    search Triangle Park, NC
Earl Brydges Library, Niagara Falls, NY
Waterfront Development Project, New York State
    Urban Development Corporation, Buffalo,
    NY
Residence for Mr. and Mrs. Richard Pistell,
    Lyford Cay, Nassau, Bahamas
Natural Science Building, State University
    College at Purchase, Purchase, NY
Apartment for Mr. and Mrs. Gardner Cowles,
    New York, NY

1970   Honorary Doctorate of Fine Arts, Florida State
                    University
                Honorary Doctorate of Fine Arts, Southeastern
                    Massachusetts University
                Fellow, American Institute of Architects
                Honor Award of New England Regional Council,
                    American Institute of Architects, for Arts
                    and Humanities Building, Southeastern
                    Massachusetts University
                Invited participant, International Conference
                    of Architects, Teheran, Iran
                Exhibit, "Work in Progress: Architects by
                    Philip Johnson, Kevin Roche and Paul
                    Rudolph," Museum of Modern Art, New
                    York, NY
                Author, "Fallingwater," introduction to Frank
                    Lloyd Wright Kaufmann House, 'Fallingwater.'
                    A.D.A. Edita: Tokyo, Japan
                Residence for Mr. and Mrs. Maurice Deane,
                    Great Neck, NY
                Moderate and Low Rent Public Housing, New
                    York State Urban Development Corporation,
                    New York, NY
                Ten Apartment Towers, DeMatteis Development
                    Company, Kew Gardens, NY
                Rockford Civic Center, Rockford Metropolitan
                    Exhibition, Auditorium and Office Building
                    Authority, Rockford, IL
                Central Suffold Office Park, Hauppauge, NY

Residence for Mr. and Mrs. Sid R. Bass, Fort
Worth, TX
Residence for Dr. and Mrs. John M. Shuey,
Bloomfield Hills, MI
Apartment for Mr. and Mrs. Maurits Edersheim,
New York, NY

1971   Elected to National Institute of Arts and Letters
Author, "Sibyl Moholy-Nagy," Architectural
Forum, June
Urban Complex, K. & S. Fakhri Brothers,
Beirut, Lebanon
Residence for Mr. and Mrs. Bert Dweck, Deal,
NJ
First National Church of Exquisite Panic, Al-
teration of 1887 work by Richard Mossis
Hunt
Office Building, Daiei House & Co., Ltd. Na-
goya, Japan
Apartment for Dorothea Elman, New York, NY
Residence for Mr. and Mrs. William Davidson,
Bloomfield Hills, MI

1972   Honorary Doctorate of Humanities, Auburn
University, Auburn, AL
Author, Paul Rudolph: Architectural Perspect-
ive Illustrations, edited by Yukio Futagawa.
Text by Paul Rudolph. A.D.A. Edita:
Tokyo, Japan
Residence for Dr. and Mrs. Louis Micheels,
Westport, CT
Residence for Mr. John Pillsbury, Cannes,
France
Office Building, Entrecancles y Tavora, Madrid,
Spain
Community Facilities Complex, New York State
Urban Development Corporation, Buffalo,
NY
Residence for Mr. and Mrs. John B. Rogers,
Houston, TX
Office, Mr. Maurits Edersheim, Drexel, Burnham
Co., New York, NY
Medical Technology, Administration, Science
and Classroom Buildings, Staten Island Com-
munity College, Staten Island, NY

1973   Award of Merit, for Tracey Towers, The Con-
              crete Industry Board of New York
            Residence for Mr. and Mrs. Erwin Staller,
              Lloyd Harbor, NY
            Addition and Master Plan, East Northport
              Jewish Center Synagogue, East Northport,
              NY
            Student Housing, Davidson College, Davidson,
              NC
            Housing, Carol Housing Corp., Miami, FL
            Residence for Joanna Steichen, New York, NY
            Modular Housing Exhibition

1974   Renovation, Pitts Theology Library, Candler
              School of Theology, Emory University, At-
              lanta, GA
            Apartment Hotel, Pan-Lon Engineering and Con-
              struction Co., Ltd., Jerusalem, Israel
            Residence for Mr. Niel C. Morgan, Aspen, CO
            Housing, Morgan Annex, New York State Urban
              Development Corporation, New York, NY
            Recreation Complex, New York State Urban
              Development Corporation, Buffalo, NY

1975   Honor Award for services to architecture, La
              Federacion Panamericana de Asociaciones de
              Arquitectos
            Honorary member, El Instituto de Arquitectos
              de Puerto Rico
            Apartment for Mr. Gary Strutin, New Rochelle,
              NY
            Residence for Miss Nancy Houston, Westerly,
              RI
            William R. Cannon Chapel, Candler School of
              Theology, Emory University, Atlanta, GA

1976   Fellowship, American Society of Interior Design-
              ers
            Addition, Residence for Mr. and Mrs. Robert
              Bernhard, Greenwich, CT
            Addition, Research Building, Burroughs Well-
              come Co., Research Triangle Park, NC

1977   Honorary Professor, La Universidad Nacional
              "Federico Villarreal," Lima, Peru

Elsie de Wolfe Award, American Society of In-
terior Designers
Author, "Enigmas of Architecture," A + U,
July--a special issue, "100 Works of Paul
Rudolph"
Addition, Residence for Mr. and Mrs. Ronald
Fein, Sands Point, NY

1978   Apartment for Dr. Vallo Benjamin, New York,
NY
Residence for Mr. and Mrs. Richard Young,
Livingston Manor, NY
Master Plan, Campus Entrance-Plaza-Pantheon
Gardens, Tuskegee Institute, Tuskegee, AL
Harrington Cancer Care Center, Panhandle
Area Cancer Council, Amarillo, TX
Apartment for Mr. and Mrs. Rafael Carrillor,
New York, NY
Residence for Mr. and Mrs. Robert Hedaya,
Deal, NJ
Apartment-Commercial Complex, Donald Zucker
Company, New York, NY
Remodeling, Housing Units, Donald Zucker
Company, New York, NY
Dance Studio and Apartments in the Northeast
Toxicology-Experimental Pathology Building,
Burroughs Wellcome Co., Research triangle
Park, NC
Remodel, residence for Mr. and Mrs. Dani
Siegel, Westhampton Beach, NY
Remodel, Townhouse for Mr. and Mrs. Donald
Zucker, New York, NY

1979   Architectural design for a Tender for urban
development sites, MARINA Centre in Singa-
pore, Hong Fok Investment Holdings Pted.,
Ltd., Singapore and Hong Kong
Residence for Mr. and Mrs. Michael Glazer, Los
Angeles, CA
City Center, Bass Brothers Enterprises, Fort
Worth, TX
Residential-Office-Shopping Complex, Hong Fok
Investment Holdings Pted. Ltd., Singapore
Apartment Building, Hong Fok Investment
Holdings Pted. Ltd., Singapore

1980   Apartment Complex, Pontiac Land Private
        Limited, Singapore
        Ten Bungalows, Hong Fok Investment Holding
        Co., Ltd., Hong Kong
        Residence for Mr. and Mrs. Henry Kwee, Singa-
        pore
        Offices, Stanley Marsh III, Amarillo, TX
        Residence for Mr. and Mrs. Wylie Tuttle, Rock
        Hall, MD
        Apartment for Dr. and Mrs. Allan Gutstein,
        New York, NY
        Electronic Data Systems Corporation, Design
        Competition, Dallas, TX
        Mr. and Mrs. Hugh Downs Residence, Connecti-
        cut
        Television Station for Stanley Marsh III, Ama-
        rillo, TX

1981   Coffee Memorial Blood Bank, Amarillo, TX
        Oxley Rise Condominium Housing for Hong Fok
        Investment Holding Co., Ltd., Singapore
        Alteration and addition to Mr. and Mrs. Kenneth
        Sherman residence, Wilton, CT
        Alteration for Cambridge Research & Develop-
        ment Group offices, Westport, CT

1982   Office Building for Pt Yamano Utama, Jakarta
        Pusat, Indonesia
        Burroughs Wellcome Co., North Office Building
        and Master Plan, Research Triangle Park,
        NC
        Alteration to Mr. and Mrs. Mark Edersheim
        residence, Mamoroneck, NY
        Beverly Park Estates residence, Beverly Hills,
        CA
        General Daniel "Chappie" James Center for
        Aerospace Science and Health Education for
        Tuskegee Institute, Tuskegee, AL

1983   Remodeling of Michael Floersheim/Dr. Strauss
        apartment, New York, NY
        Addition to John B. Rogers residence, Palm
        Beach, FL
        Bristol-Myers Research Laboratory, Design
        competition, Connecticut

Remodeling of Dr. and Mrs. Hillel Tobias residence, Remsenburg, NY

1984   Remodeling of Mr. and Mrs. Eisner residence, Westport, CT
Science Building, Southeastern Massachusetts University, Boston, MA
Mr. and Mrs. Michael Glazer residence, Los Angeles, CA
Mr. and Mrs. George Pavarini residence, Greenwich, CT
Mr. and Mrs. Wylie Tuttle residence, Rock Hall, MD
Office Complex, Jakarta, Indonesia
Office and Commercial Building, Hong Kong

1985   Addition to Mr. and Mrs. Licht residence, Hewlett Harbor, NY
Macy's Department Store, Danbury, CT
Macy's Department Store, Riverchase, Birmingham, AL
Hotel and Condominiums, Fisher Island, Miami, FL

PART II

LOUIS I. KAHN

Fig. 9: Richards Research Building at the University of
Pennsylvania

BIBLIOGRAPHIC CHRONOLOGY OF WORKS

MONUMENTAL ENTRANCE

Student Competition, 17th Paris Prize, Society of Beaux-Arts
    Architects. Project, 1923.

"First preliminary competition for the 17th Paris Prize of the
    Society of Beaux-Arts Architects: a monumental entrance
    to a thoroughfare." il. American Architect 125 (27 Feb-
    ruary 1924): 207-210.

SHOPPING CENTER

Student Competition, Beaux-Arts Institute of Design. Project,
    1923.

"Class 'A'-III project--a shopping center." il. American
    Architect 125 (9 April 1924): 366.

UNITED STATES VETERAN'S HOSPITAL

Student Competition, Society of Beaux-Arts Architects. Pro-
    ject, 1924.

"Second preliminary competition for the 17th Paris Prize,
    Society of Beaux-Arts Architects." il. American Archi-
    tect 125 (7 May 1924): 446.

ARMY POST

Student Competition, Beaux-Arts Institute of Design. Project,
    1924.

"Class 'Λ'-V project--an army post." il. American Architect
    126 (24 September 1924): 297.

EUROPEAN TRAVEL SKETCHES

1928-1959.

"Arcane Kahn." il. Architect's Journal 169 (6 June 1979):
    1148.
Kahn, Louis I. Drawings. Los Angeles: Access Press, 1981.
    il. pp. 1-18.
_____. The Notebooks and Drawings of Louis I. Kahn,
    edited and designed by Richard Saul Wurman and Eugene
    Feldman. Philadelphia: Falcon, 1962. il. fig. 7-25.
_____. The Notebooks and Drawings of Louis I. Kahn,
    edited and designed by Richard Saul Wurman and Eugene
    Feldman. Cambridge: M.I.T., 1973. il. fig. 7-25.
_____. The Travel Sketches of Louis I. Kahn. An exhi-
    bition organized by the Pennsylvania Academy of the Fine
    Arts, 1978-1979, designed by Kurt Wiener. Philadelphia:
    Pennsylvania Academy of the Fine Arts, 1978. il. (pt.
    col.). 63 p.
"Louis I. Kahn: silence and light." il. (pt. col.). Archi-
    tecture and Urbanism 3 (January 1973): 4, 13-16, 25,
    191-194.
Nevins, Deborah. The Architect's Eye. New York: Pantheon,
    1979. col. il. pp. 20-21, 152-153.
Osman, Mary E. "Travel sketches of Louis Kahn." il. (pt.
    col.). AIA Journal 67 (May 1978): 46-55.
"Pencil drawings." il. Architecture, New York 63 (January
    1931): 15-17.
Scully, Vincent. Louis I. Kahn. New York: Braziller, 1962.
    il., plates 1, 9, 21-23.
Smithson, Alison. "Louis Kahn." col. il. Architects' Year-
    book 9 (1960): 103.
"Temple interior, Karnak, Egypt, 1951." il. Perspecta 19
    (1982): 88.
"Value and aim in sketching." il. T-Square Club Journal
    1 (May 1931): 4, 18-21.
Wilson, Janet. "Travel sketches of Louis I. Kahn." col. il.
    Art News 77 (September 1978): 183.

AHAVATH ISRAEL SYNAGOGUE

6735 North 16th Street, Philadelphia, Pennsylvania. 1935-1939.

Ronner, Heinz. Louis I. Kahn: Complete Works, 1935-74.

Boulder, Colo.: Westview, 1977. il. p. 47.
Scully, Vincent. Louis I. Kahn. New York: Braziller, 1962.
il. plate 12, p. 14.

JERSEY HOMESTEADS COOPERATIVE DEVELOPMENT

Hightstown, New Jersey. 1935-1937. In association with Alfred Kastner.

Scully, Vincent. Louis I. Kahn. New York: Braziller, 1962.
il., plan. plate 13, p. 15.

JESSE OSER RESIDENCE

688 Stetson Road, Melrose Park, Pennsylvania. 1940.

"House in Melrose Park, Pennsylvania provides spaciousness
in a compact plan." il., plan. Architectural Forum 83
(August 1945): 132-134.
Ronner, Heinz. Louis I. Kahn: Complete Works, 1935-74.
Boulder, Colo.: Westview, 1977. il., plan. p. 49.

PINE FORD HOUSING

Pine Ford Acres, Middletown, Pennsylvania. 1941-1942. In
association with George Howe.

"Defense housing at Middletown, Pa." il., plans. Architectural Forum 75 (October 1941): 216-217.
"450 permanent units-rental, Middletown, Pa." il., plans.
Architectural Forum 76 (May 1942): 306-307.
"Pine Ford acres, Pa." il., plan. Architectural Forum 84
(January 1946): 110-111.
Stern, Robert A. M. George Howe: Toward a Modern American Architecture. New Haven: Yale, 1975. il. pp.
193-194, fig. 122-123.

CARVER COURT HOUSING DEVELOPMENT

Coatesville, Pennsylvania. 1941-1943. In association with
George Howe and Oscar Stonorov.

"Carver court, Coatesville, Pa." il., plans, sec., elev.
  Architectural Forum 81 (December 1944): 109-116.
"Carver court, Coatesville, Pa. 1941." il., plan, elev.
  Architettura 18 (June 1972): 100-101.
Scully, Vincent. Louis I. Kahn. New York: Braziller, 1962.
  il. plate 14, p. 15.
Sheppard, Richard. "U.S. wartime housing." il., plan.
  Architectural Review 96 (August 1944): 33, 44, 48.
Smithson, Alison and Peter Smithson. "Louis Kahn." il.
  Architects' Yearbook 9 (1960): 103.
Stern, Robert A. M. George Howe: Toward a Modern Ameri-
  can Architecture. New Haven: Yale, 1975. il., plan.
  pp. 197-198, fig. 124-127.

WARTIME HOUSING

Pennypack Woods, Philadelphia, Pennsylvania. 1943-1944. In
  association with George Howe and Oscar Stonorov.

Sheppard, Richard. "U.S. wartime housing." il. Architect-
  ural Review 96 (August 1944): 46, 51.
Teitelman, Edward. Architecture in Philadelphia: A Guide.
  Cambridge: M.I.T., 1974. il. p. 169.

LILY PONDS HOUSING

National Public Housing Authority, Washington, D.C. Project,
  1943. In association with George Howe and Oscar Stonorov.

Stern, Robert A. M. George Howe: Towards a Modern American Architecture. New Haven: Yale, 1975. il., plan.
  pp. 197-198, fig. 128-129.

TOWN OF WILLOW RUN

Ypsilanti, Michigan. 1943. In association with Oscar Stonorov.

"Town of Willow Run." il., plan, map. Architectural Forum
  78 (March 1943): 52-54.

HOTEL FOR 194X

Hypothetical town of 70,000.   Project, 1943.   In association
with Oscar Stonorov.

"New buildings for 194X: hotel." il., plans, sec., elcv.
Architectural Forum 78 (May 1943): 74-79.

MILL CREEK DEVELOPMENT

Area of 4600 Lancaster, Philadelphia, Pennsylvania. 1946-
1962. In association with Kenneth Day, Louis McAllister,
Anne Tyng, and Christopher Tunnard。

Bacon, Edmund N. "Urban designs of today: Philadelphia."
il., plan. Progressive Architecture 37 (August 1956):
108-109.
"Genetrix: personal contributions to American architecture;
Louis Kahn." il. Architectural Review 121 (May 1957):
344-345.
Giurgola, Romaldo. Louis I. Kahn. Boulder, Colo.: Westview,
1975. il., plans. pp. 27-32.
Meyerson, Martin. Face of the Metropolis. New York: Rand-
om House, 1963. il., plan. pp. 156-157.
"Millcreek redevelopment project." plan. Perspecta 2 (1953):
20.
"Philadelphia's redevelopment." il. Architectural Forum 105
(December 1956): 134.
"Ristrutturozione di Mill Creek." il., plans. Casabella 260
(February 1962): 25.
Ronner, Heinz. Louis I. Kahn: Complete Works, 1935-74.
Boulder, Colo.: Westview, 1977. il., plan, elev. pp. 38-
45.
Scully, Vincent. Louis I. Kahn. New York: Braziller, 1962.
il., plan. plates 39, 82-84, pp. 31-32.
Stern, Robert A. M. New Directions in American Architecture.
Revised ed. New York: Braziller, 1977. il. pp. 13-15.
Tyng, Alexandra. Beginnings: Louis I. Kahn's Philosophy
of Architecture. New York: John Wiley and Sons, 1984.
il., plan. pp. 88-91.

SOLAR HOUSE

Pennsylvania. Project, 1947.

Simon, Maron J. Your Solar House. New York: Simon and
    Schuster, 1947. il., plan. pp. 42-43.

PHILADELPHIA PLANS

Includes all urban plans. 1952-1974.

"American architectural drawings." il. Progressive Archi-
    tecture 58 (August 1977): 54-55.
"Architecture visionnaires." il., plan, sec. L'Architecture
    D'Aujourd'hui 33 (June-July 1962): 4, 12.
Baker, Geoffrey. Parking. New York: Reinhold, 1958. il.,
    plan. pp. 42-43.
Banham, Reyner. Megastructure: Urban Futures of the Re-
    cent Past. London: Thames and Hudson, 1976. il., plan.
    pp. 38-41.
"A city tower." il., plan, sec. Architecture and Urbanism
    3 (January 1973): 145-149.
"A city tower: a concept of natural growth," in Universal
    Atlas Cement Company, United States Steel Corporation
    Publication No. ADUAC-707-57 (5-BM-WP), 1957.
Cook, John Wesley. Conversations With Architects. New
    York: Praeger, 1973. il., plan. pp. 184-186.
Coombs, Robert. "Philadelphia architecture after Kahn:
    Philadelphia's phantom school." il., plan (not Kahn's).
    Progressive Architecture 57 (April 1976): 58-63.
Crane, David A. "Philadelphia tomorrow," in Philadelphia
    Architecture, prepared by A.I.A., Philadelphia Chapter.
    New York: Reinhold, 1961. il. pp. 63-69.
Frateili, Enzo. "Louis Kahn." il. Zodiac 8 (1961): 16-19.
"Genetrix: personal contributions to American architecture;
    Louis Kahn." il. Architectural Review 121 (May 1957):
    344-345.
Giurgola, Romaldo. Louis I. Kahn. Boulder, Colo.: West-
    view, 1975. il., plan (pt. col.), sec. p. 226-239, 241.
Gruen, Victor. The Heart of Our Cities; The Urban Crisis:
    Diagnosis and Cure. New York: Simon and Schuster,
    1964. il. pp. 223-224.
Harms, Hans H. "Trends in architektur: USA-Louis I. Kahn."
    il., plan. Bauwelt 54 (28 October 1963): 1252-1261.
"Imaginative study of Philadelphia done over on modernistic
    planning principles." Philadelphia Evening Bulletin (17
    May 1941): 3.

Kahn, Louis I. Drawings. Los Angeles: Access Press, 1981.
    il. pp. 61-70.
_____. "Toward a plan for midtown Philadelphia." il.
    (pt. col.), plans, maps. Perspecta 2 (1953): 10-27.
_____. The Notebooks and Drawings of Louis I. Kahn,
    edited and designed by Richard Saul Wurman and Eugene
    Feldman. Philadelphia: Falcon, 1962. il., plan, sec.
    endpapers, fig. 4-5, 28-31, 39-47, 71-74.
_____. The Notebooks and Drawings of Louis I. Kahn,
    edited and designed by Richard Saul Wurman and Eugene
    Feldman. Cambridge: M.I.T., 1973. il., plan, sec.
    endpapers, fig. 4-5, 28-31, 39-47, 71-74.
LeRicolais, Robert. "An approach to architectural education."
    Pennsylvania Triangle 42 (January 1956): 28-32.
Lewis, David, ed. The Pedestrian in the City. Princeton:
    Van Nostrand, 1965. il., plan. pp. 33-35, 168-171.
"Louis Kahn." il., plan, sec., elev. L'Architecture
    D'Aujourd'hui 33 (December 1962): 12-13.
"Louis Kahn and the living city." il., plan, port. Archi-
    tectural Forum 108 (March 1958): 114-119.
"Louis I. Kahn; oeuvres 1963-1969." il., plan. L'Architecture
    D'Aujourd'hui 40 (February-March 1969): 8, 11, 30-31.
"Louis Kahn: order in architecture." il., plan, sec. Per-
    specta 4 (1957): 60-65.
"Louis Kahn urbaniste." il., plan, elev. L'Architecture
    D'Aujourd'hui 33 (December 1962): 35-39.
"The mind of Louis Kahn." plan. Architectural Forum 137
    (July-August 1972): 84-85.
Molitor, John. "How the sesqui-centennial was designed."
    American Architect 130 (1926): 377-382.
Nevins, Deborah. The Architect's Eye. New York: Pantheon,
    1979. il. pp. 150-151.
"The Philadelphia cure: clearing slums with penicillin, not
    surgery." il., plans, port. Architectural Forum 96
    (April 1952): 112-119.
Pierson, William Harvey. American Buildings and Their Archi-
    tects: The Impact of European Modernism in the Mid-
    Twentieth Century, v. 4. Garden City, N.Y.: Double-
    day, 1972. il., plan. pp. 422-423, 426.
"Planning studies of Penn Center." il., plan, sec., elev.
    Architecture and Urbanism 3 (January 1973): 40, 141,
    144.
"Proposed city hall building." il., plan, sec., elev. Perspecta
    2 (1953): 23-27.

Reichley, James。 "Philadelphia does it: the battle for Penn
    Center." Harper's Magazine 214 (February 1957):   49-56.
Ronner, Heinz. Louis I. Kahn: Complete Works, 1935-74.
    Boulder, Colo。: Westview, 1977. il., plans (pt。 col.),
    maps, sec., elev. pp。 11-33, 73-77, 443-445.
Scully, Vincent. American Architecture and Urbanism. New
    York: Praeger, 1969. il., plan. p。 224.
_____. Louis I. Kahn. New York: Braziller, 1962. il.,
    plan. plates 60, 120-130. pp. 27, 40-42.
Sky, Alison. Unbuilt America; Forgotten Architecture in the
    United States, From Thomas Jefferson to the Space Age.
    New York: McGraw-Hill, 1976. plan. p. 258.
Smithson, Alison. "Louis Kahn." il. (pt. col.), plan (pt.
    col.). Architects' Yearbook 9 (1960):   102, 108-111.
_____. Urban Structuring. New York: Reinhold, 1967.
    il. pp. 77-79.
"Spatial triangulation. City hall, Phila., Pa." il., elev.
    Progressive Architecture 35 (June 1954): 102.
Stern, Robert A. M. New Directions in American Architecture.
    New York: Braziller, 1969. il., plans. pp。 13-15.
Tentori, Francesco. "L'architetto Louis I. Kahn; ordine de
    forma nell'opera di Louis Kahn." il., plan, sec. Casabella
    241 (July 1960): 2, 10, 12-13.
Tyng, Alexandra. Beginnings: Louis I. Kahn's Philosophy
    of Architecture. New York: John Wiley and Sons, 1984.
    il., plan。 pp. 35, 77-87, 92-94, 102-109.

WINSLOW T. TOMPKINS RESIDENCE

Apalogen Road and School House Lane, Germantown, Pennsyl-
    vania. 1947-1949.

Ronner, Heinz. Louis I. Kahn: Complete Works, 1935-74.
    Boulder, Colo。: Westview, 1977. plan, elev. p。 51.

MORTON WEISS RESIDENCE

White Hall Road, Norristown, Pennsylvania. 1948-1949.

Ford, Katherine Morrow. The American House Today. New
    York: Reinhold, 1951. il., plan. pp。 232-234.
Giurgola, Romaldo. Louis I. Kahn. Boulder, Colo.: Westview,
    1975. il., plan. pp。 18-19, 21.

"Modern space framed with traditional artistry." il., plan,
    sec., elev. Architectural Forum 93 (September 1950):
    101-105.
Ronner, Heinz. Louis I. Kahn: Complete Works, 1935-74.
    Boulder, Colo.: Westview, 1977. il., plan, diag. pp.
    53-55.
Scully, Vincent. Louis I. Kahn. New York: Braziller, 1962.
    il., plan. plates 16-17, pp. 16-17.
Smithson, Alison. "Louis Kahn." il., plan, elev. Architects'
    Yearbook 9 (1960): 102, 106-107.

COWARD SHOE STORE

1118-20 Chestnut, Philadelphia, Pennsylvania. 1949. In as-
    sociation with Oscar Stonorov.

"Glass front store in Philadelphia." il., plan, sec. Archi-
    tectural Forum 91 (December 1949): 94-95.

SAMUEL GENEL RESIDENCE

Indian Creek Road and Lancaster, Overbrook, Lower Merion
    Township, Pennsylvania. 1949.

Ronner, Heinz. Louis I. Kahn: Complete Works, 1935-74.
    Boulder, Colo.: Westview, 1977. il., plan, elev. pp.
    57-59.
Scully, Vincent. Louis I. Kahn. New York: Braziller, 1962.
    il. plate 18.

PINCUS THERAPY BUILDING and RADBILL PSYCHIATRIC
HOSPITAL

Ford Road and Monument Avenue, Philadelphia, Pennsylvania.
    1949-1950 and 1950-1953.

"Mental hospital." il. Architectural Forum 95 (September
    1951): 198-200.
"New hospital type brings the spark of good architecture to
    the mentally ill, substitutes glass for bars." il., plan,
    sec. Architectural Forum 98 (January 1953): 118-121.

Fig. 10:   Coward Shoe Store in Philadelphia, Pennsylvania

Olgyay, Aladar. <u>Solar Control and Shading Devices</u>. Princeton, N.J.: Princeton University, 1957. il. pp. 100-101.
Ronner, Heinz. <u>Louis I. Kahn: Complete Works, 1935-74</u>. Boulder, Colo.: Westview, 1977. il., plan, sec. pp. 61-63.
Rosenfield, Isadore. "Philadelphia psychiatric hospital, Philadelphia, Pa." il., plan, diag. <u>Progressive Architecture</u> 27 (November 1946): 81-88.
Scully, Vincent. <u>Louis I. Kahn</u>. New York: Braziller, 1962. il. plate 20, p. 17.
Tentori, Francesco. "Ordine e forma nell'opera di Louis Kahn." il. <u>Casabella</u> 241 (July 1960): 14-15.
Tyng, Alexandra. <u>Beginnings: Louis I. Kahn's Philosophy of Architecture</u>. New York: John Wiley and Sons, 1984. il. pp. 137-138.

TEMPLE AND POPLAR PUBLIC HOUSING

Philadelphia, Pennsylvania. 1950-1953. In association with Christopher Tunard.

Ronner, Heinz. <u>Louis I. Kahn: Complete Works, 1935-74</u>. Boulder, Colo.: Westview, 1977. il., plan, map. pp. 35-37.
Scully, Vincent. <u>Louis I. Kahn</u>. New York: Braziller, 1962. plan, elev., sec. plate 7, pp. 10-11.

Fig. 11: Mellon Center for British Art and Studies

Fig. 12:   Yale Art Gallery on the Yale University campus

YALE ART GALLERY

Yale University, New Haven, Connecticut. 1951-1953. In
association with Douglas Orr.

Banham, Reyner. "The new brutalism." il., plan. Archi-
tectural Review 118 (December 1955): 355-361.
Brawne, Michael. The Museum Interior. London: Thames
and Hudson, 1982. il. pp. 57-59, 64, 79, 122, 132.
The British Art Center at Yale: An Introduction for Visitors
and Students. New Haven: Yale Center for British Art,
1979. il. 40p.
Bush-Brown, Albert. "Architect's hero. Louis Kahn." il.
Horizon 5 (September 1962): 57-59, 61.
Cook, John Wesley. Conversations With Architects. New York:
Praeger, 1973. pp. 179-181, 210-212.
Filler, M. "Opus posthumous." Progressive Architecture
59 (May 1978): 76-81.
Frampton, Kenneth. Modern Architecture: A Critical History.
New York: Oxford University, 1980. il., plan. pp.
242-243.
"Genetrix, personal contributions to American architecture;
Louis Kahn." il. Architectural Review 121 (May 1957):
344-345.
Giurgola, Romaldo. Louis I. Kahn. Boulder, Colo.: West-
view, 1975. il., plan, sec. pp. 60, 62-64.
Harms, Hans H. "Trends in architektur: U.S.A.--Louis I.
Kahn." plan. Bauwelt 54 (28 October 1963): 1252-1261.
Huff, Williams S. "Kahn and Yale." il., port. Journal of
Architectural Education 35 (Spring 1982): 22-31.
"Institute: Kahn's gallery at Yale wins 25-year award." il.
AIA Journal 68 (May 1979): 11, 14.
"Ivyless halls of Yale." col. port. Holiday 37 (May 1965):
76-77.
Jacob, Eva. New Architecture in New England. Lincoln,
Mass.: De Cordova Museum, 1974. il. p. 12.
Jacobus, John. Twentieth Century Architecture: The Middle
Years, 1940-1965. New York: Praeger, 1966. il., plan.
pp. 119-122.
Joedicke, Jurgen. Architecture Since 1945; Sources and
Directions. New York: Praeger, 1969. il. p. 128.
Kahn, Louis I. The Notebooks and Drawings of Louis I. Kahn,
edited and designed by Richard Saul Wurman and Eugene
Feldman. Philadelphia: Falcon, 1962. il., plan, sec.
fig. 27.

_____. The Notebooks and Drawings of Louis I. Kahn,
   edited and designed by Richard Saul Wurman and Eugene
   Feldman. Cambridge: M.I.T., 1973. il., plan, sec. fig.
   27.
_____. Yale University Art Gallery; New Haven, Connecti-
   cut, 1951-1953. Kimbell Art Museum; Fort Worth, Texas,
   1966-1972, by Marshall D. Meyers. Tokyo: A.D.A. Edita,
   1976. il., plans, sec. pp. 2-17, 42-45.
"Louis I. Kahn; oeuvres 1963-1969." "Plans. 1953-1958."
   plan. Architecture D'Aujourd'hui 40 (February-March
   1969): 8.
"Louis Kahn." il., plan, sec. Architecture D'Aujourd'hui
   33 (December 1962): 4-5.
Mee, Charles L. "Louis Kahn," in Three Centuries of Notable
   American Architects, edited by Joseph J. Thorndike. New
   York: American Heritage, 1981. pp. 286-287.
McQuade, Walter. "Architect Louis Kahn and his strong-boned
   structures." il. Architectural Forum 107 (October 1957):
   138-139.
"P/A views." Letters to the editor from Robert W. McLaughlin,
   Leopold Arnaud, H. Holmes Perkins, Frederick Gutheim,
   Jose Luis Sert and C. Clark Macomber. Progressive Archi-
   tecture 35 (May 1954): 15-16, 22, 24.
Pushkarev, Boris. "Order and form: Yale Art Gallery and
   design center." il. (pt. col.), plan, sec., diag. Per-
   specta 3 (1955): 46-59.
Raafat, Aly Ahmed. Reinforced Concrete in Architecture.
   New York: Reinhold, 1958. il. pp. 180-181, 194-195.
Ragon, Michel. "Power of doubt." col. il. Connaissance des
   Arts 346 (December 1980): 84-91.
Rice, Norman. "Kahn." il. Architectural Plus 2 (May-June
   1974): 105.
Ronner, Heinz. Louis I. Kahn: Complete Works, 1935-74.
   Boulder, Colo.: Westview, 1977. il., plan, sec., elev.,
   diag. pp. 65-71.
Sanderson, George A. "Extension: university art gallery
   and design center." il., plan, sec., elev., diag. Pro-
   gressive Architecture 35 (May 1954): 88-101, 130-131.
Scully, Vincent. American Architecture and Urbanism.
   New York: Praeger, 1969. il. pp. 203, 214.
_____. "Archetype and order in recent American archi-
   tecture." il. Art in America 42 (December 1954): 250-
   257.
_____. "Doldrums in the suburbs." il. Society of Archi-
   tectural Historians. Journal 24 (March 1965): 47.

_____. Louis I. Kahn. New York: Braziller, 1962. il.
    plates 30-38, pp. 20-22.
_____. "Le Musée des Beaux-Arts de l'Université Yale, New
    Haven." il., plan, diag. Museum 9 (1956): 101-109
    (French), 110-113. (English).
Smith, G. E. Kidder. The Architecture of the United States.
    Garden City, N.Y.: Anchor, 1981, v. 1, il. pp. 34-35.
Smithson, Alison. "Louis Kahn." plan, sec., diag. Archi-
    tects' Yearbook 9 (1960): 112-114.
Spiker, David. "The Yale Center for British Art." il., plans,
    sec. Perspecta 16 (1980): 50-61.
Stern, Robert A. M. New Directions in American Architecture.
    New York: Braziller, 1969. il. pp. 11-12.
_____. New Directions in American Architecture. Revised
    ed. New York: Braziller, 1977. il. pp. 11-12.
Tentori, Francesco. "L'architetto Louis I. Kahn; ordine de
    forma nell'opera di Louis Kahn." il., plan. Casabella
    241 (July 1960): 4, 6-7, 9.
"Tetrahedral floor system: Yale's new design laboratory con-
    ceals lighting and ductwork within a 31-inch-deep floor
    structure." il., diag. Architectural Forum 97 (November
    1952): 148-149.
"Three-dimensional concrete floor system." il. Progressive
    Architecture 35 (June 1954): 103.
Tyng, Alexandra. Beginnings: Louis I. Kahn's Philosophy
    of Architecture. New York: John Wiley and Sons, 1984.
    il., plan, diag. pp. 31-35.
"Yale University Art Gallery." il., sec., diag. Architecture
    and Urbanism 3 (January 1973): 103-105.

ADATH JESHURUN SYNAGOGUE

York and Ashburne Roads, Elkins Park, Pennsylvania. 1954.

Coombs, Robert. "Light and silence: the religious architecture
    of Louis Kahn." plan, elev. Architectural Association
    Quarterly 13 (October 1981): 26-36.
Franteili, Enzo. "Louis Kahn." plans. Zodiac 8 (1961): 21.
Kahn, Louis I. "A Synagogue." plan. Perspecta 3 (1955):
    62-63.
"Louis Kahn." plan. Architecture D'Aujourd'hui 33 (December
    1962): 18.
Ronner, Heinz. Louis I. Kahn: Complete Works, 1935-74.

Boulder, Colo.: Westview, 1977. il., plan, sec., elev.
pp. 79-81.
Scully, Vincent. Louis I. Kahn. New York: Braziller, 1962.
il., plan. plates 40-41, p. 22.

WEBER DE VORE RESIDENCE

Montgomery Avenue, Springfield Township, Pennsylvania.
1954.

Ronner, Heinz. Louis I. Kahn: Complete Works, 1935-74.
Boulder, Colo.: Westview, 1977. plan, elev. p. 83.
Scully, VIncent. Louis I. Kahn. New York: Braziller, 1962.
plan. plate 44, p. 23.
Smithson, Alison. "Louis Kahn." il., plan. Architects'
Yearbook 9 (1960): 114.
Tentori, Francesco. "L'architetto Louis I. Kahn; ordine de
forma nell' opera di Louis Kahn." il., plan. Casabella
241 (July 1960): 8-10.
"Two houses." plan, sec., elev. Perspecta 3 (1955): 60-61.

FRANCIS ADLER RESIDENCE

8870 Towanda, Philadelphia, Pennsylvania. 1954.

Castex, Jean. "De Louis Kahn à Robert Venturi." Architec-
ture D'Aujourd'hui 163 (August-September 1972): 86-87.
Giurgola, Romaldo. Louis I. Kahn. Boulder, Colo.: Westview,
1975. plan. pp. 18, 20.
Ronner, Heinz. Louis I. Kahn: Complete Works, 1935-74.
Boulder, Colo.: Westview, 1977. plan, elev. pp. 84-85.
Scully, Vincent. Louis I. Kahn. New York: Braziller, 1962.
plan, elev. plates 42-43, p. 23.
Tentori, Francesco. "L'architetto Louis I. Kahn; ordine de
forma nell' opera di Louis Kahn." plan, elev. Casabella
241 (July 1960): 8-10.
"Two houses." plan, elev. Perspecta 3 (1955): 60-61.

AFL-CIO MEDICAL SERVICE BUILDING

1326 Vine Street, Philadelphia, Pennsylvania. 1954-1956.
Demolished 1973.

Donohoe, Victoria. "Downtown Philadelphia loses its only Kahn
building." il. Progressive Architecture 54 (November
1973): 23, 26.
"Genetrix: Personal contributions to American architecture;
Louis Kahn." il. Architectural Review 121 (May 1957):
344-345.
Jones, Cranston. "Louis Kahn, the esthetic of space," in
Architecture Today and Tomorrow. New York: McGraw-
Hill, 1961. p. 182.
"Louis Kahn." il., plan. Architecture D'Aujourd'hui 33
(December 1962): 6-7.
McBride, Richard D. "A new mode or an old manner? Decision
for Louis Kahn." il. Architecture and Urbanism 81
(August 1977): 77-90.
McQuade, Walter. "Architect Louis Kahn and his strong-boned
structures." il., port. Architectural Forum 107 (October
1957): 134-137.
_____. "The Exploded landscape." il., plan. Perspecta
7 (1961): 89-90.
Philadelphia Architecture. Prepared by American Institute of
Architects, Philadelphia Chapter. New York: Reinhold,
1961. p. 29.
Ronner, Heinz. Louis I. Kahn: Complete Works, 1935-74.
Boulder, Colo.: Westview, 1977. il., plans. pp. 87-89.
Scully, Vincent. Louis I. Kahn. New York: Braziller, 1962.
il. plates 45-46, p. 23.
Tentori, Francesco. "L'architetto Louis I. Kahn; Ordine e
forma nell' opera di Louis Kahn." il. Casabella 241 (July
1960): 4-5.

JEWISH COMMUNITY CENTER

909 Lower Ferry Road, Trenton, New Jersey. 1954-1959.

Cook, John Wesley. Conversations With Architects. New
York: Praeger, 1973. plan, sec. pp. 212-216.
Frateili, Enzo. "Louis Kahn." il., plan. Zodiac 8 (1961):
15, 24-25.
"Genetrix: personal contributions to American architecture;
Louis Kahn." il., plan, sec. Architectural Review 121
(May 1957): 344-345.
Giurgola, Romaldo. Louis I. Kahn. Boulder, Colo.: Westview,
1975. il., plan. pp. 112, 114-116.

Harms, Hans H. "Trends in architektur: U.S.A.—Louis I. Kahn." il., plan. Bauwelt 54 (28 October 1963): 1252-1261.

Jencks, Charles. Modern Movements in Architecture. Garden City, N.Y.: Anchor, 1973. il. pp. 230-231.

"Louis I. Kahn and the living city." Architectural Forum 108 (March 1958): 114-119.

"Louis I. Kahn; oeuvres 1963-1969." "Plan. 1953-1958." plan. Architecture D'Aujourd'hui 40 (February-March 1969): 8.

"Louis Kahn." il., plan. Architecture D'Aujourd'hui 33 (December 1962): 8-9.

"Louis Kahn: order in architecture." il., plans. Perspecta 4 (1957): 58-59.

McQuade, Walter. "Architect Louis Kahn and his strong-boned structures." il., plan, sec. Architectural Forum 107 (October 1957): 140-142.

Ronner, Heinz. Louis I. Kahn: Complete Works, 1935-74. Boulder, Colo.: Westview, 1977. il. (pt. col.), plan, sec. pp. 91-97.

Scully, Vincent. Louis I. Kahn. New York: Braziller, 1962. il., plan. plates 47-56, pp. 25-26.

_____. Modern Architecture. New York: Braziller, 1964. il., sec. plate 119, pp. 38-39.

_____. "Wright, International Style and Kahn." Arts 36 (March 1962): 67-71, 77.

Solomon, Susan G. "Beginnings." il. (pt. col.), plan. Progressive Architecture 65 (December 1984): 68-73.

Tentori, Francesco. "L'architetto Louis I. Kahn; ordine de forma nell'opera di Louis Kahn." il., plan. Casabella 241 (July 1960): 10-11.

_____. "Il passato come un amico." il., plan, elev. Casabella 275 (May 1963): 29.

MARTIN RESEARCH INSTITUTE

Fort Meade, Maryland. 1955-1957.

"Louis Kahn." il., plan. Architecture D'Aujourd'hui 33 (December 1962): 15.

Ronner, Heinz. Louis I. Kahn: Complete Works, 1935-74. Boulder, Colo.: Westview, 1977. il., plan. p. 99.

Scully, Vincent. Louis I. Kahn. New York: Braziller, 1962. il. plate 59, p. 26.

Tentori, Francesco. "Il passato come un amico." il., plan.
   Casabella 275 (May 1963): 31.

WASHINGTON UNIVERSITY LIBRARY

Saint Louis, Missouri. Project, 1956.

Kahn, Louis I. Drawings. Los Angeles: Access Press, 1981.
   il. pp. 57-59.
"P/A news survey: St. Louis architects win Washington Uni-
   versity competition." elev. Progressive Architecture 37
   (July 1956): 76-77.
"Record reports: Murphy and Mackey design wins Washington
   University competition." il. Architectural Record 120
   (July 1956): 16.
Ronner, Heinz. Louis I. Kahn: Complete Works, 1935-74.
   Boulder, Colo.: Westview, 1977. il., plan, sec., elev.
   pp. 101-107.
Scully, Vincent. Louis I. Kahn. New York: Braziller, 1962.
   il., elev. plates, 57-58, p. 26.
"Space, form, use." Pennsylvania Triangle (December
   1956): 43-47.
Tentori, Francesco. "Il passato come un amico." il., plan,
   elev. Cassabella 275 (May 1963): 30.

UNIVERSAL ATLAS CEMENT COMPANY, CITY TOWER

New York, New York. Project, 1957.

Cook, John Wesley. Conversations With Architects. New
   York: Praeger, 1973. plan, sec. pp. 179, 182.
Scully, Vincent. Louis I. Kahn. New York: Braziller, 1962.
   il., plan, diag. plates 61-63, p. 27.

FRED E. CLEVER RESIDENCE

Delaware Township, New Jersey. 1957-1961.

Ronner, Heinz. Louis I. Kahn: Complete Works, 1935-74.
   Boulder, Colo.: Westview, 1977. il. p. 109.

Fig. 13:   Richards Research Building on the campus of the
           University of Pennsylvania

ALFRED NEWTON RICHARDS RESEARCH BUILDINGS

3700 Hamilton Walk, University of Pennsylvania, Philadelphia,
   Pennsylvania.   1957-1964.

"Alfred Newton Richards Medical Research Building."   il., plan.
   Architecture and Urbanism 3 (January 1973):   29, 60, 67-
   70.
"Alfred Newton Richards Medical Research Building, Philadel-
   phia (1957-1961)."   il., plan.   Werk 7 (1974):   798-799.
"American rebuilding: a theory for the future."   il., plan.
   Architectural Forum 112 (January 1960):   138-140.
"Arcaismo technologico."   il., plan.   Architettura 6 (October
   1960):   410-411.
Aregger, Hans.   Highrise Building and Urban Design.   New
   York: Praeger, 1967.   il., plans.   pp. 90-91.
"Art serves science: Alfred Newton Richards Medical Research
   Building, University of Pennsylvania, Philadelphia, Pa."
   il., plan.   Architectural Record 128 (August 1960):   149-
   156.

Fig. 14:   Richards Research Building

Banham, Reyner. Age of the Masters; a Personal View of
    Modern Architecture. New York: Harper and Row, 1975.
    il. pp. 86-87.
_____. Guide to Modern Architecture. Princeton: Van
    Nostrand, 1962. il. pp. 72, 74-75.
_____. Guide to Modern Architecture. London: Archi-
    tectural Press, 1962. il. pp. 72, 74-75.
_____. "On trial 2: Louis Kahn; the buttery-hatch aesthet-
    ic." diags. Architectural Review 131 (March 1962):
    203-205.
Boyd, Robin. "The new vision in architecture." il. Harper's
    Magazine 223 (July 1961): 80-81.
_____. The Puzzle of Architecture. London: Cambridge,
    1965. il. pp. 50, 132-134, 143.
"Building skeletons: an investigation of ten buildings." diags.
    North Carolina State University. School of Design. Stu-
    dent Publication. 17 (January 1967): 3a-3b.
Bush-Brown, Albert. "Architect's hero: Louis Kahn." il.
    Horizon 5 (September 1962): 57-63.
Chermayeff, Ivan. Observations on American Architecture.
    New York: Viking, 1972. col. il. pp. 138-139.
Cook, John Wesley. Conversations With Architects. New York:
    Praeger, 1973. il. pp. 210-211.
Donat, John. World Architecture Today. New York: Viking,
    1964. il., plan. pp. 34-37.
Drew, Philip. Third Generation: The Changing Meaning of
    Architecture. New York: Praeger, 1972. il., plan. pp.
    37-38.
Drexler, Arthur. Transformations in Modern Architecture.
    New York: Museum of Modern Art, 1979. il. pp. 102-
    103.
"Form evokes function." il. Time 75 (6 June 1960): 76.
Fitch, James Marston. "A building of rugged fundamentals."
    il., plan, elev. Architectural Forum 113 (July 1960):
    82-87, 185.
Frampton, Kenneth. Modern Architecture: A Critical History.
    New York: Oxford, 1980. plan. pp. 244-245.
Frateili, Enzo. "Louis Kahn." il. Zodiac 8 (1961): 14-17,
    22-23.
Giurgola, Romaldo. Louis I. Kahn. Boulder, Colo.: Westview,
    1975. il., plan. pp. 194-202.
Green, Wilder. "Louis I. Kahn, architect: Alfred Newton
    Richards Medical Research Building, University of Penn-
    sylvania, Philadelphia, 1958-60." il., plan, sec., elev.,
    port. Museum of Modern Art Bulletin 28 (1, 1961): 1-24.

_____. "Medical research buildings--Louis Kahn." il.,
    plan, sec., elev. Arts and Architecture 78 (July 1961):
    14-17, 28.
Harms, Hans H. "Trends in architektur: USA--Louis I.
    Kahn." il., plan, diag. Bauwelt 54 (28 October 1963):
    1252-1261.
Hennessy, Richard. "Prototype and progeny; some recent
    monumental architecture." il. Artforum 17 (November
    1978): 68-70.
Hitchcock, Henry Russell. "Notes of a traveller: Wright and
    Kahn." Zodiac 6 (1960): 20-21.
Hofmann, Werner. Modern Architecture in Color. New York:
    Viking, 1970. col. il., plan. pp. 382-385.
Huxtable, Ada Louise. "In Philadelphia, an architect." il.
    New York Times (11 June 1961): II, 14: 3.
Jacobus, John. Twentieth Century Architecture; The Middle
    Years, 1940-1965. New York: Praeger, 1966. il., plan.
    pp. 158, 190-192.
Jencks, Charles. Modern Movements in Architecture. Garden
    City, N.Y.: Anchor, 1973. il. p. 230.
Joedicke, Jurgen. Architecture Since 1945; Sources and
    Directions. New York: Praeger, 1969. il., plan. p.
    128.
Johnson, Philip. "Great reputations in the making: three
    architects." il. Art in America 48 (Spring 1960): 70-71.
Jordy, William H. "Medical research building for Pennsylvania
    University, Philadelphia." il., plans, sec. Architectural
    Review 129 (February 1961): (98-106.
Kahn, Louis I. Drawings. Los Angeles: Access Press, 1981.
    il. p. 71.
_____. "Form and design." plan, elev. Architectural
    Design 31 (April 1961): 145.
_____. "The Lewis Richards Medical Research Building at
    the University of Pennsylvania. il., plan, port. South
    African Architectural Record 48 (April 1963): 23-26.
_____. The Notebooks and Drawings of Louis I. Kahn,
    edited and designed by Richard Saul Wurman and Eugene
    Feldman. Philadelphia: Flacon, 1962. il. fig. 32-37.
_____. The Notebooks and Drawings of Louis I. Kahn,
    edited and designed by Richard Saul Wurman and Eugene
    Feldman. Cambridge: M.I.T., 1973. il. fig. 32-37.
_____. Richards Medical Research Building, Pennsylvania,
    1961; Salk Institute for Biological Studies, California, 1965,
    edited and photographed by Yukin Futagawa, text by

Fumihiko Maki. Tokyo: A.D.A. Edita, 1971. (Global
Architecture, 5). il. (pt. col.), plans, sec. pp. 26-40.
"Kahn's medical science building dedicated at University of
Pennsylvania." il. Progressive Architecture 41 (June
1960): 61.
"Kahn's second phase at Pennsylvania; new biology building."
il., plan. Progressive Architecture 45 (September 1964):
208-213.
Komendant, August E. 18 Years With Architect Louis I. Kahn.
Englewood, N.J.: Aloray, 1975. il., plan, diag. pp. 7-24.
Kulski, Julian Eugene. Architecture in a Revolutionary Era.
Nashville, Tenn.: Aurora, 1971. il. pp. 232-235.
"Laboratoires a l'Université de Pennsylvanie, Etats-Unis."
il., plan, elev., diag. Architecture D'Aujourd'hui 31
(September 1960): 66-67.
"Laboratoires de recherches médicales Alfred Newton à l'Univer-
sité de Pennsylvanie." il., plan, elev. Architecture
D'Aujourd'hui 6 (February 1962): 76-81.
Ligo, Larry L. The Concept of Function in Twentieth-Century
Architectural Criticism. Ann Arbor, Mich.: UMI Research
Press, 1984. il., plan, elev. pp. 30, 52, 62, 79, 82,
84, 163-167.
Lobell, John. Between Silence and Light. Boulder, Colo.:
Shambhala, 1979. il., plan, elev. p. 72-75.
"Logic and art in precast concrete." il., plan, elev., diag.
Architectural Record 134 (September 1959): 232-238.
"Louis I. Kahn; oeuvres 1963-1969." "Plans. 1953-1958."
Architecture D'Aujourd'hui 142 (February-March 1969): 8.
"Louis Kahn." il., plan, diag. Architecture D'Aujourd'hui
33 (December 1962): 10-11.
McQuade, Walter. "Architect Louis Kahn and his strong-boned
structures." il., plan, elev. Architectural Forum 107
(October 1957): 143.
_____. "The exploded landscape." plan, elev. Perspecta
7 (1961): 88.
Magnago Lampugnani, Vittorio. Architecture of the 20th Cen-
tury in Drawings. New York: Rizzoli, 1982. il. p. 161.
Maki, Fumihiko. "American architecture," in Contemporary
Architecture of the World, 1961. Tokyo: Shokokusha,
1961. col. il. pp. 324-325.
Mee, Charles L. "Louis Kahn," in Three Centuries of Notable
American Architects, edited by Joseph J. Thorndike. New
York: American Heritage, 1981. col. il. pp. 287-291.
Moholy-Nagy, Sibyl. "The future of the past; doctor mira-
bilis." il. Perspecta 7 (1961): 73-76.

New York. Museum of Modern Art. Louis I. Kahn, Alfred
   Newton Richards Medical Research Building, University
   of Pennsylvania, Philadelphia, 1958-1960. New York: The
   Museum, 1961. il., plans. 22p.
Norberg-Schulz, Christian. Meaning in Western Architecture.
   New York: Praeger, 1975. il., plan, elev., diag. pp.
   418-420.
Obrogon, Jose. Medical research center, University of Penn-
   sylvania. Cambridge: Harvard University, Department
   of Architecture, 1961. il., plans, sec. unp. Thesis.
Onobayasi, Hiroki. "Louis I. Kahn and Alfred Newton Rich-
   ards Medical Research Building." il., plan. Kokusai-
   Kentiku 28 (March 1961): 64-69.
Peters, Paulhans. "Zum tod von Peter Celsing, Hans Dollgast,
   und Louis Kahn." il. Baumeister 71 (May 1974): 488-
   489.
Philadelphia Architecture, prepared by AIA, Philadelphia
   Chapter. New York: Reinhold, 1961. il., plan. pp. 41-
   43.
Pierson, William Harvey. American Buildings and their Archi-
   tects: The Impact of European Modernism in the Mid-
   Twentieth Century, v. 4. Garden City, N.Y.: Doubleday,
   1972. il., plan, elev., diag. pp. 361-426, 444-445.
Ragon, Michel. "Power of doubt." col. il. Connaissance des
   Arts 346 (December 1980): 84-91.
Rice, Norman. "Kahn." il. Architectural Plus 2 (May-June
   1974): 104.
"Richards Medical Research Building." il. Arts 35 (September
   1961): 66.
"Richards research laboratories." il. Architectural Forum
   113 (October 1960): 2-3.
Ronner, Heinz. Louis I. Kahn: Complete Works, 1935-74.
   Boulder, Colo.: Westview, 1977. il., plan, sec., elev.,
   diag. pp. 111-117.
Roth, Leland M. A Concise History of American Architecture.
   New York: Harper and Row, 1979. il. pp. 299-300.
Roth, Ueli. "Amerikanische architektur-gestern." il. DU 24
   (June 1964): 25, 42, 44.
_____. "Louis Kahn and the medical towers in Philadelphia."
   il., plans, elev. Werk 49 (January 1962): 22-25.
Scully, Vincent. American Architecture and Urbanism. New
   York: Praeger, 1969. il., plan, elev. pp. 214-215.
_____. "Light, form and power: new work of Louis Kahn."
   il. Architectural Forum 121 (August-September 1964):
   162-163.

_____. Louis I. Kahn. New York: Braziller, 1962. il.,
    plan, elev. plates 2, 64-74, pp. 27-30.
_____. "The precisionist strain in American architecture."
    il. Art in America 48 (Summer 1960): 53.
_____. "Recent works by Louis Kahn." il., plan, elev.,
    diag. Zodiac 17 (1967): 58-67.
_____. "Wright, International Style, and Kahn." Arts 36
    (March 1962): 67-71, 77.
"Shapes of tomorrow, two buildings in diverging directions."
    il. Interiors 120 (July 1961): 41, 116.
Smith, G. E. Kidder. The Architecture of the United States.
    Garden City, N.Y.: Anchor, 1981, v. 1. il., pp. 635-
    637.
_____. A Pictorial History of Architecture in America.
    New York: American 1976. il. pp. 258-259.
Smithson, Alison. "Louis Kahn." il., plan, elev. Architects'
    Yearbook 9 (1960): 102, 104-105.
Stern, Robert A. M. New Directions in American Architecture.
    New York: Braziller, 1969. il. pp. 11-12.
_____. New Directions in American Architecture. Revised
    ed. New York: Braziller, 1977. il. pp. 11-12.
Tatum, George B. Penn's Great Town. Philadelphia: Uni-
    versity of Pennsylvania, 1961. il. plate 145, pp. 139,
    206-207.
Tentori, Francesco. "L'architetto Louis I. Kahn; ordine de
    forma nell'opera di Louis Kahn." il., plan, elev., diag.
    Casabella 241 (July 1960): 15-17.
Tyng, Alexandra. Beginnings: Louis I. Kahn's Philosophy
    of Architecture. New York: John Wiley and Sons, 1984.
    il., plan. pp. 37-40, 72-73, 140.
"Ulkomaat." il. Arkkitechti 71 (February 1974): 23.
Von Eckardt, Wolf. A Place to Live: The Crises of the
    Cities. New York: Delacorte, 1967. il. pp. 142-144,
    198-199.
Whiffen, Marcus. American Architecture, 1607-1976. Cam-
    bridge: M.I.T., 1981. il., plan. pp. 426-433.
Wilson, Colin St. John. "Open and Closed." il. Perspecta
    7 (1961): 101-102.
World Architecture. New York: McGraw-Hill, 1963. il. pp.
    337-338, 341.

LAWRENCE MORRIS RESIDENCE

Mount Kisco, New York. 1958.

Giurgola, Romaldo. Louis I. Kahn. Boulder, Colo.: Westview,
   1975. il., plan. pp. 18-19, 21.
"Louis I. Kahn." il., plan. Architecture D'Aujourd'hui 33
   (December 1962): 23.
Ronner, Heinz. Louis I. Kahn: Complete Works, 1935-74.
   Boulder, Colo.: Westview, 1977. il., plan, elev. pp.
   119-121.
Scully, Vincent. Louis I. Kahn. New York: Braziller, 1962.
   il. plate 77, p. 31.
Smithson, Alison. "CIAM, Team 10." Architectural Design
   30 (May 9160): 192-193.
_____. "Louis Kahn." il., plan. Architects' Yearbook 9
   (1960): 118.
Tentori, Francesco. "L'architetto Louis Kahn; ordine de forma
   nell'opera di Louis Kahn." il. Casabella 241 (July 1960):
   15.

TRIBUNE REVIEW BUILDING

Greensburg, Pennsylvania. 1958-1961.

Giurgola, Romaldo. Louis I. Kahn. Boulder, Colo.: Westview,
   1975. il., plan, sec., elev. pp. 194, 203-205.
"Imprimérie d'un journal à Pittsburgh, Pennsylvanie." il.,
   plan, sec., elev. Architecture D'Aujourd'hui 105 (Decem-
   ber 1962): 12-13.
"Kahn newspaper shop." il., plan, sec., elev. Architectural
   Forum 116 (April 1962): 82-85.
Komendant, August E. 18 Years With Architect Louis I. Kahn.
   Englewood, N.J.: Aloray, 1975. il., plan. pp. 25-31.
Ronner, Heinz. Louis I. Kahn: Complete Works, 1935-74.
   Boulder, Colo.: Westview, 1977. il., plan, sec., elev.
   pp. 123-125.
Scully, Vincent. "Light, form and power: new work of Louis
   Kahn." il. Architectural Forum 121 (August-September
   1964): 165.
_____. Louis I. Kahn. New York: Braziller, 1962. il.
   plates 78-81, p. 31.
"Tribune Review Publishing Company building." il., plan.
   Architecture and Urbanism 3 (January 1973): 127-129.

ROBERT H. FLEISHER RESIDENCE

Elkins Park, Pennsylvania. 1959.

Giurgola, Romaldo. Louis I. Kahn. Boulder, Colo.: Westview,
    1975. il., plan. pp. 18-19.
"Louis Kahn." il., plan. Architecture D'Aujourd'hui 33
    (December 1962): 22.
Ronner, Heinz. Louis I. Kahn: Complete Works, 1935-74.
    Boulder, Colo.: Westview, 1977. il., plan. p. 127.
Scully, Vincent. Louis I. Kahn. New York: Braziller, 1962.
    il., plan. plates 97-98, p. 35.
Smithson, Alison. "Louis Kahn." il., plan, diag. Architects'
    Yearbook 9 (1960): 117.
_____. "CIAM, Team 10." il. Architectural Design 30
    (May 1960): 192-193.
Tentori, Francesco. L'architetto Louis I. Kahn; ordine de
    forma nell'opera di Louis Kahn." il. Casabella 241 (July
    1960): 15.

MORTON GOLDENBERG RESIDENCE

Frazer Road, Rydal, Pennsylvania. 1959.

Boyd, Robin. The Puzzle of Architecture. London: Cam-
    bridge, 1965. plan. p. 147.
Kahn, Louis I. Drawings. Los Angeles: Access Press, 1981.
    plan, sec. p. 56.
_____. "Kahn." il., plan. Perspecta 7 (1961): 12-14,
    19-20.
"Louis Kahn." il., plan. Architecture D'Aujourd'hui 33
    (December 1962): 24.
"Louis I. Kahn; oeuvres 1963-1969." "Plans, 1953-1959."
    plan. Architecture D'Aujourd'hui 40 (February-March
    1969): 9.
Ronner, Heinz. Louis I. Kahn: Complete Works, 1935-74.
    Boulder, Colo.: Westview, 1977. il., plan. pp. 129-131.
Scully, Vincent. Louis I. Kahn. New York: Braziller, 1962.
    il., plan. plates, 92-94, pp. 34-35.
Smithson, Alison. "Louis Kahn." il., plan, diag. Architects'
    Yearbook 9 (1960); 115-116.

MARGARET ESHERICK RESIDENCE

204 Sunrise Lane, Chestnut Hill, Pennsylvania. 1959-1961.

"Architectural changes forecast new adventures in living."
col. il. House and Garden 122 (October 1962): 158-159.
Castex, Jean. "De Louis Kahn à Robert Venturi." plan.
Architecture D'Aujourd'hui 163 (August 1972): 87.
Giurgola, Romalda. Louis I. Kahn. Boulder, Colo.: Westview, 1975. il., plan. pp. 18, 20-21.
"A house by Louis Kahn--a timeless sense of light and space."
il. (pt. col.), plan. House Beautiful 108 (September
1966): 170-175.
Kahn, Louis I. Drawings. Los Angeles: Access Press, 1981.
plan, elev. pp. 33-47.
"Louis I. Kahn: oeuvres 1963-1969." "Plan, 1953-1958."
plan. Architecture D'Aujourd'hui 40 (February-March
1969): 8.
"Louis Kahn." il., plan, sec. Architecture D'Aujourd'hui
33 (December 1962): 25.
Overland, Orm. "Louis I. Kahn as philosopher." il., plan.
Byggekunst 48, no. 5 (1966): 116-127.
Ronner, Heinz. Louis I. Kahn: Complete Works, 1935-74.
Boulder, Colo.: Westview, 1977. il. (pt. col.), plan,
sec. pp. 133-135.
Scully, Vincent. "Light, form and power: new work of
Louis Kahn." il. Architecture Forum 121 (August-
September 1964): 165.
_____. Louis I. Kahn. New York: Braziller, 1962. il.
plates 95-96, p. 35.
Tyng, Alexandra. Beginnings: Louis I. Kahn's Philosophy
of Architecture. New York: John Wiley and Sons, 1984.
il. p. 145.

BERNARD SHAPIRO RESIDENCE

Hidden River Road, Narberth, Pennsylvania. 1959-1961.

Ronner, Heinz. Louis I. Kahn: Complete Works, 1935-74.
Boulder, Colo.: Westview, 1977. il., plan. p. 137.

UNITED STATES CONSULATE BUILDINGS

Luanda, Angola. 1959-1961.

Campajola, Viviana. "Architettura bioclimatica: en/arch 83."

il. Architettura 29 (August–September 1983): 613.
Giurgola, Romaldo. Louis I. Kahn. Boulder, Colo.: West-
view, 1975. il., plan, sec., elev. pp. 194, 206-209.
Kahn, Louis I. Drawings. Los Angeles: Access Press, 1981.
il., plan, elev. pp. 48-55.
_____. "Form and design." plan, sec., elev., diag.
Architectural Design 31 (April 1961): 150-151.
_____. "Kahn." plan, sec., diag. Perspecta 7 (1961):
9-12, 21-22.
"Louis Kahn." plan, sec., elev. Architecture D'Aujourd'hui
33 (December 1962): 14.
Ronner, Heinz. Louis I. Kahn: Complete Works, 1935-74.
Boulder, Colo.: Westview, 1977. il., plan, sec., elev.,
diag. pp. 139-141.
Rowan, Jan C. "Wanting to be: the Philadelphia School."
il., plan, sec., elev., diag. Progressive Architecture
42 (April 1961): 140-141.
Scully, Vincent. Louis I. Kahn. New York: Braziller, 1962.
il., plan, diag. plates 99-103, pp. 35-36.
Tyng, Alexandra. Beginnings: Louis I. Kahn's Philosophy
of Architecture. New York: John Wiley and Sons, 1984.
il. pp. 145-146, 163.
"U.S. consulate building for Angola." il., plan, diag. Architecture and Urbanism 3 (January 1973): 33, 130-131.

SALK INSTITUTE

10010 North Torrey Pines Road, La Jolla, California. 1959-
1965.

"Academic ratrace." il. Architectural Review 139 (March
1966): 168-169.
"Address by Louis I. Kahn; April 5, 1966." il. Boston
Society of architects. Journal 1 (1967): 7-20.
Anderson, Stanford. "Louis I. Kahn in the 1960's." il., plan,
sec. Boston Society of Architects. Journal 1 (1967):
21-30.
Andrews, Wayne. Architecture in America. New York: Athe-
neum, 1977. il. p. 161.
Borck, F. K. "Planung mit installationsgeschossen Dargestellt
an Bauten des Cesundheitswesens in USA und Kanada.
il. Bauwelt 64 (18 June 1963): 1033.
Frampton, Kenneth. Modern Architecture: A Critical History.
New York: Oxford, 1980. sec. pp. 244-246.

Giurgola, Romaldo. Louis I. Kahn. Boulder, Colo.: Westview,
    1975. il., plan, sec. pp. 60, 66-75.
Hall, Mary Harrington. "Gifts from the sea and the high
    hopes of Jonas Salk." San Diego Magazine 14 (February
    1962): 41-45, 105-106.
Hammett, Ralph Warner. Architecture in the United States:
    A Survey of Architectural Styles Since 1776. New York:
    Wiley, 1976. p. 306.
Harms, Hans H. "Trends in architektur: USA-Louis I. Kahn."
    il., plan, sec., diag. Bauwelt 54 (28 October 1963):
    1252-1261.
Hughes, Robert. "Brick is stingy, concrete is generous:
    Salk Institute." il. Horizon 16 (Autumn 1974): 36-37.
_____. "Building with spent light." il., port. Time
    101 (15 January 1973): 60-65.
Jencks, Charles. Modern Movements in Architecture. Garden
    City, N.Y.: Anchor, 1973. il., diag. pp. 213-233.
"Jonas Salk: der Sinn des Menschen fur Ordnung." Werk
    (July 1974): 806.
Jordy, William H. "Symbolic essence of modern European ar-
    chitecture of the twenties and its continuing influence."
    il. Society of Architecture Historians. Journal 22 (Octo-
    ber 1963): 186-187.
Kahn, Louis I. Drawings. Los Angeles: Access Press, 1981.
    il., plan, elev. pp. 27-32.
_____. "Form and design." il., plan, elev., sec., diag.
    Architectural Design 31 (April 1961): 152-154.
_____. The Notebooks and Drawings of Louis I. Kahn,
    edited and designed by Richard Saul Wurman and Eugene
    Feldman. Philadelphia: Falcon, 1962. il., plan, elev.
    fig. 48-61.
_____. The Notebooks and Drawings of Louis I. Kahn,
    edited and designed by Richard Saul Wurman and Eugene
    Feldman. Cambridge, Massachusetts: M.I.T., 1973. il.,
    plan, elev. fig. 48-61.
_____. "Remarks." il., plan, sec. Perspecta 9/10 (1965):
    332-335.
_____. Richards Medical Research Building, Pennsylvania
    1961; Salk Institute for Biological Studies, California, 1965,
    edited and photographed by Yukio Futagawa, text by Fumi-
    hiko Maki. Tokyo: A.D.A. Edita, 1971. (Global Archi-
    tecture, 5). il. (pt. col.), plans. pp. 9-25.
_____. "Ten buildings that point the future." il. Fortune
    72 (December 1965): 174-179.

"Kahn not for the faint-hearted." il. AIA Journal 55 (June 1971): 28-29.

Komendant, August E. 18 Years With Architect Louis I. Kahn. Englewood, N.J.: Aloray, 1975. il., plan, diag. pp. 41-73.

"Laboratory 1: precession of massive forms." il., plan, sec. Architectural Forum 122 (May 1965): 36-45.

"Labs slab." il. Architectural Review 143 (March 1968): 173-174.

Lobell, John. Between Silence and Light. Boulder, Colo.: Shambhala, 1979. il., plan, sec. pp. 7, 25, 34, 76-85.

"Louis I. Kahn exhibit." il. Arts and Architecture 82 (July 1965): 36-37.

"Louis I. Kahn; oeuvres 1963-1969." il., plan, sec. Architecture D'Aujourd'hui 142 (February-March 1969): 10, 80-87, 100.

"Louis Kahn." il., plan, sec., elev. Architecture D'Aujourd'hui 33 (December 1962): 29-34.

"Louis Kahn--en Ameridansk Arkitekt." Arkitekten 8 (August 1966): 149-160.

"Louis Kahn: Institut Salk." il., plan, sec. Architecture D'Aujourd'hui (January 1967): 4-10.

McCoy, Esther. "Buildings in the United States: 1966-1967." il. Lotus 4 (1967-1968): 50-57.

_____. "Dr. Salk talks about his institute." il., plan, sec. Architectural Forum 127 (December 1967): 27-35.

Magnago Lampugnani, Vittorio. Architecture of the 20th Century in Drawings. New York: Rizzoli, 1982. il. p. 162.

"The man behind Mikveh Israels new building." The Jewish Exponent, Philadelphia (30 March 1962): 21.

Mee, Charles L. "Louis Kahn." Three Centuries of Notable American Architects, edited by Joseph J. Thorndike. New York: American Heritage, 1981. col. il. pp. 288-289, 292, 294.

"The mind of Louis Kahn." il., plan. Architectural Forum 127 (July-August 1972): 42, 45, 85-87.

Nairn, Janet. "Conference dissects works of five very different architects." Architecture 73 (October 1984): 16, 18, 21.

"An old master's footnote preserves an early idea." il. Fortune 74 (July 1966): 126.

Pierson, William Harvey. American Buildings and Their Architects: The Impact of European Modernism in the Mid-Twentieth Century, v. 4. Garden City, N.Y.: Doubleday, 1972. il., plan, sec. pp. 383-387, 389-390, 411-412.

Ragon, Michel. "Power of doubt." col. il. Connaissance des
     Arts 346 (December 1980): 84-91.
Ronner, Heinz. Louis I. Kahn: Complete Works, 1935-74.
     Boulder, Colo.: Westview, 1977. il., plan, sec., elev.,
     diag. pp. 143-167.
Roth, Leland M. A Concise History of American Architecture.
     New York: Harper and Row, 1979. il. pp. 301-303.
Roth, Ueli. "Zwei Forschungslaboratorien." il., plan, diag.
     Werk 54 (April 1967): 193-204.
Rowan, Jan C. "Wanting to be: the Philadelphia school."
     il., plan, sec., elev., diag. Progressive Architecture
     42 (April 1961): 142-149.
"Il Salk institute di Louis Kahn." il., plan, sec. Architettura
     11 (November 1965): 462-463.
"Salk institute for biological studies." il., plan, elev. Archi-
     tecture and Urbanism 3 (January 1973): 28-29, 61, 79-88.
"Salk institute for biological studies, La Jolla (San Diego)."
     il., plan, diag. Werk (July 1974): 804-805.
"Salk institute, La Jolla." il., plan, sec. World Architecture
     4 (1967): 40-47.
Scully, Vincent. American Architecture and Urbanism. New
     York: Praeger, 1969. il. pp. 221-222.
_____. "Light, form and power; new work of Louis Kahn."
     il., plan, sec. Architectural Forum 121 (August-September
     1964): 166.
_____. Louis I. Kahn. New York: Braziller, 1962. il.,
     plan, sec., elev., diag. plates 105-114, p. 36.
_____. "Recent works by Louis Kahn." il., plan, sec.,
     elev. Zodiac 17 (1967): 80-103.
Smith, G. E. Kidder. The Architecture of the United States.
     Garden City, N.Y.: Anchor, 1981. il. pp. 94-97.
_____. A Pictorial History of Architecture in America.
     New York: American Heritage, 1976. il. pp. 818-819.
Stern, Robert A. M. New Directions in American Architecture.
     New York: Braziller, 1969. il. pp. 19-21.
_____. New Directions in American Architecture. Revised
     ed. New York: Braziller, 1977. il., pp. 19-21.
Temko, Allan. "Evaluation: Louis Kahn's Salk Institute after
     a dozen years; what it is and what it might have been."
     il., sec. AIA Journal 66 (March 1977): 42-49.
"Ten buildings that point the future." col. il. Fortune 72
     (December 1965): 174-175, 178.
Tentori, Francesco. "Il passato come un amico." il., plan,
     sec., elev., diag. Casabella 275 (May 1963): 34-40.

Tyng, Alexandra. Beginnings: Louis I. Kahn's Philosophy
     of Architecture. New York: John Wiley and Sons, 1984.
     il., plan, sec. pp. 40-43, 74-75, 140-142, 147-148, 165.
"Ulkomaat." il. Arkkitehti 71 (February 1974): 23.
Weeks, John. "A design approach," in Design for Research;
     Principles of Laboratory Architecture, edited by Susan
     Braybrooke. il., plan. pp. 4-8.
West, Don. "Doctor Salk's bold new venture." Pageant Maga-
     zine 17 (February 1962): 156-161.
Whiffen, Marcus. American Architecture, 1606-1976. Cam-
     bridge: M.I.T., 1981. il. pp. 426-433.
Wilson, Richard Guy. "Gold Medal for 1971; Louis Isidore
     Kahn," in The AIA Gold Medal. New York: McGraw-Hill,
     1984. il., plan, port. pp. 123, 212.

FIRST UNITARIAN CHURCH

220 South Winton, Rochester, New York. 1959-1967.

Andrews, Wayne. Architecture in New York: A Photographic
     History. New York: Atheneum, 1969. il. p. 167.
"Architecture of Louis Kahn." Interiors 125 (May 1966): 10.
Cook, John Wesley. Conversations With Architects. New
     York: Praeger, 1973. il. pp. 189-190.
Coombs, Robert. "Light and silence: the religious architect-
     ure of Louis Kahn." plan, sec. Architectural Association
     Quarterly 13 (October 1981): 26-36.
Coulin, Claudius. Drawings by Architects: From the Ninth
     Century to the Present Day. New York: Reinhold, 1962.
     il. pp. 130-131.
Drexler, Arthur. Transformations in Modern Architecture.
     New York: Museum of Modern Art, 1979. il. p. 102.
"Form and design." plan, sec., elev., diag. Architectural
     Design 31 (April 1961): 146-147.
"Four Unitarian churches." il., plan, sec. Architecture
     Canada 45 (February 1968): 39-40.
Friedman, Arnold. Interior Design: An Introduction to Archi-
     tectural Interiors. Revised ed. New York: Elsevier,
     1976. col. il. pp. 156-157.
Giurgola, Romaldo. Louis I. Kahn. Boulder, Colo.: West-
     view, 1975. il., plans, sec., elev. pp. 38-43.
Harms, Hans H. "Trends in Architecktur: U.S.A.--Louis I.
     Kahn." il., plan, sec., diag. Bauwelt 54 (28 October
     1963): 1252-1261.

Jacobs, John. Twentieth Century Architecture: The Middle
    Years, 1940-1965. New York: Praeger, 1966. il., plan.
    pp. 192-193.
Jencks, Charles. Modern Movements in Architecture. Garden
    City, N.Y.: Anchor, 1973. il., diag. pp. 233-235.
"Kahn." il., plan, sec., elev., diag. Perspecta 7 (1961):
    14-18, 23-28.
Kennedy, Roger G. American Churches. New York: Stewart,
    Tabori and Chang, 1982. il. pp. 38-39.
Komendant, August E. 18 Years With Architect Louis I. Kahn.
    Englewood, N.J.: Aloray, 1975. il., plan, sec., diag.
    pp. 33-40.
"Komendant on concrete." Progressive Architecture 47 (Octo-
    ber 1966): 208-214.
"Louis I. Kahn; oeuvres 1963-1969." "Plans. 1953-1958."
    plan. Architecture D'Aujourd'hui 40 (February-March
    1969): 9.
"Louis Kahn." il., plan, sec., elev. Architecture
    D'Aujourd'hui 33 (December 1972): 16-17.
Malo, Paul. Landmarks of Rochester and Monroe County:
    A Guide to Neighborhoods and Villages. Syracuse: Syra-
    cuse, 1974. il. pp. 45, 47, 55.
Monk, Anthony J. "First Unitarian Church, Rochester, New
    York." il., plan, sec., elev. Royal Institute of British
    Architects. Journal 71 (July 1964): 315-316.
Overland, Orm. "Louis I. Kahn as philosopher." il., plan.
    Byggekunst 48 (1966): 116-127.
Piene, Nan R. "New York: gallery notes." il. Art in
    America 54 (March-April 1966): 124-125.
Ragon, Michel. The Aesthetics of Contemporary Architecture,
    translated by Haalson Chevalier. Neuchatel: Ed. du
    Griffon, 1968. il. p. 100.
_____. "Power of doubt." col. il. Connaissance des Arts
    346 (December 1980): 84-91.
Rice, Norman. "Kahn." col. il. Architectural Plus 2 (May-
    June 1974): 106-107.
Ronner, Heinz. Louis I. Kahn: Complete Works, 1935-74.
    Boulder, Colo.: Westview, 1977. il., plan, sec., elev.,
    diag. pp. 169-179.
Roth, Leland M. A Concise History of American Architecture.
    New York: Harper & Row, 1979. il. p. 301.
Rowan, Jan C. "Wanting to be: the Philadelphia school."
    il., plan, sec., elev., diag. Progressive Architecture
    42 (April 1961): 134-139.

Scully, Vincent. American Architecture and Urbanism. New
    York: Praeger, 1969. il., plan. pp. 216-217.
_____. "Light, form and power: new work of Louis Kahn."
    il., plan, sec. Architectural Forum 121 (August-September
    1964): 164-165.
_____. Louis I. Kahn. New York: Braziller, 1962. il.,
    plan, sec., elev., diag. plates 88-91, pp. 32-34.
_____. "Wright, International style and Kahn." Arts 36
    (March 1962): 67-71, 77.
Smith, G. E. Kidder. The Architecture of the United States,
    v. 1. Garden City, N.Y.: Anchor, 1981. il. pp. 456-
    457.
_____. A Pictorial History of Architecture in America. New
    York: American Heritage, 1976. il. p. 259.
Tyng, Alexandra. Beginnings: Louis I. Kahn's Philosophy
    of Architecture. New York: John Wiley and Sons, 1984.
    il., plan. pp. 17-19, 43-45, 70-71, 142.
Whiffen, Marcus. American Architecture, 1607-1976. Cam-
    bridge: M.I.T., 1981. il., plan. pp. 426-433.

NORMAN FISHER RESIDENCE

Mill Road, Philadelphia, Pennsylvania. 1960.

Giurgola, Romaldo. Louis I. Kahn. Boulder, Colo.: Westview,
    1975. il., plan. pp. 18, 20-22.
Ronner, Heinz. Louis I. Kahn: Complete Works, 1935-74.
    Boulder, Colo.: Westview, 1977. il., plan. p. 181.

MUNICIPAL BUILDING

Mill Creek at Bath Road, Bristol, Levittown, Pennsylvania.
1960.

Ronner, Heinz. Louis I. Kahn: Complete Works, 1935-74.
    Boulder, Colo.: Westview, 1977. plan. p. 183.
Scully, Vincent. Louis I. Kahn. New York: Braziller, 1962.
    plan. plate 104.

ROOSEVELT MEMORIAL

Washington, D.C. Project, 1960-1961.

Ronner, Heinz. Louis I. Kahn: Complete Works, 1935-74.
Boulder, Colo.: Westview, 1977. il., plan, sec. p. 185.

ERDMAN HALL DORMITORIES

Bryn Mawr College, Bryn Mawr, Pennsylvania. 1960-1965.

"Academic ratrace." il., plan. Architectural Review 139
(March 1966): 168-169.
Cook, John Wesley. Conversations With Architects. New
York: Praeger, 1973. il., plan. pp. 206-209.
Dixon, John Morris. "Another kind of castle." il., plans.
Architectural Forum 123 (November 1965): 58-65.
"Dormitories, Bryn Mawr College." il., plan. Architecture
and Urbanism 3 (January 1973): 38, 57-58, 71-74.
Giurgola, Romaldo. Louis I. Kahn. Boulder, Colo.: West-
view, 1973. il., plan, sec. pp. 23-26.
Jacobus, John. Twentieth Century Architecture: The Middle
Years, 1940-1965. New York: Praeger, 1966. il. pp.
198-199.
Kahn, Louis I. Drawings. Los Angeles: Access Press, 1981.
plan. p. 75.
_____. The Notebooks and Drawings of Louis I. Kahn,
edited and designed by Richard Saul Wurman and Eugene
Feldman. Philadelphia: Falcon, 1962. plans. fig. 2-3.
_____. The Notebooks and Drawings of Louis I. Kahn,
edited and designed by Richard Saul Wurman and Eugene
Feldman. Cambridge: M.I.T., 1973. plans. fig. 2-3.
Komendant, August. "Komendant on concrete." il., diag.
Progressive Architecture 47 (October 1966): 208-214.
Koyama, Hisao. "Dormitories, Bryn Mawr College." il. (pt.
col.), plans, sec. Architecture and Urbanism 152 (May
1983): 11-18.
"Louis I. Kahn; oeuvres 1963-1969." "Plans 1953-1958."
plan. Architecture D'Aujourd'hui 40 (February-March 1969):
9.
"Louis Kahn; internat de Jeunes Filles au College de Bryn
Mawr, Pennsylvania, 1960-1962." il., plan, sec. Archi-
tecture D'Aujourd'hui 33 (December 1962): 20-21.
Overland, Orm. "Louis I. Kahn as philosopher." il., plan.
Byggekunst 48 (1966): 116-127.
Piene, Nan R. "New York: gallery notes." il. Art in America 54 (March-April 1966): 124-125.

Ronner, Heinz. Louis I. Kahn: Complete Works, 1935-74.
    Boulder, Colo.: Westview, 1977. il., plan, sec., elev.
    pp. 187-195.
Scholz, Lynn. "Architecture alive on campus: Erdman Hall."
    il., plans. Bryn Mawr Alumnae Bulletin 47 (Fall 1965):
    2-9.
Scully, Vincent. American Architecture and Urbanism. New
    York: Praeger, 1969. il. pp. 218-219.
_____. "Light, form and power: new work of Louis Kahn."
    il., plan. Architectural Forum 121 (August-September
    1964): 165.
_____. Louis I. Kahn. New York: Braziller, 1962. plan.
    plate 117, p. 39.
_____. "Recent works by Louis Kahn." il., plan, sec.,
    elev. Zodiac 17 (1967): 68-79.
Smith, G. E. Kidder. The Architecture of the United States,
    v. 1. Garden City, N.Y.: Anchor, 1981. il. pp. 600-
    601.
Stern, Robert A. M. New Directions in American Architecture.
    New York: Braziller, 1969. il. pp. 16, 18-19.
_____. New Directions in American Architecture. Revised
    ed. New York: Braziller, 1977. il. pp. 16-19.
"Ten buildings that point the future." col. il. Fortune 72
    (December 1965): 174-175.
Tentori, Francesco. "Il passato come un amico." il., plan.
    Casabella 275 (May 1963): 32.
Tyng, Alexandra. Beginnings: Louis I. Kahn's Philosophy
    of Architecture. New York: John Wiley and Sons, 1984.
    il., plan. pp. 17-19, 44, 46-47, 73-74, 143.

THAMES BARGE

London, England. 1961.

Ronner, Heinz. Louis I. Kahn: Complete Works, 1935-74.
    Boulder, Colo.: Westview, 1977. il. p. 197.
Scully, Vincent. Louis I. Kahn. New York: Braziller, 1962.
    il. plate 118, p. 39.

WAREHOUSE AND REGIONAL SALES OFFICE BUILDING

Niagara Falls, New York. 1961.

Ronner, Heinz. Louis I. Kahn: Complete Works, 1935-74.
    Boulder, Colo.: Westview, 1977. il., sec., elev. p. 199.

GENERAL MOTORS EXHIBITION

1964 World's Fair, New York, New York. Project, 1961.

Kahn, Louis I. Drawings. Los Angeles: Access Press, 1981.
    il. p. 26.
    _____. The Notebooks and Drawings of Louis I. Kahn,
    edited and designed by Richard Saul Wurman and Eugene
    Feldman. Philadelphia: Falcon, 1962. il., plan. fig.
    38.
    _____. The Notebooks and Drawings of Louis I. Kahn,
    edited and designed by Richard Saul Wurman and Eugene
    Feldman. Cambridge: M.I.T., 1973. il., plan. fig. 38.
Ronner, Heinz. Louis I. Kahn: Complete Works, 1935-74.
    Boulder, Colo.: Westview, 1977. il., plan, elev. p. 201.
Scully, Vincent. Louis I. Kahn. New York: Braziller, 1962.
    il. plate 119.
Tentori, Francesco. "Il passato come un amico." il. Casa-
    bella 275 (May 1963): 41.

CHEMISTRY BUILDING, UNIVERSITY OF VIRGINIA

Charlottesville, Virginia. 1961.

Kahn, Louis I. The Notebooks and Drawings of Louis I. Kahn,
    edited and designed by Richard Saul Wurman and Eugene
    Feldman. Philadelphia: Falcon, 1962. plan. fig. 75.
    _____. The Notebooks and Drawings of Louis I. Kahn,
    edited and desinged by Richard Saul Wurman and Eugene
    Feldman. Cambridge: M.I.T., 1973. plan. fig. 75.

ADELE LEVY MEMORIAL PLAYGROUND

Riverside Park, New York, New York. 1961-1964. In asso-
    ciation with Isamu Noguchi.

"Giocare con la terra." il. Architettura 10 (September 1964):
    338.

Kahn, Louis I. "Remarks." plans. Perspecta 9/10 (1965):
    330-331.
"Kahn-Noguchi playground proposed for New York." il.
    Progressive Architecture 45 (March 1964): 65, 67.
Ronner, Heinz. Louis I. Kahn: Complete Works, 1935-74.
    Boulder, Colo.: Westview, 1977. il., plan. p. 203.

THEATER OF PERFORMING ARTS AND FINE ARTS CENTER

232½ West Wayne Street, Fort Wayne, Indiana. 1961-1974.

Giurgola, Romaldo. Louis I. Kahn. Boulder, Colo.: Westview,
    1975. il., plan, sec. pp. 112, 117-125.
Herrera, Philip. "U.S. architecture: a progress report."
    il. Fortune 81 (1 September 1967): 124-125.
Kahn, Louis I. "Remarks." il. Perspecta 9/10 (1965): 318-
    319.
"Louis I. Kahn; oeuvres 1963-1969." plan. Architecture
    D'Aujourd'hui 40 (February-March 1969): 24-25.
Lym, Glenn Robert. A Psychology of Building. Englewood
    Cliffs, N.J.: Prentice-Hall, 1980. diag. pp. 78-80.
Ronner, Heinz. Louis I. Kahn: Complete Works, 1935-74.
    Boulder, Colo.: Westview, 1977. il. (pt. col.), plan,
    sec., elev. pp. 205-219.
Scully, Vincent. "Light, form and power: new work of Louis
    Kahn." il. Architectural Forum 121 (August-September
    1964): 170.
Stewart, H. Michael. American Architecture for the Arts,
    v. 1. Dallas: Handel and Sons, 1978. il. pp. 122-123.
Tyng, Alexandra. Beginnings: Louis I. Kahn's Philosophy
    of Architecture. New York: John Wiley and Sons, 1984.
    plan, sec. pp. 97-99, 115-117.

MIKVEH ISRAEL SYNAGOGUE

Church Walk, between 4th and 5th Streets, Philadelphia,
    Pennsylvania. Project, 1961-1970.

Coombs, Robert. "Light and silence: the religious architect-
    ure of Louis Kahn." plan, sec. Architectural Association
    Quarterly 13 (October 1981): 26-36.
Giurgola, Romaldo. Louis I. Kahn. Boulder, Colo.: West-
    view, 1975. il., plan, sec. pp. 38, 44-47.

Giurgola, Romaldo and Jaimini Mehta. "Mikveh Israel, Phila-
delphia." il. AIA Journal 65 (November 1976): 57.
Jewish Theological Seminary of America. Jewish Museum.
Recent American Synagogue Architecture. New York: The
Jewish Museum, 1963. il., plan. pp. 44-45.
Kahn, Louis I. Drawings. Los Angeles: Access Press, 1981.
il. p. 25.
_____. The Notebooks and Drawings of Louis I. Kahn,
edited and designed by Richard Saul Wurman and Eugene
Feldman. Philadelphia: Falcon, 1962. il., plan, elev.
fig. 62-70.
_____. The Notebooks and Drawings of Louis I. Kahn,
edited and designed by Richard Saul Wurman and Eugene
Feldman. Cambridge: M.I.T., 1973. il., plan, elev.
fig. 62-70.
_____. "Remarks." il., plan. Perspecta 9/10 (1965):
320-321.
Kampf, Avram. Contemporary Synagogue Art: Developments
in the United States, 1945-1965. New York: Union of
American Hebrew Congregations, 1966. il., pp. 37, 40.
"Louis I. Kahn exhibit." il., plan. Arts and Architecture
82 (July 1965): 36-37.
"Louis I. Kahn; oeuvres 1963-1969." "Plans, 1953-1958."
plan. Architecture D'Aujourd'hui 40 (February-March
1969): 10.
"Louis Kahn." il., plan, elev. Architecture D'Aujourd'hui
33 (December 1962): 18-19.
"Mikveh Israel Synagogue." il., plan. Architecture and Ur-
banism 3 (January 1973): 32-33, 62, 98-99.
Pile, John. Drawings of Architectural Interiors. New York:
Whitney Library of Design, 1967. il. pp. 80-81.
Ronner, Heinz. Louis I. Kahn: Complete Works, 1935-74.
Boulder, Colo.: Westview, 1977. il., plan, sec., elev.
pp. 221-227.
Scully, Vincent. "Light, form, and power: new work of
Louis Kahn." il., plan. Architectural Forum 121 (August-
September 1964): 166-167.
Sky, Alison. Unbuilt America: Forgotten Architecture in the
United States from Thomas Jefferson to the Space Age.
New York: McGraw-Hill, 1976. il. pp. 145-146.
Tentori, Francesco. "Il passato come un amico." il., plan,
elev. Casabella 275 (May 1963): 33.
Tyng, Alexandra. Beginnings: Louis I. Kahn's Philosophy
of Architecture. New York: John Wiley and Sons, 1984.
il., plan. pp. 148-150, 167.

SHER-E-BANGLANAGAR

Dacca, Bangladesh. 1962-

"Address by Louis I. Kahn; April 5, 1966." il. Boston
Society of Architects Journal 1 (1967): 7-20.
"American architectural drawings." il. Progressive Archi-
tecture 58 (August 1977): 56.
Banerji, Anupam. "Learning from Bangladesh." il., plan.
Canadian Architect 25 (October 1980): 34-39.
Berg, Erik. "Louis I. Kahn: Indien og Pakistan." il., plan.
Arkitekten 70 (1968): 337-349.
Bonfanti, Ezio. "Una risporta su Kahn." Controspazio
(September-October 1969): 42-43.
Campajola, Viviana. "Architettura bioclimatica: en/arch 83"
il., sec. Architettura 29 (August-September 1983): 613.
Cook, John Wesley. Conversations With Architects. New
York: Praeger, 1973. pp. 178, 180, 192-198.
Curtis, William J. R. "Authenticity, abstraction and the
ancient sense: Le Corbusier's and Louis Kahn's ideas of
parliament." il., plan. Perspecta 20 (1983): 181-194.
"Dacca, capital of Bangladesh, national assembly hall." il.,
plan, sec. Architecture and Urbanism 3 (January 1973):
34-35, 166-182.
"Dacca, die Hauptstadt von Bangladesch." il., plan. Werk
(July 1974): 810-811.
"Dacca-Kahn." il., plan, maps. Architecture D'Aujourd'hui
167 (May 1973): 24-29.
"Development drawings: impression of the mosque at Dacca."
il. Architecture Review 137 (February 1965): 148.
Drexler, Arthur. Transformations in Modern Architecture.
New York: Museum of Modern Art, 1979. il. pp. 102-
104, 116.
Dunnett, James. "City of the tiger: work of Louis Kahn at
Dacca, Bangladesh." il., plans, sec. Architectural Review
167 (April 1980): 229-234.
_____. "Work is moving again to complete Louis Kahn's
great monument at Dacca." il. Architect's Journal 171
(13 February 1980): 323.
Giurgola, Romaldo. Louis I. Kahn. Boulder, Colo.: Westview,
1975. il., plan, sec., elev. pp. 112, 130-157.
Gubler, Jacques. "La campata e un tipo?/Is the bay a type?"
il (pt. col.). Casabella 509-510 (January -February 1985):
76-83.

Hubert, Bruno J.   "Government centre in Dacca, 1962-1983:
    the last work of Louis Kahn."   il., plan, sec.   Techniques
    and Architecture 350 (November 1983):   155-165.
_____.   "Kahn's epilogue."   il (pt. col.), plan, sec.   Pro-
    gressive Architecture 65 (December 1984):   56-67.
Hughes, Robert.   "Brick is stingy, concrete is generous:
    Dacca, Bangladesh."   il.   Horizon 16 (Autumn 1974):   42-
    45.
_____.   "Building with spent light."   col. il., port.   Time
    101 (15 January 1973):   60-65.
"Indian Kahn."   il., plan.   Architectural Review 140 (November
    1966):   315.
"Islamabad, capital of Pakistan, presidential plan."   il.   Archi-
    tecture and Urbanism 3 (January 1973):   163-165.
Jencks, Charles.   Modern Movements in Architecture.   Garden
    City, N.Y.:   Anchor, 1973.   il.   pp. 235-237.
"Kahn a Dacca lavori in corso: Louis Kahn's Decca capital
    buildings; documents des travoux à Dacca."   col. il.
    Domus 548 (July 1975):   9-13.
Kahn, Louis I.   "The development by Louis I. Kahn of the
    design for the second capital of Pakistan at Dacca."   il.,
    plan, map, sec., elev., port.   North Carolina University
    at Raleigh.   School of Design.   Student Publications 14
    (1964, 3):   entire issue.
_____.   Drawings.   Los Angeles: Access Press, 1981.   il.,
    sec.   p. 24.
_____.   "Remarks."   il., plans, sec.   Perspecta 9/10 (1965):
    306-317.
"Kahn not for the faint-hearted."   il.   AIA Journal 55 (June
    1971):   27.
Komendant, August E.   18 Years With Architect Louis I. Kahn.
    Englewood, N.J.:   Aloray, 1975.   il., plan, sec.   pp. 75-
    90, 167-170.
L'Amato, Caludio and Sergio Petrini.   "Kahn Dakha venezia."
    il., plans, port.   Controspazio 1 (January 1969):   8-19.
Langford, Fred.   "Concrete in Dacca."   il., diag.   Mimar 6
    (October-December 1982):   50-55.
Lobell, John.   Between Silence and Light.   Boulder, Colo.:
    Shambhala, 1979.   il., plan, sec.   pp. 37, 89-93.
"Louis I. Kahn.   Banglanagar.   Dacca, Bangladesh.   Design:
    1969-74."   plans.   GA Document.   Special Issue 1970-
    1980:   224-225.
"Louis I. Kahn exhibit."   il.   Arts and Architecture 82 (July
    1965):   36-37.

"Louis I. Kahn; oeuvres 1963-1969." il., plan, sec., elev.
    Architecture D'Aujourd'hui 142 (February-March 1969):
    LXXXV, 12, 17, 26-29, 44-59.
"Louis Kahn. Dacca, seconde capitale du Pakistan; études
    préliminaries." il., plan, sec., elev. Architecture
    D'Aujourd'hui 122 (September 1965): 92-93.
"Louis Kahn's Dacca capital buildings." col. il. Domus 548
    (July 1975): 9-13, i-ii.
Maki, Fumihiko. "National assembly hall and ayub national
    hospital." il. (pt. col.), plan, sec. Architecture and
    Urbanism 148 (January 1983): 11-30.
"The mind of Louis Kahn." il., plan, sec., elev. Architec-
    tural Forum 137 (July-August 1972): 46-55.
"The new capital in Dacca." il. Design, Bombay 17 (January
    1972): 29-32.
Nilsson, Sten. "Palaces, camps, capitals." Lotus 34 (1982):
    125-127.
Nilsson, Sven Ake. "Dacca-huvudstad for Bangladesh?" il.,
    plan, map. Arkitektur: The Swedish Review of Archi-
    tecture 72 (August 1972): 12-15, 25-26.
Norbert-Schulz, Christian. Meaning in Western Architecture.
    New York: Praeger, 1972. il., plan. p. 404.
Pakistan. Public Works Department. The Second Capital of
    Pakistan in Dacca. Dacca: Pakistan Public Works Depart-
    ment, 1966. il., plan, sec., diag. 26p.
Perez de Arce, Rodrigo. "Urban transformations: Dacca
    citadel of the assembly." plans, diags. AD: Architectu-
    ral Design 48 (April, 1978): cover, 261, 263, 265.
Piene, Nan R. "New York: gallery notes." il. Art in
    America 54 (March-April 1966): 124-125.
Pieper, Jan. "A look at India." il., plan, sec. Bauwelt 74
    (29 July 1983): 1084-1108.
Pile, John. Drawings of Architectural Interiors. New York:
    Whitney Library of Design, 1967. il., sec. pp. 76-79.
Ragon, Michel. "Power of doubt." il. (pt. col.). Connais-
    sance des Arts 346 (December 1980): 84-91.
Ronner, Heinz. Louis I. Kahn: Complete Works, 1935-74.
    Boulder, Colo.: Westview, 1977. il., plan, sec., elev.,
    diag. p. 229-263.
Scully, Vincent. American Architecture and Urbanism. New
    York: Praeger, 1969. il., elev. p. 220.
_____. "Light, form and power: new work of Louis Kahn.:
    il., plan, sec. Architectural Forum 121 (August-September
    1964): 168-169.

_____. "Recent works by Louis Kahn." il., plan, sec.,
   elev. Zodiac 17 (1967): 104-117.
"Selearchitettura: Louis Kahn à Dacca." il., plan, sec.
   Architettura 29 (August-September 1983): 644-645.
Smithson, Alison. "Review of recent work: Louis Kahn."
   Architectural Design 43 (August 1973): 530.
Stern, Robert A. M. New Directions in American Architecture.
   New York: Braziller, 1969. il., plan, sec. pp. 15-16.
_____. New Directions in American Architecture. Revised
   ed. New York: Braziller, 1977. il., plan, sec. pp. 15-
   17.
Taylor, Brian Bruce. "National assembly hall, Dacca." il.
   (pt. col.), plan, sec., port. Mimar 6 (October-December
   1982): 1, 40-49.
_____. "Report from Dacca: Kahn's assembly building."
   il. Progressive Architecture 60 (December 1979): 41.
_____. "Visions of grandeur." col. il. Mimar 6 (October-
   December 1982): 37-39.
Tyng, Alexandra. Beginnings: Louis I. Kahn's Philosophy
   of Architecture. New York: John Wiley and Sons, 1984.
   il., plan. pp. 44, 46, 48-50, 94-97, 117-119, 167, 169.
"The urban redevelopment of the city: Chandigarh and Dacca." il., plan. Lotus 19 (1978): 98-101.
Waisman, Marina. "Futuro senza nostalgia." il., plan. Casabella 45 (November-December 1981): 50.

INSTITUTE OF MANAGEMENT

Ahmedabad, India. 1962-1974. In association with Anant
   Raje.

"Address by Louis I. Kahn; April 5, 1966." il., sec. Boston
   Society of Architects 1 (1967): 7-20.
"Ahamedabad; business college." il., plans. Architectural
   Review 150 (December 1971): 358.
Bailey, James. "Louis Kahn in India; an old order on a new
   scale." il., plan. Architectural Forum 125 (July-August
   1966): 39-47.
Banerji, Anupam. "The last form-maker: Louis Kahn in In-
   dia." il., plans. Canadian Architect 23 (March 1978):
   60-69.
Berg, Erik. "Louis I. Kahn: Indien og Pakistan." il., plan.
   Arkitekten 70 (1968): 337-349.

Bottero, Maria. "Louis Kahn revisited in Ahmedabad." il., por., plan. Domus 592 (March 1979): 1-5.

_____. "Viaggio in India: da le Corbusier a Kahn." il. Zodiac 16 (1966): 127-135.

Cook, John Wesley. Conversations With Architects. New York: Praeger, 1973. il. pp. 194-201.

Doshi, Balkrishna V. "Louis Kahn in India." il., port. Architectural Association Quarterly 13 (October 1981): 23-25.

Giurgola, Romaldo. Louis I. Kahn. Boulder, Colo.: Westview, 1975. il., plan, sec. pp. 60, 76-85.

Hughes, Robert. "Building with spent light." col. il., port. Time 101 (15 June 1973): 60-65.

"Indian Institute of Management." il., plan, sec. Architecture and Urbanism 3 (January 1973): 150-162.

"Indian Kahn." il., plan. Architectural Review 140 (November 1966): 315.

Kahn, Louis I. Indian Institute of Management, Ahmedabad, India, 1963-: Exeter Library, Phillips Exeter Academy, Exeter, New Hampshire, U.S.A., 1972. (Global Architecture, 35). Tokyo: A.D.A. Edita, 1975. il., plan, sec. pp. 2-4, 9-27, 42-45.

_____. "Remarks." il., plan. Perspecta 9/10 (1965): 322-329.

Kulski, Julian Eugene. Architecture in a Revolutionary Era. Nashville, Tenn.: Aurora, 1971. il., plans, sec., diag. pp. 240-241, 245-247.

Lobell, John. Between Silence and Light. Boulder, Colo.: Shambhala, 1979. il. pp. 17, 53, 57.

"Louis I. Kahn; oeuvres 1963-1969." il., plan, sec. Architecture D'Aujourd'hui 40 (February-March 1969): LXXXV, 32, 60-67.

Lym, Glenn Robert. A Psychology of Building. Englewood Cliffs, N.J.: Prentice-Hall, 1980. diag. pp. 77-80.

Martinelli, Antonio. "Louis I. Kahn: the Indian Institute of Management, Ahmedabad, Inde, 1962-74." il. (pt. col.), plan. Architecture D'Aujourd'hui 226 (April 1983): 85-94.

Mein, Philip. "Kahn." il. Architects' Journal 155 (9 February 1972): 277.

"The mind of Louis Kahn." il., plan, sec. Architectural Forum 137 (July-August 1972): 62-67.

"Not for the faint-hearted." il. AIA Journal 55 (June 1971): 30.

Peters, Paulhans. "Zum Tod von Peter Celsing, Hans Dollgast and Louis Kahn." il. Baumeister 71 (May 1974): 488-489.

Ragon, Michel. "Power of doubt." col. il. Connaissance des
    Arts 346 (December 1980): 84-91.
Ronner, Heinz. Louis I. Kahn: Complete Works, 1935-74.
    Boulder, Colo.: Westview, 1977. il., plan, sec., elev.,
    diag. pp. 265-305.
Russell, Beverly. "An architect speaks his mind: Louis Kahn
    talks about color, light, the ideal house, the street, and
    other inspirations for living." il. House and Garden 142
    (October 1972): 124-125.
Scully, Vincent. American Architecture and Urbanism. New
    York: Praeger, 1969. il. p. 221.
Stern, Robert A. M. New Directions in American Architecture.
    New York: Braziller, 1969. il. pp. 15-16, 18.
    _____. New Directions in American Architecture. Revised
    ed. New York: Braziller, 1977. il. pp. 15-18.
Tyng, Alexandra. Beginnings: Louis I. Kahn's Philosophy
    of Architecture. New York: John Wiley and Sons, 1984.
    il., plan. pp. 50, 119, 151-152, 175.

PRESIDENT'S ESTATE

Islamabad, Pakistan. 1963.

"Islambad, presidential plan." il. Architecture and Urbanism
    3 (January 1973): 163-165.
Ronner, Heinz. Louis I. Kahn: COmplete Works, 1935-74.
    Boulder, Colo.: Westview, 1977. il., plan, sec., elev.
    pp. 307-311.

PHILADELPHIA COLLEGE OF ART

Broad Street between Spruce and Pine, Philadelphia, Pennsylvania. Project, 1964-1967.

Giurgola, Romaldo. Louis I. Kahn. Boulder, Colo.: Westview,
    1975. il., plan, sec. pp. 61, 86-89.
"Louis I. Kahn; oeuvres 1963-1969." il., plan, sec. Archi-
    tecture D'Aujourd'hui 40 (February-March 1969): LXXXVI,
    76-79.
"Philadelphia College of Art: the third wave." il. Progres-
    sive Architecture 47 (May 1966): 51.
Pierson, William Harvey. American Buildings and Their Archi-
    tects: The Impact of European Modernism in the Mid-

   Twentieth Century. Garden City, N.Y.: Doubleday, 1972,
   v. 4. il. pp. 390-392.
Ronner, Heinz. Louis I. Kahn: Complete Works, 1935-74.
   Boulder, Colo.: Westview, 1977. il., plan, sec., elev.
   pp. 313-317.
Scully, Vincent. American Architecture and Urbanism. New
   York: Praeger, 1969. il. pp. 222-224.

INTERAMA, PANAMERICAN CENTER

Miami, Florida. 1964-1967.

Giurgola, Romaldo. Louis I. Kahn. Boulder, Colo.: Westview,
   1975. plan, sec. pp. 112, 126-129.
"Interama exposition hailed as 'full-scale experiment in urban
   design.'" il., plan. Architectural Record 141 (March
   1967): 40-41.
Ronner, Heinz. Louis I. Kahn: Complete Works, 1935-74.
   Boulder, Colo.: Westview, 1977. il., plan, sec. p. 319.

MEMORIAL TO SIX MILLION JEWS

New York, New York. 1964-1972.

Giurgola, Romaldo. Louis I. Kahn. Boulder, Colo.: Westview,
   1975. il. pp. 158-159.
Huxtable, Ada Louise. Will They Ever Finish Bruckner Boulevard? Reprints from the New York Times, October 17,
   1968. New York: Macmillan, 1970. il. pp. 108-110.
"Louis I. Kahn: oeuvres 1963-1969." il. Architecture
   D'Aujourd'hui 40 (February-March 1969): LXXXVI, 21,
   74-75.
Ronner, Heinz. Louis I. Kahn: Complete Works, 1935-74.
   Boulder, Colo.: Westview, 1977. il., plan, sec., elev.
   pp. 321-323.

DOMINICAN SISTERS' CONVENT

Media, Pennsylvani. 1965-1968.

Coombs, Robert. "Light and silence: the religious architec-

ture of Louis Kahn." plan, elev. Architectural Associa-
tion Quarterly 13 (October 1981): 26-36.
Giurgola, Romaldo. Louis I. Kahn. Boulder, Colo.: Westview,
1975. il., plan, elev. pp. 38, 48-50.
"Louis I. Kahn; oeuvres 1963-1969." il. Architecture
D'Aujourd'hui 40 (February-March 1960): 20.
"Motherhouse for the Dominican sisters." il., plan. Archi-
tecture and Urbanism 3 (January 1973): 40, 75-78.
Ronner, Heinz. Louis I. Kahn: Complete Works, 1935-74.
Boulder, Colo.: Westview, 1977. il., plan, sec., elev.
pp. 325-329.

SAINT ANDREW'S PRIORY

Valyermo, California. 1966.

Coombs, Robert. "Light and silence: the religious architec-
ture of Louis Kahn." plan. Architectural Association
Quarterly 13 (October 1981): 26-36.
Giurgola, Romaldo. Louis I. Kahn. Boulder, Colo.: Westview,
1975. il., plan. pp. 38, 51-53.
Ronner, Heinz. Louis I. Kahn: Complete Works, 1935-74.
Boulder, Colo.: Westview, 1977. il., plan. pp. 330-331.

OLIVETTI-UNDERWOOD FACTORY

Harrisburg, Pennsylvania. 1966-1970.

Dixon, John Morris. "More than just a volume; Pennsylvania
Olivetti plant." il. (pt. col.), plan, sec. Architectural
Forum 134 (April 1971): 20-25.
"Fabbrica Olivetti Underwood." il., diags. Zodiac 22 (1973):
135.
Giurgola, Romaldo. Louis I. Kahn. Boulder, Colo.: West-
view, 1975. il., plan. pp. 194, 210-211.
"Industriegebaude der Olivetti in Harrisburg, Pennsylvania."
il., plan. Werk (July 1974): 814-815.
Komendant, August E. 18 Years With Architect Louis I. Kahn.
Englewood, N.J.: Aloray, 1975. il., diag. pp. 91-104.
Pica, Agnoldomenico. "Una nuova opera di Louis I. Kahn."
il. (pt. col.), plan. Domus 493 (December 1970): 2-9.
Ronner, Heinz. Louis I. Kahn: Complete Works, 1935-74.

Boulder, Colo.:   Westview, 1977. il., plan, sec., elev.
    pp. 333-341.
Smith, G. E. Kidder. The Architecture of the United States.
    Garden City, N.Y.:   Anchor, 1981, v. 1. il. pp. 606-
    607.
Tyng, Alexandra. Beginnings: Louis I. Kahn's Philosophy
    of Architecture. New York: John Wiley and Sons, 1984.
    il. p. 43.
"USA 71, usine Olivetti." il., plans. Architecture
    D'Aujourd'hui 43 (August-September 1971):   86-87.

KIMBELL ART MUSEUM

Will Rogers Road West, Fort Worth, Texas. 1966-1972. In
    association with Preston M. Geren.

American Institute of Architects. Dallas Chapter. Dallasight.
    Dallas: AIA. Dallas Chapter, 1978. il., map. pp. 171,
    176-177.
Brawne, Michael. The Museum Interior. London: Thames
    and Hudson, 1982. il. pp. 48, 110-111.
"Building boom in Texas." il. Museum News 54 (December
    1974):   18-19.
Davern, Jeanne M., ed. Architecture 1970-1980: A Decade
    of Change. New York: McGraw-Hill, 1980. il. pp. 54-
    55.
Dean, Andrea O. "Kimbell Art Museum. Fort Worth, Texas."
    il. AIA Journal 63 (May 1975):   38-39.
Dillon, David. "The buildings that house Fort Worth's museums
    rival the fine quality of their collections." il. Portfolio
    3 (March-April 1981):   91.
"Eyes on Texas: Fort Worth." il. Interiors 131 (April 1972):
    124-125.
"Fort Worth's Kimbell: art housing art." il. Progressive Ar-
    chitecture 42 (November 1972):   25, 29.
Gleeson, Larry. "Texas: new center of art museum activity."
    il. Facets: Journal of the Texas Fine Arts Society 4
    (Spring 1973):   cover, 10-13.
Giurgola, Romaldo. Louis I. Kahn. Boulder, Colo.: Westview,
    1975. il., plan, sec. pp. 61, 94-98.
Holmes, Ann. "From the panhandle to the gulf coast: the
    museum boom in Texas." Artnews 72 (May 1973):   34-38.
Hoving, Thomas. "Gem of a museum." il. Connoisseur 210
    (May 1982):   86-95.

Fig. 15:   Kimbell Art Museum in Fort Worth, Texas

Hughes, Robert. "Brick is stingy, concrete is generous."
     il., elev. Horizon 16 (Autumn 1974): 34-35.
_____. "Building with spent light." col. il., port. Time
     101 (15 January 1973): 60-65.
Jordy, William H. "Criticism: Kimbell Art Museum." il.
     Architectural Review 155 (June 1974): 330-335.
Kahn, Louis I. Light is the Theme: Louis I. Kahn and the
     Kimbell Art Museum. Fort Worth: Kimbell Art Foundation,
     1975. il., plans, sec. 79p.
_____. Louis I. Kahn: Sketches for the Kimbell Art Mu-
     seum, organized by David M. Robb; essay by Marshall D.
     Meyers. Fort Worth: Kimbell Art Foundation, 1978. il.,
     plan, sec., elev., diag. [27]p.
_____. Yale University Art Gallery, New Haven, Connecti-
     cut, 1951-53. Kimbell Art Museum, Fort Worth, Texas,
     1966-1972, by Marshall D. Meyers. Tokyo: A.D.A. Edita,
     1976. il. (pt. col.), plans, sec. pp. 2-7, 18-40, 46-47.
"Kahn: Kimbell: Kimbell Art Museum, Fort Worth, Texas."
     il., plan, sec. Architectural Review 155 (June 1974):
     320-329.
"Kahn's Kimbell: a building in praise of nature and light."
     il. (pt. col.), plan, sec., diag., port. Interiors 132
     (March 1973): 84-91.
"Kahn's museum: an interview with Richard F. Brown." il.,
     port. Art in America 60 (September-October 1972): 44-
     48.
"Kimbell Art Museum." il. Architectural Record 152 (Novem-
     ber 1972): 43.
"Kimbell Art Museum." il., plan, sec., diag. Architecture
     and Urbanism 3 (January 1973): 36, 65, 106-112.
"Kimbell Art Museum." il., plans. Studio 189 (May 1975):
     216.
Komendant, August E. 18 Years With Architect Louis I. Kahn.
     Englewood, N.J.: Aloray, 1975. il., plan, sec. pp. 115-
     131.
Lam, William M. C. Sunlighting as Formgiver for Architecture.
     New York: Van Nostrand Reinhold, 1986. il. pp. 145,
     340, 342.
Lobell, John. Between Silence and Light. Boulder, Colo.:
     Shambhala, 1979. il., plan, sec. pp. 15, 39, 94-99.
"Louis I. Kahn, Kimbell Art Museum, Fort Worth, Texas.
     Design: 1967, Completion: 1972." il. (pt. col.), plan,
     sec. GA Document. Special Issue 1970-1980 (1980): 74-
     77.

"Louis I. Kahn; oeuvres 1963-1969." il., plan, sec. Architecture D'Aujourd'hui 40 (February-March 1969): LXXXVI,
    23, 68-69.
"Louis Kahn: Kimbell Art Museum." il. (pt. col.), elev.
    Oeil 214 (October 1972): 32-37.
"Louis Kahn un museo, a Fort Worth nel Texas; les noutes et
    la lumière." col. il., plan, sec. Domus 561 (August
    1976): 17-19.
Mee, Charles L. "Louis Kahn," in Three Centuries of Notable
    American Architects, edited by Joseph J. Thorndike. New
    York: American Heritage, 1981. il. pp. 296-298.
Meyers, Marshall. "Masters of light: Louis Kahn." col. il.,
    diag. AIA Journal 68 (September 1979): 60-62.
Miller, Robert L. "Case Studies," in Building Systems Integration Handbook, edited by Richard D. Rush. New York:
    Wiley, 1986. il., plan, sec. pp. 54, 64-67, 209-211, 240-
    241, 256-257, 364, 404-405.
"The mind of Louis Kahn." il. (pt. col.), plan, sec. Architectural Forum 137 (July-August 1972): 56-61.
"Musée Kimbell: Fort Worth, Etats-Unis." il., plan, diag.
    Architecture 402 (April 1977): 52-55.
"The new treasure-houses of Texas." col. il. Fortune 89
    (May 1974): 206-209.
Plagens, Peter. "Louis Kahn's new museum in Fort Worth."
    il., plan, diag., port. Artforum 6 (February 1968): 18-
    23.
"Product review: lead innovations." il., sec. Architectural
    Forum 137 (July-August 1972): 92.
Rice, Norman. "Kahn." col. il. Architectural Plus 2 (May-
    June 1974): 102-103.
Ronner, Heinz. Louis I. Kahn: COmplete Works, 1935-74.
    Boulder, Colo.: Westview, 1977. il., plan (pt. col.),
    sec., diag. pp. 343-351.
Russell, Beverly. "An architect speaks his mind: Louis Kahn
    talks about color, light, the ideal house, the street, and
    other inspirations for living." il. House and Garden
    142 (October 1972): 125.
Seymour, A. T. "Immeasurable made measurable: building
    the Kimbell Art Museum." il. VIA 7 (1984): 76-85.
Shepard, Richard F. "After a six-year honeymoon, the Kimbell
    Art Museum." il., port. Art News 71 (October 1972):
    22-31.
Smith, C. Roy. "The great museum debate." il., elev.
    Progressive Architecture 50 (December 1969): 84-85.

Smith, G. E. Kidder. The Architecture of the United States.
    Garden City, N.Y.: Anchor, 1981. il. pp. 661–663.
_____. A Pictorial History of Architecture in America.
    New York: American Heritage, 1976. il. pp. 614–615.
Speck, Lawrence W. "Evaluation: the Kimbell Museum." il.
    (pt. col.), plan. American Institute of Architects.
    Journal 71 (August 1982): 36–43.
_____. Landmarks of Texas Architecture. Austin: Uni-
    versity of Texas Press, 1986. col. il. pp. 7, 98–103.
Stewart, H. Michael. American Architecture for the Arts,
    v. 1. Dallas: Handel and Sons, 1978. il. pp. 218–219.
Tyng, Alexandra. Beginnings: Louis I. Kahn's Philosophy
    of Architecture. New York: John Wiley and Sons, 1984.
    il., plan, sec. pp. 53–55, 153–155, 170, 175–176.
Weiss, Barbara. "American museums: three examples." il.
    Lotus 35 (1982): 102–106.
Whiffen, Marcus. American Architecture, 1607–1976. Cam-
    bridge: M.I.T., 1981. il. pp. 426–433.

TEMPLE BETH-EL SYNAGOGUE

Chappaqua, New York. 1966–1972.

"Louis I. Kahn; oeuvres 1963–1969." plan. Architecture
    D'Aujourd'hui 40 (February–March 1969): 22.
"The mind of Louis Kahn." il., plan. Architectural Forum
    137 (July–August 1972): 43, 47.
Ronner, Heinz. Louis I. Kahn: Complete Works, 1935–74.
    Boulder, Colo.: Westview, 1977. il., plan, sec., elev.
    pp. 353–355.

OFFICE BUILDING

Kansas City, Kansas. Project, 1966–1973.

Cook, John Wesley. Conversations With Architects. New
    York: Praeger, 1973. il. pp. 190–193.
Giurgola, Romaldo. Louis I. Kahn. Boulder, Colo.: Westview,
    1975. il., plan, sec. pp. 194, 212–215.
"Kahn sospeso." il., plan, sec. Architettura 18 (January
    1973): 614–615.
"Kansas City office building." il., plan, sec., elev. Archi-
    tecture and Urbanism 3 (January 1973): 133–135.

Komendant, August E. 18 Years With Architect Louis I. Kahn.
Englewood, N.J.: Aloray, 1975. il., plan, sec., elev.,
diag. pp. 133-159.
"Louis I. Kahn; oeuvres 1963-1969." il., plan, sec., elev.
Architecture D'Aujourd'hui 40 (February-March 1969):
LXXXV, 36-37.
"The mind of Louis Kahn." il., plan, sec. Architectural
Forum 137 (July-August 1972): 74-75.
Ronner, Heinz. Louis I. Kahn: Complete Works, 1935-74.
Boulder, Colo.: Westview, 1977. il., plan, sec., elev.
pp. 357-361.

BROADWAY CHURCH OF CHRIST, OFFICE AND CHURCH
BUILDING

Block east of Broadway between 56th and 57th Streets,
New York, New York. 1967-1968.

Ronner, Heinz. Louis I. Kahn: Complete Works, 1935-74.
Boulder, Colo.: Westview, 1977. plan, elev. p. 363.

PHILLIPS EXETER LIBRARY AND DINING HALL

Phillips Exeter Academy, Exeter, New Hampshire. 1967-1972.

"Ancora sulla biblioteca di Exeter." il., plan, sec. Archi-
tettura 20 (September 1974): 325-327.
Andrews, Wayne. Architecture in America. New York: Athe-
neum, 1977. il. p. 160.
Dednar, Michael J. The New Atrium. New York: McGraw-
Hill, 1986. il., plan, sec. pp. 172-173.
Drexler, Arthur. Transformations in Modern Architecture.
New York: Museum of Modern Art, 1979. il. pp. 102-
105.
"Exeter library." il., plan, sec. Architecture and Urbanism
3 (January 1973): 66, 118-126.
Giurgola, Romaldo. Louis I. Kahn. Boulder, Colo.: Westview,
1975. il., plan, sec. pp. 61, 90-93.
Hennessy, Richard. "Prototype and progeny: some recent
monumental architecture." il. Artforum 17 (November
1978): 68-72.
Hughes, Robert. "Brick is stingy, concrete is generous,

Exeter Library." il. Horizon 16 (Autumn 1974): 38-41.
———————. "Building with spent light." col. il., port. Time
   101 (15 January 1973): 60-65.
Jacob, Eva. New Architecture in New England. Lincoln,
   Mass.: De Cordova Museum, 1974. il. pp. 18-19, 68-69.
Jordy, William H. "Criticism; library, Phillips Exeter Academy,
   Exeter." il., plan. Architectural Review 155 (June 1974):
   330-335.
Kahn, Louis I. Indian Institute of Management, Ahmedabad,
   India, 1963--Exeter Library, Phillips Exeter Academy, Exe-
   ter, New Hampshire, U.S. (Global architecture 35).
   Tokyo: A.D.A. Edita, 1975. il., plan. pp. 5-7, 28-40,
   46-47.
"Kahn a doppio guscio." il., plan. Architettura 18 (January
   1973): 615.
"Kahn: Phillips Exeter." il., plan, sec. Architectural Re-
   view 155 (June 1974): 336-342.
LeCuyer, Annette. "Evaluation: Kahn's powerful presence
   at Exeter." il. (pt. col.), plan. Architecture 74 (Feb-
   ruary 1985): 74-79.
Lobell, John. Between Silence and Light. Boulder, Colo.:
   Shambhala, 1979. il., plan, sec. pp. 100-105.
"Louis I. Kahn. Exeter Library, Phillips Exeter Academy,
   Exeter, New Hampshire. Design: 1967, Completion:
   1972." il., plan. GA Document, Special Issue 1970-1980
   (1980): 78-79.
"Louis I. Kahn; oevures 1963-1969." il., plan, sec. Archi-
   tecture D'Aujourd'hui 40 (February-March 1969): LXXXVI,
   70-73.
Lym, Glenn Robert. A Psychology of Building. Englewood
   Cliffs, N.J.: Prentice-Hall, 1980. il., diag. pp. 82-93.
Marlin, William. "Within the folds of construction: Louis
   Kahn's work at Exeter Academy evinces an ongoing search
   for the essential elements of architecture." il. (pt. col.),
   plan, sec. Architectural Forum 139 (October 1973): 26-
   35.
Mee, Charles L. "Louis Kahn," in Three Centuries of Notable
   American Architects, edited by Joseph J. Thorndike. New
   York: American Heritage, 1981. il. pp. 292-294, 296.
"The mind of Louis Kahn." il., plan, sec. Architectural
   Forum 137 (July-August 1972): 76-77.
Rice, Norman. "Kahn." il. Architectural Plus 2 (May-June
   1974): 104.
Ronner, Heinz. Louis I. Kahn: Complete Works, 1935-74.

Boulder, Colo.: Westview, 1977. il., plan, sec., elev.,
 diag. pp. 365-373.
Russell, Beverly. "An architect speaks his mind: Louis Kahn
 talks about color, light, the ideal house, the street, and
 other inspirations for living." il. House and Garden
 142 (October 1972): 124-125.
Smith, G. E. Kidder. A Pictorial History of Architecture in
 America. New York: American Heritage, 1976. il. p.
 115.
_____. The Architecture of the United States. Garden
 City, N.Y.: Anchor, 1981, v. 1. il. 341-343.
Tyng, Alexandra. Beginnings: Louis I. Kahn's Philosophy
 of Architecture. New York: John Wiley and Sons, 1984.
 il., plan, sec. pp. 18, 51-52, 175.
"Ulkomaat." il., elev. Arkkitehti 71 (February 1974): 23.
Whiffen, Marcus. American Architecture, 1607-1976. Cam-
 bridge: M.I.T., 1981. il. pp. 426-433.
Wilson, Richard Gus. "Gold Medal for 1971; Louis Isidore
 Kahn," in The AIA Gold Medal. New York: McGraw-Hill.
 1984. il. (pt. col.), plan, port. oppos. p. 87, pp. 212-
 213.

HILL CENTRAL AREA REDEVELOPMENT

New Haven, Connecticut. 1968-1973.

Ronner, Heinz. Louis I. Kahn: Complete Works, 1935-74.
 Boulder, Colo.: Westview, 1977. il., plan. pp. 375-377.

HURVA SYNAGOGUE

Jerusalem, Israel. 1968-1974.

Coombs, Robert. "Light and silence: the religious architecture
 of Louis Kahn." plan. Architectural Association Quarterly
 13 (October 1981): 26-36.
Giurgola, Romaldo. Louis I. Kahn. Boulder, Colo.: Westview,
 1975. il., plan. pp. 38, 54-56.
"Hurva Synagogue." il., plan, sec. Architecture and Urbanism 3 (January 1973): 100-102.
"Louis I. Kahn; oeuvres 1963-1969." il., plan. Architecture
 D'Aujourd'hui 40 (February-March 1969): LXXXV, 18-19,
 38-43.

"The mind of Louis Kahn." il., plan, sec. Architectural
     Forum 137 (July-August 1972): 68-69.
"Not for the faint-hearted." il. AIA Journal 55 (June 1971):
     31.
Ronner, Heinz. Louis I. Kahn: Complete Works, 1935-74.
     Boulder, Colo.: Westview, 1977. il., plan, sec. pp.
     379-385.
Tyng, Alexandra. Beginnings: Louis I. Kahn's Philosophy
     of Architecture. New York: John Wiley and Sons, 1984.
     il., plan, sec. pp. 155-158, 175.

PALACE OF CONGRESS

Venice, Italy. 1968-1974.

Bonfanti, Ezio. "Una risposta su Kahn." Controspazio 1
     (September-October 1969): 42-43.
"Conference center for Venice." il., plan, sec. Architectural
     Record 145 (March 1969): 40.
Cook, John Wesley. Conversations With Architects. New
     York: Praeger, 1973. plan, sec. pp. 202-204.
Giurgola, Romaldo. Louis I. Kahn. Boulder, Colo.: Westview,
     1975. il., plan, sec. pp. 113, 160-164.
"Incoerenza: scelte per Venezia." il., plans, sec. Casabella
     334 (March 1969): 54.
"Kahn in Venice." il., plan, sec., port. Architectural Forum
     130 (March 1969): 64-67.
"Kahn in Venice." il. Architectural Review 145 (April 1969):
     304, 306.
"Kahn not for the faint-hearted." il., plan, sec. AIA Journal
     55 (June 1971): 26.
Komendant, August E. 18 Years with Architect Louis I. Kahn.
     Englewood, N.J.: Aloray, 1975. il., plan, sec., elev.
     pp. 107-114.
"Louis I. Kahn; oeuvres 1963-1969." il., plan, sec. Archi-
     tecture D'Aujourd'hui 40 (February-March 1969): LXXXV,
     12, 33-35.
"Louis Kahn in Venedig." il., plan, sec., port. Werk 56
     (April 1969): 221-226.
Mazzariol, Giuseppe. "Un progetto per Venezia." il. (pt.
     col.), plans, sec., port. Lotus 6 (1969): 6-39.
"The mind of Louis Kahn." il., plan, sec. Architectural
     Forum 137 (July-August 1972): 70-73.

"Palace of congress for Venice." il., plan, sec. Progressive
Architecture 50 (April 1969): 42-43.
"Palazzo dei congressi, Venice." il. (pt. col.), plan, sec.
Architecture and Urbanism 3 (January 1973): 89-94.
Pica, Agnoldomenico. "Louis Kahn a Venezia: mouve sedi per
la biennale." il., plan, sec., port. Domus 472 (March
1969): 1-6.
_____. "Quattro progetti per Venezia alla XXXVI biennale."
il. Domus 515 (October 1972): 1-3.
Ronner, Heinz. Louis I. Kahn: Complete Works, 1935-74.
Boulder, Colo.: Westview, 1977. il., plan (pt. col.),
sec., elev., diag. pp. 387-393.
Silipo, Andrea. "Kahn Dakka Venezia." il., plan. Controspazio 1 (January 1969): 8-19.
"3 projects." il. Architectural Review 149 (May 1971): 318-
319.

WOLFSON CENTER

University of Tel Aviv, Tel Aviv, Israel. 1968-1974. In association with Con J. Mochly and E. I. Eldar.

Giurgola, Romaldo. Louis I. Kahn. Boulder, Colo.: Westview,
1975. il., plan, sec. pp. 61, 103-105.
"L'ultima opera di Louis Kahn: il Wolfson Engineering Building
a Tel Aviv." il. (pt. col.), plans, sec., port. Architettura 27 (January 1981): 30-36.
Ronner, Heinz. Louis I. Kahn: Complete Works, 1935-74.
Boulder, Colo.: Westview, 1977. il., plan, sec., elev.
pp. 395-399.
"Scuola d'ingegneria: l'ultimo progetto di Kahn a Tel Aviv."
il., plan, sec., elev. Domus 557 (April 1976): 28-29.
"University of Tel aviv." plan, sec. Architecture and Urbanism 3 (January 1973): 26-27, 51, 95-97.

PAUL MELLON CENTER FOR BRITISH ART AND STUDIES

1080 Chapel Street, Yale University, New Haven, Connecticut.
1969-1977. Completed by Pellecchia and Meyers.

Abercrombie, Shanley. "Yale Center for British Art." il.
(pt. col.), plan, sec., diag. Contract Interiors 136 (July
1977): 52-59.

Fig. 16: Mellon Center for British Art and Studies, Yale
          University

Banham, Reyner. "Kahn's warehouse of art." il. New So-
    ciety 62 (18 November 1982): 307-308.
Bednar, Michael J. The New Atrium. New York: McGraw-
    Hill, 1986. il., plan, sec. pp. 86, 184-185.
Brawne, Michael. The Museum Interior. London: Thames
    and Hudson, 1982. il. pp. 48-49, 71-72, 115, 142-145.
Cook, John Wesley. Conversations With Architects. New
    York: Praeger, 1973. il. pp. 204-206.
Coombs, Robert. "Report from New Haven." il. Progressive
    Architecture 55 (November 1974): 38.
Cormack, Malcolm. "Selective promenade." Apollo 105 (April
    1977): 286-291.
Crosbie, Michael J. "Evaluation: Monument before its time."
    col. il., plan. Architecture 75 (January 1986): 64-67.
Davern, Jeanne M., ed. Architecture; 1970-1980: A Decade
    of Change. New York: McGraw-Hill, 1980. il. (pt.
    col.). pp. iv, 174-175.
Davis, Douglas. "A new stately home." col. il. Newsweek
    89 (18 April 1977): 90-91.
Dean, Andrea O. "Legacy of light." il. (pt. col.) AIA
    Journal 67 (Mid-May 1978): 80-89.
Filler, Martin. "Yale Center for British Art, Yale University,
    New Haven; opus posthumous." il. (pt. col.), plans, sec.
    Progressive Architecture 59 (May 1978): 76-81. Discus-
    sion, "More light on Kahn," Progressive Architecture 59
    (July 1978): 10.
Frankenstein, Alfred. "Lords, ladies and common folk at
    Yale." il. (pt. col.). Art News 76 (Summer 1977): 40-
    43.
Giurgola, Romaldo. Louis I. Kahn. Boulder, Colo.: Westview,
    1975. il., plan, sec. pp. 60, 90-102.
Goldberger, Paul. "Louis Kahn's legacy of silence and light,"
    in On the Rise. New York: Times Books, 1983. il. pp.
    150-153.
Hoyt, Charles K. Interior Spaces Designed by Architects.
    New York: McGraw-Hill, 1981. il., plan, sec., diag.
    pp. 184-189.
Huff, William S. "Kahn and Yale." il., port. Journal of
    Architectural Education 35 (Spring 1982): 22-31.
"In the philosophy of Louis Kahn, engineering and architecture
    were inseparable parts of total form." il., diag. Archi-
    tectural Record 156 (Mid-August 1974): 84-85.
Jordy, William. "Kahn at Yale: art centre, Yale University."
    il., plans, sec., diag. Architectural Review 162 (July
    1977): 37-44.

_____ . "Monotonie 1962-1977: Yale Center for British Art."
    il., plans. Werk 65 (May-June 1978): 50-52.
"Kahn's last work opens at Yale." il. Progressive Architec-
    ture 58 (May 1977): 21.
"Kahn's last work; the Yale Center for British Art." il.
    Interiors 136 (May 1977): 4.
Leoni, Fulvio. "Lo Yale Center for British Art di New Haven."
    il., plan. Casabella 43 (January 1979): 38-39.
Lobell, John. Between Silence and Light. Boulder, Colo.:
    Shambhala, 1979. il., plan, sec. pp. 11, 106-111.
"Louis I. Kahn, Pellecchia and Meyers; Yale Center for British
    Art, Yale University, New Haven, Connecticut. Comple-
    tion: 1977." il. (pt. col.), plan. GA Document. Special
    Issue 1970-1980 (1980): 252-255.
"Louis Kahn un museo." col. il., plan, sec. Domus 561
    (August 1976): 17-19.
Lynes, Russell. "Mastery of architect Louis I. Kahn; the Yale
    Center for British Art." il. Architectural Digest 35 (July
    1978): 26, 30.
Magnago Lampugnani, Vittorio. Architecture of the 20th Cen-
    tury in Drawings. New York: Rizzoli, 1982. il. p. 163.
Mee, Charles L. "Louis Kahn," in Three Centuries of Notable
    American Architects, edited by Joseph J. Thorndike. New
    York: American Heritage, 1981. il. (pt. col.). pp.
    280-281, 290, 298-299.
"Mellon Art Center at Yale." il. Interiors 131 (April 1972):
    30.
"The mind of Louis Kahn." il., plan, sec. Architectural
    Forum 137 (July-August 1972): 82-83.
"Paul Mellon Center for British Art and British Studies." il.,
    plan. Architecture and Urbanism 3 (January 1973): 37,
    113-117.
"Paul Mellon Center for British Art, Yale." il. Architectural
    Record 152 (July 1972): 41.
Pica, A. D. "Pittura inglese at Yale: Kahn for the Mellon
    collection." il., plan, sec. Domus 579 (February 1978):
    1-5.
Prown, Jules David. "Architecture of the Yale Center for
    British Art." il., plan. Apollo 105 (April 1977): 234-237.
_____ . Architecture of the Yale Center for British Art.
    New Haven: Yale University, 1977, 1982. il., plan, sec.,
    elev. 68p.
_____ . "On being a client." il. Society of Architectural
    Historians. Journal 42 (March 1983): 11-14.

Ronner, Heinz. Louis I. Kahn: Complete Works, 1935-74.
    Boulder, Colo.: Westview, 1977. il., plan, sec., elev.
    pp. 401-417.
Roth, Leland M. A Concise History of American Architecture.
    New York: Harper & Row, 1979. il. pp. 355-357.
Schur, S. E. "Museum profile: Yale Center for British Art."
    il. Technology and Conservation 4 (Spring 1979): 18-23+.
Scully, Vincent. "Yale Center for British Art." il. (pt.
    col.), plans, sec., diag. Architectural Record 161 (June
    1977): 95-104.
Searing, Helen. New American Art Museums. New York:
    Whitney Museum of American Art, 1982. il., plan. pp.
    65-68.
Smith, G. E. Kidder. The Architecture of the United States.
    Garden City, N.Y.: Anchor, 1981, v. 1. il. pp. 35-37.
Smithson, Peter. "Louis Kahn's Centre for British Art and
    British Studies at Yale University." il., plan. RIBA
    Journal 83 (April 1976): 149-151.
Spiker, David. "Yale Center for British Art." il., plan, map,
    sec. Perspecta 16 (1980): 50-61.
Tyng, Alexandra. Beginnings: Louis I. Kahn's Philosophy
    of Architecture. New York: John Wiley and Sons, 1984.
    il., plan. pp. 56-58.
Weiss, Barbara. "American museums; three examples." il.
    Lotus 35 (1982): 102-106.
Yale Center for British Art. The British Art Center at Yale:
    An Introduction for Visitors and Students. New Haven:
    Yale Center for British Art, 1979. il., plan, map. 40 p.
"Yale Center for British Art, New Haven, Conn." il. (pt.
    col.), plans, sec. Architecture D'Aujourd'hui 193 (October
    1977): 70-74.
"Yale Center for British Art opened." il. College and Re-
    search Libraries News 38 (July-August 1977): 193-194.

DUAL MOVIE THEATER

2021-23 Sansom Street, Philadelphia, Pennsylvania. 1970.

Ronner, Heinz. Louis I. Kahn: Complete Works, 1935-74.
    Boulder, Colo.: Westview, 1977. il. p. 419.

FAMILY PLANNING CENTER

Khatmandu, Nepal. 1970-1974.

Giurgola, Romaldo. Louis I. Kahn. Boulder, Colo.: Westview,
    1975. il., plan, sec. pp. 113, 172-175.
"HMG family planning and material child health project." il.,
    plan, sec. Architecture and Urbanism 3 (January 1973):
    183-185.
Ronner, Heinz. Louis I. Kahn: Complete Works, 1935-74.
    Boulder, Colo.: Westview, 1977. il., plan, sec. p. 421.

INNER HARBOR PROJECT

Baltimore, Maryland. 1971-1973.

"Baltimore Inner Harbor project." il., plan, sec. Architec-
    ture and Urbanism 3 (January 1973): 136-140.
Giurgola, Romaldo. Louis I. Kahn. Boulder, Colo.: West-
    view, 1975. il., plan, sec. pp. 113, 165-171.
"The mind of Louis Kahn." il., plan, sec. Architectural
    Forum 137 (July-August 1972): 78-81.
Ronner, Heinz. Louis I. Kahn: Complete Works, 1935-74.
    Boulder, Colo.: Westview, 1977. il., plan, sec. pp.
    423-425.

GOVERNMENT HILL DEVELOPMENT

Jerusalem, Israel. 1972-1974.

Ronner, Heinz. Louis I. Kahn: Complete Works, 1935-74.
    Boulder, Colo.: Westview, 1977. il., plan. pp. 427-429.

THEOLOGICAL LIBRARY

University of California, Berkeley, California. 1973-1974.

Ronner, Heinz. Louis I. Kahn: Complete Works, 1935-74.
    Boulder, Colo.: Westview, 1977. il., plan, sec. p. 431.

ROOSEVELT MEMORIAL

New York, New York. 1973-1974.

Giurgola, Romaldo. Louis I. Kahn. Boulder, Colo.: Westview,
    1975. il., plan. pp. 113, 178-179.
Rice, Norman. "Kahn." il. Architectural Plus 2 (May-June
    1974): 106.
Ronner, Heinz. Louis I. Kahn: Complete Works, 1935-74.
    Boulder, Colo.: Westview, 1977. il., plan, sec. p. 433.

POCONO ARTS CENTER

Luzerne County, Pennsylvania. 1973-1974.

Giurgola, Romaldo. Louis I. Kahn. Boulder, Colo.: Westview,
    1975. il., plan. pp. 113, 176-177.
Ronner, Heinz. Louis I. Kahn: Complete Works, 1935-74.
    Boulder, Colo.: Westview, 1977. il., plan, col. sec. pp.
    435-437.

ABBASABAD DEVELOPMENT

Teheran, Iran. 1974. In association with Kenzo Tange.

"Abbasabad new city center, 1974-Teheran, Iran." il., map,
    plan. Japan Architect 51 (August-September 1976): 104-
    109.
Giurgola, Romaldo. Louis I. Kahn. Boulder, Colo.: Westview,
    1975. il., plan. pp. 242-243.
Ronner, Heinz. Louis I. Kahn: Complete Works, 1935-74.
    Boulder, Colo.: Westview, 1977. il., plan. p. 439.

FLOATING CONCERT HALL

Ohio, Mississippi and Allegheny Rivers. 1974.

"Nave-concerto, ultima opera di Louis Kahn." il. Architettura
    25 (March 1979): 132.

KORMAN RESIDENCE

Whitemarsh Township, Pennsylvania. 1974.

"Focus on Kahn." il. (pt. col.), ports. Interior Design 45
    (November 1974): 128-135.
Ronner, Heinz. Louis I. Kahn: Complete Works, 1935-74.
    Boulder, Colo.: Westview, 1977. plan, sec., elev. p.
    441.

OBITUARIES

Born February 20, 1901
Died March 17, 1974

"Der architekt Louis Kahn." Kunstwerk 27 (May 1974): 88.

Branzi, Andrea. "Louis Kahn superstar. Casabella 38 (July 1974): 8.

Brunner, Conrad U. "Eine haltung gegenuber menschen."
il. Werk (July 1974): 807-809.

"Credo." port. Architectural Design 44 (May 1974): 279-281.

Debuyst, Frederic. "In memoriam Louis I. Kahn." il., port.
Art D'Eglise 168-169 (July-December 1974): 205-206.

Dixon, John Morris. "Louis I. Kahn, 1901-1974." Progressive
Architecture 55 (April 1974): 51.

Donat, John. "Obituary." port. Design 306 (June 1974):
81.

Giurgola, Romaldo. "Louis I. Kahn, 1901-1974." port. Progressive Architecture 55 (May 1974): 4-5. Reply by Macy
DuBois, "Kahn: more to be said." 55 (October 1974):
10.

Goldberger, Paul. "Louis I. Kahn, 1901-1974: an almost
metaphysical quest for 'what a building wants to be.'"
port. Art News 73 (Summer 1974): 46.

Hoesli, Bernhard. "Louis I. Kahn: Findling im Flussbett
der Moderne." col. il. Werk (July 1974): 794-797, 871.

Komendant, August E. 18 Years With Architect Louis I. Kahn.
Englewood, N.J.: Aloray, 1975. pp. 191-192.

Korzeniwski, Svetikic. "Louis I. Kahn: a tribute." Architecture in Australia 63 (December 1974): 55.

Le-Ricolais, Robert. "Louis I. Kahn." port. Architecture
D'Aujourd'hui 173 (May-June 1974): v.

"Louis I. Kahn." il., port. Architecture in Australia 63
(December 1974): 54-57.

"Louis I. Kahn, FAIA; 1901-1974." AIA Journal 61 (April
1974): 8.

"Louis I. Kahn, 1900-1974." Industrial Design 21 (May 1974):
12.

"Louis Kahn dead at 73." port. Memo: Newsletter of the
American Institute of Architects 481 (29 March 1974): 7.

Matsushita, Kazuzuki. "Louis Kahn, going to the better world
of silence and light; on receipt of the obituary of Louis
Kahn." (In Japanese). port. Architecture and Urbanism
4 (May 1974): 6-7.

"La morte di Louis Kahn." port. Architettura 20 (May 1974):
5.

Moser-Khalili, Moira. "Louis Kahn in Iran. AIA Journal 62
(July 1974): 70.

Peverelli, Diego. "Hommage à Louis I. Kahn (1901-1974)."
port. Werk (July 1974): 793.

Rice, Norman. "Kahn." il., port. Architecture Plus 2 (May
-June 1974): 102-107.

Roth, Ueli. "Begegnungen mit Louis I. Kahn." Werk (July
1974): 812-813.

Salk, Jonas. "An homage to Louis I. Kahn." Architecture
D'Aujourd'hui 173 (May 1974): vi.

Scully, Vincent J. "Education and inspiration." Architecture
D'Aujourd'hui 173 (May 1974): vi.

_____. "Louis I. Kahn, 1901–1974." il., port. Yale University Art Gallery Bulletin 35 (Summer 1974): 6–7.

Shimizu, Hideki. "Recalling Louis Kahn." (In Japanese).
Architecture and Urbanism 4 (May 1974): 8.

Winter, John. "Louis I. Kahn: 1901–1974." port. Architectural Review 155 (May 1974): 313.

_____. "Obituary: Louis Kahn 1901–74." il. Riba Journal 81 (May 1974): 9.

EXHIBITIONS AND AWARDS

"Aalto, Kahn, Tange; laurea honoris causa, a Milano." port. Domus 416 (July 1964): 16.

"Architecture of Louis Kahn." il., port. Interiors 125 (May 1966): 10.

"Attualita: le lauree honoris causa conferite dalla facolta di architettura di Milano." il., port. Casabella 286 (April 1964): 54-55.

"Broadcast journalists are honored with silver sculpture by Kahn." il. AIA Journal 53 (February 1970): 22.

Davies, Marfyn. "Something in the heart (RIBA Gold Medal)." il., port. Architect 2 (June 1972): 52-55.

"Duct-hater Kahn is RIBA gold-medallist." port. Design 278 (February 1972): 22.

"Homage: Kahn enshrined (an exhibition at the Museum of Modern Art of Kahn's works)." il. Architectural Forum 124 (June 1966): 30.

"Institut's '71 gold medalist to receive similar honor from British architects." AIA Journal 57 (March 1972): 11.

"Kahn at MOMA." il. Progressive Architecture 47 (June 1966): 47, 49.

"Kahn honored (Metal of Achievement by the Philadelphia Art Alliance)." American Institute of Architects Journal 38 (July 1962): 20.

"Louis I. Kahn honored by Columbia University." Architectural Record 155 (June 1974): 34.

"Louis I. Kahn honored by Danish architects (Danish Architects Association's Medal of Honor)." port. Architectural Record 138 (December 1965): 36.

"Louis I. Kahn: royal gold medallist." il. RIBA Journal 79 (August 1972): 324-326.

"Louis Kahn honored (National Institute of Arts and Letters, Arnold W. Brunner Award)." Architectural Record 127 (May 1960): 25.

"Louis Kahn to receive 1971 gold medal." port. AIA Memo 427 (February 1971): 1.

"Louis Kahn to receive RIBA gold medal." Progressive Architecture 53 (April 1972): 35.

"Made fellow of American Institute of Architects." port. AIA Journal 19 (June 1953): 267.

"People: gold medals '71." port. Architectural Forum 134 (March 1971): 72.

"People in the arts (National Institute and American Academy of Arts and Letters, Brunner Award)." Arts 34 (May 1960): 12.

"People in the news: Louis I. Kahn honored (Philadelphia Art Alliance Medal of Achievement)." port. Architectural Forum 116 (May 1962): 13.

"Photograph exhibit of works of Louis Kahn (at Tokyo department store)." il. Japan Architect 48 (March 1973): 16.

Piene, Nan R. "New York: gallery notes." il. Art in America 54 (March 1966): 124-125.

"Royal Gold Medallists; 1848-1984." port. Royal Institute of British Architects. Journal 91 (May 1984): 78.

"Scelte dure per gli architetti americani (AIA gold medal)." Architettura 17 (November 1971): 424-425.

Winter, John. "Louis Kahn (RIBA gold medal)." il., port.
    Royal Institute of British Architects. Journal 79 (Feb-
    ruary 1972): 61–62.

"World-renowned 'sculptural' architect to receive AIA gold
    medal in June." AIA Journal 55 (March 1971): 10.

BIOGRAPHY, PHILOSOPHY, WRITINGS,
CRITIQUES AND PORTRAITS

"Architects in the news." port. Architectural Record 131
(may 1962): 58.

"Architecture--fitting and befitting: the new art of urban
design--are we equipped?" port. Architectural Forum
114 (June 1961): 88.

"Behind the blueprints: Louis Kahn." port. Architectural
Forum 93 (September 1950): 79.

Blake, Peter. "Are you illiterate about modern architecture?"
port. Vogue 138 (15 September 1961): 180-181, 214, 218.

Boles, Daralice D. "After Kahn." col. il., plans (not
Kahn's). Progressive Architecture 65 (December 1984):
74-77.

_____. Legacy of Louis Kahn." col. il., port. Progressive
Architecture 65 (December 1984): 53-55.

Bonnefoi, Christian. "Louis Kahn and minimalism." il., plan.
Oppositions 24 (Spring 1981): 2-25.

Bottero, Maria. "Louis Kahn e l'incontro fra morfologia organ-
ica e razionale." Zodiac 17 (1967): 47-53, English pp.
240-245.

Brown, Denise Scott. "Team 10, Perspecta 10, and the present state of architectural theory." American Institute of
Planners. Journal 33 (January 1967): 46, 48-49.

_____. "Worm's eye view of recent architectural history."
Architectural Record 172 (February 1984): 69-81.

Burton, Joseph. "Notes from volume zero: Louis Kahn and the language of God." il., plan, diag. Perspecta 20 (1983): 69-90.

Bush-Brown, Albert. "Architects' hero: Louis Kahn." il. Horizon 5 (September 1962): 57-63.

_____. "Exemplary essays." Progressive Architecture 44 (October 1963): 218, 222.

Cagnoni, Giovanni. "Espressioni nuove per isituzioni antiche." Casabella 45 (June 1981): 6.

Castex, Jean. "De Louis Kahn à Robert Venturi." il., plan, sec. L'Architecture D'Aujourd'hui 44 (August-September 1972): 86-89.

"City structures: Louis Kahn on learning." port. Design Quarterly 86-87 (1972): 40-44.

"Clearing: interviews with Louis I. Kahn." VIA 2 (1973): 158-161.

"The connectors." il. Architecture and Urbanism 3 (January 1973): 38.

Cook, John Wesley. "Louis Kahn," in Conversations With Architects. New York: Praeger, 1973. il., plans, port., sec. pp. 178-217.

Coombs, Robert. "Philadelphia architecture after Kahn: Philadelphia's phantom school." il., plans, sec., elev. Progressive Architecture 57 (April 1976): 58-63.

"Education for urban design, part I: the changing role of the architect." Journal of Architectural Education 16 (Autumn 1961): entire issue. Published as a part of American Institute of Architects. Journal 36 (December 1961): 85-104. The 1961 AIA-ASCA Seminar discussions at the Cranbrook Academy of Art. "The nature of nature." pp. 95-97.

Farrell, Terence. "The Louis Kahn studio at the University of Pennsylvania." il., plan. Arena, Architectural Association Journal 82 (March 1967): 216-219.

"Form evokes function." il. Time 75 (6 June 1960): 76.

Frampton, Kenneth. "Botta's paradign." il. (pt. col.), plans (not Kahn's). Progressive Architecture 65 (December 1984): 82-90.

_____. "Louis Kahn and the French connection." il., plan, sec., elev. Oppositions 22 (Fall 1980): 20-53.

_____. "Notes on American architectural education from the end of the nineteenth century until the 1970's." Lotus 27 (1980): 25-27.

Frateili, Enzo. "Louis Kahn." port. Zodiac 8 (1961): 14-25.

"Genetrix; personal contributions to American architecture; Louis Kahn." il., plans, sec., port. Architectural Review 121 (May 1957): 344-345.

Giurgola, Romaldo. "Giurgola on Kahn." il. (pt. col.), plan, port. American Institute of Architects. Journal (August 1982): 26-35.

_____. "Romaldo Giurgola on Louis Kahn." Zodiac 17 (1967): 119.

Gorlin, Alexander C. "Biblical imagery in the work of Louis I. Kahn." il., plan, port. Architecture and Urbanism 176 (May 1985): 83-92.

Gowan, James. "Notes on American architecture." Perspecta 7 (1961): 81-82.

"Great builders of the 1960's." il., port. Japan Architect 45 (July 1970): 68.

Group for the Research of Social and Visual Inter-relationships. "Louis Kahn, Philadelphia-Pennsylvania/USA--talk at the conclusion of the Otterlo Congress," in CIAM'59 in Otterlo. il., plan, port. pp. 205-217.

Gubler, Jacques. "La campata e un tipo?/Is the bay a type?" il. (pt. col.). Casabella 509-510 (January-February 1985): 76-83.

Howe, George, Oscar Stonorov and Louis I. Kahn. "'Stand-
ards' versus essential space: comments on unit plans for
war housing." il., plans, sec. Architectural Forum 76
(May 1942): 308-311.

Hughes, Robert. "Brick is stingy, concrete is generous."
il., port. Horizon 16 (Autumn 1974): 30-35.

Jacobus, John M. "Kahn, Louis I.," in Encyclopedia of Modern Architecture. New York: Abrams, 1964. il. pp.
167-169.

Jencks, Charles. Modern Movements in Architecture. Garden
City, N.Y.: Anchor, 1973. pp. 228-229.

Katan, Elleda. "Le fondamentalisme dans l'oeuvre de Louis
Kahn." port. L'Architecture D'Aujourd'hui 33 (December
1962): 1-3.

"Kahn collection at Pennsylvania gets $21,000 from bricklayers."
American Institute of Architects. Journal 68 (November
1979): 88, 92.

"Kahn in Italia." Casabella 350-351 (July-August 1970): 2.

Kahn, Louis I. "L'accord de l'homme et l'architecture: une
conférence de Louis Kahn." il., port. La Construction
Moderne (July-August 1973): 10-21.

_____. "Address to Boston Society of Architects, April
5, 1966." il., sec. Boston Society of Architects. Journal
(1967, 1): 7-20.

_____. "Architecture fitting and befitting." port. Archi-
tectural Forum 114 (June 1961): 88.

_____. "Architecture is the thoughtful making of spaces.
The continual renewal of architecture comes from changing
concepts of space." Perspecta 4 (1957): 2-3.

_____. "Architecture: silence and light." il. Design,
Bombay 16 (October 1971): 26-30.

_____. "City structures." port. Design Quarterly 86-87
(1973): 40-44.

_____. "Don't let war plants scare you." Nation's Business 32 (April 1944): 27, 70.

_____. "Form and design." il. Architecture and Urbanism 3 (January 1973): 28.

_____. "Form and design." Paper given in a "Voice of America" broadcast. il., plan, elev. Architectural Design 31 (April 1961): 4, 145-154.

_____. "Form and design," in Louis I. Kahn, by Vincent Scully. New York: Braziller, 1962. pp. 114-121.

_____. "I have taught self rewarded." Journal of Architectural Education 27 (February 1974): 10.

_____. "Kahn: dialoghi di architettura--conversazioni con gli studenti della Rice University." port. Casabella 350-351 (July-August 1970): 18-23.

_____. "L. I. Kahn, form and design, and other writings: 1957-62," in America Builds, edited by Leland M. Roth. New York: Harper and Row, 1983. pp. 574-580.

_____. "L. I. Kahn, order is: 1955," in America Builds, edited by Leland M. Roth. New York: Harper and Row, 1983. pp. 571-573.

_____. "Law and rule in architecture." Public lecture by Louis I. Kahn at Princeton University, November 29, 1961. Unpublished.

_____. "Louis I. Kahn, architect FAIA." Philadelphia Museum of Art. Bulletin 309 (Spring 1974): 56-57.

_____. "Louis I. Kahn: Gesprache mit Studenten." port. Bauwelt 62 (11 January 1971): 13-17.

_____. "Louis I. Kahn; order is," in Programs and Manifestoes on 20th-Century Architecture, edited by Ulrich Conrads. Cambridge: M.I.T., 1970. pp. 169-170.

_____. "Louis I. Kahn: silence and light." port. Architecture and Urbanism 3 (January 1973): 6.

_____. "Louis I. Kahn; talks with students. il., ports. Architecture at Rice 26 (1969): 53 pp.

_____. "Louis I. Kahn: the room, the street and human agreement." col. il. Architecture and Urbanism 3 (January 1973): 7-22.

_____. "Louis Kahn: statements on architecture from a talk given at the Politecnico di DMilano in January 1967." il. Zodiac 17 (1967): 54-57. Italian translation, pp. 226-227.

_____. "Man and nature." Architecture and Urbanism 3 (January 1973): 23.

_____. "Monumentality," in New Architecture and City Planning, edited by Paul Zucker. New York: Philosophical Library, 1944. il. pp. 577-588.

_____. "1973: Brooklyn, New York." il. Perspecta 19 (1982): 88-100.

_____. "Not for the fain-hearted." il., plan, port, diag. American Institute of Architects. Journal 55 (June 1971): 25-31.

_____. "Notes in passing." Arts and Architecture 80 (April 1963): 9.

_____. "On philosophical horizons." American Institute of Architects. Journal 33 (June 1960): 99-100.

_____. "Man is the measure: room, window and sun." il. Canadian Architect 18 (June 1973): 52-55.

_____. The Notebooks and Drawings of Louis I. Kahn, edited and designed by Richard Saul Wurman and Eugene Feldman. Philadelphia: Falcon, 1962. port. between illus. 6 and 7.

_____. The Notebooks and Drawings of Louis I. Kahn, edited and designed by Richard Saul Wurman and Eugene Feldman. Cambridge: M.I.T., 1973. port. between illus. 6 and 7.

_____. "On the responsibility of the architect." Perspecta 2 (1953): 45-47.

_____. "Order is." Perspecta 3 (1955): 59.

_____. "Order is," in Louis I. Kahn, by Vincent Scully. New York: Braziller, 1962. pp. 113-114.

_____. "Order of space." Architecture and Urbanism 3 (January 1973): 24.

_____. Portrait. Architectural Forum 78 (May 1943): 72.

_____. "Remarks." il., plans. Perspecta 9/10 (1965): 303-335.

_____. "The room, the street, and human agreement." port. American Institute of Architects. Journal. 56 (September 1971): 33-34.

_____. "The room, the street, and human agreement." il. Architecture and Urbanism 3 (January 1973): 40.

_____. "The room, the street, and human agreement." il. Architecture in Australia 63 (December 1974): 55-57.

_____. "Silence." il. VIA 1 (1968): 88-89.

_____. "Silence and light." Architecture and Urbanism 3 (January 1973): 24.

_____. "Silence and light---Louis I. Kahn at ETH," in Louis I. Kahn: Complete Works, 1935-74, by Heinz Ronner. Boulder, Colo.: Westview, 1977. port. pp. 447-449.

_____. "A statement by Louis I. Kahn." Arts and Architecture 78 (February 1961): 14-15, 28-30.

_____. "A statement by Louis I. Kahn." Arts and Architecture 81 (May 1964): 18-19, 33. Paper delivered at the Internaitonal Design Conference, Aspen, Colorado.

_____. "Statements by Kahn." Architecture and the University (1954): 27, 29, 67-68.

_____. "Toward a plan for midtown Philadelphia." Per-
specta 2 (1953): 10-27.

_____. "War plants after the war." American Institute
of Architects. Journal 2 (August 1944): 59-62.

_____. "World design conference." port. Industrial
Design 7 (July 1960): 46-49.

"Kahn's movement notation. plan. Design Quarterly 80 (1971):
80.

Koenig, G. K. "Un colosso inedito. An unpublished colos-
sus." il. (pt. col.). Casabella 382 (October 1973): 30-
36.

Komendant, August E. "Kahn as poet-philosopher and
architect-teacher," in 18 Years With Architect Louis I.
Kahn. Englewood, N.J.: Aloray, 1975. il. pp. 161-190.

_____. "Komendant on concrete." il., diag. Progressive
Architecture 47 (October 1966): 208-214.

Koyama, Hisao. "Hisao Koyama talks on Louis Kahn." Architecture and Urbanism 155 (August 1983): 113-118.

Kramer, Paul R. "Ein Gesprach mit Louis I. Kahn." plan,
ports. Werk (July 1974): 800-803.

"The Legacy of Louis Kahn..." port. American Institute of
Architects. Journal 67 (September 1978): 39.

Lobell, John. "The Beaux-Arts: a reconsideration of meaning
in architecture." il., plan (not Kahn's) American Institute
of Architects. Journal 64 (November 1975): 32-37.

_____. Between Silence and Light. Boulder, Colo.: Sham-
bhala, 1979. il., port. pp. 1-70, 114-115.

_____. "Kahn and Venturi; an architecture of being-in-
context." il., plan. Artforum 16 (1978, 6): 46-52.

"Louis I. Kahn." port. Architecture in Australia 63 (December 1974): 54.

"Louis I. Kahn; oeuvres 1963-1969." L'Architecture
    D'Aujourd'hui 40 (February-March 1969): LXXXIV-LXXXV,
    4-7. Includes "Architecture," "A Propos de Louis Kahn"
    by Le Ricolais and Aldo Giurgola, "Silence," and "Space
    and the Inspirations."

"Louis I. Kahn to receive A.I.A. gold medal." port. Archi-
    tectural Record 149 (February 1971): 36.

"Louis Kahn." L'Architecture D'Aujourd'hui 33 (December
    1962): LXXX.

"Louis Kahn, Philadelphia, Pennsylvania/USA--talk at the con-
    clusion of the Otterlo Congress," in New Frontiers in Ar-
    chitecture. New York: Universe Books, 1961. il., plan,
    port. pp. 205-216.

Lucan, Jacques. "Da Guadet a Kahn: il tema della stanza."
    Casabella 49 (January/February 1986): 72-75.

Lym, Glenn Robert. A Psychology of Building. Englewood
    Cliffs, N.J.: Prentice-Hall, 1980. il. pp. 77-93.

McBride, Richard D. "A new mode or an old manner? Decision
    for Louis Kahn." il., plan, port. Architecture and Ur-
    banism 81 (August 1977): 77-90.

McQuade, Walter. "Architect Louis Kahn and his strong-
    boned structures." Architectural Forum 107 (October 1957):
    134-143. A Russian language version was published in
    America Illustrated 48: 21-23 by the U.S.I.A. for distri-
    bution in the Soviet Union.

_____. "The exploded landscape. Perspecta 7 (1961):
    83-90.

"Man and nature." il. Architecture and Urbanism 3 (January
    1973): 25.

"Marin City redevelopment." il. Progressive Architecture
    41 (November 1960): 149-153.

Mee, Charles L. "Louis Kahn," in Three Centuries of Notable
    American Architects, edited by Joseph J. Thorndike. New

York: American Heritage, 1981. il. (pt. col.), port.
pp. 280-299.

Mein, Philip. "Kahn." il., port. The Architects' Journal
155 (9 February 1972):   276-279.

"The mind of Louis Kahn." port. Architectural Forum 137
(July-August 1972):   88.

Moholy-Nagy, Sibyl.   "The future of the past; Louis Kahn,
doctor mirabilis." il. Perspecta 7 (1961):   73-76.

Norberg-Schulz, Christian.   "Kahn, Heidegger and the language
of architecture." il., plan, sec., elev. Oppositions 18
(Fall 1979):   28-47.   Also in Arquitectura: Madrid 223
(March/April 1980):   51-61.

Oechslin, Werner.   "Measurable, Unmeasurable." Daidalos 5
(15 September 1982):   16-17.

"On the responsibility of the architect." Perspecta 2 (1953):
45-57.

"Order and space." il. Architecture and Urbanism 3 (January
1973):   26.

"P/A design awards seminars 1960." il. Progressive Architecture 41 (November 1960):   149-164.

Pollock, Randle.   "Louis I. Kahn." port. American School
and University 56 (November 1983):   10.

Rowan, Jan C.   "Wanting to be; the Philadelphia School."
il., plan, port, sec., elev., diag. Progressive Architecture 42 (April 1961):   130-149.

Russell, Beverly.   "An architect speaks his mind; Louis Kahn
talks about color, light, the ideal house, the street, and
other inspirations for living." il., plan, port. House
and Garden 142 (October 1972):   124-125, 219.

Scully, Vincent.   "Louis I. Kahn in the Soviet Union." il.
(pt. col.), port. Architectural Digest 43 (May 1986):   62,
66, 71.

_____ . The Shingle Style Today; Or the Historian's Revenge. New York: Braziller, 1974. pp. 16-17, 19.

Sekler, Eduard F. "Formalism and the polemical use of history." il., plan (not Kahn's). Harvard Architecture Review 1 (Spring 1980): 32-39.

Serneek, Willy. "Louis Kahn as a teacher." L'Architecture D'Aujourd'hui 40 (February-March 1969): 88-91.

"Served space and servant space." il. Architecture and Urbanism 3 (January 1973): 29.

Shimizu, Hideki. "Context of man: Louis I. Kahn, F.A.I.A." il., ports. Utah Architect 53 (Summer 1973): 1, 8-12.

Siravo, Francesco. "Luis Kahn e gli anni dell'apprendistato." il. Casabella 45 (October 1981): 4.

Smith, C. Ray. Supermannerism: New Attitudes in Post-Modern Architecture. New York: Dutton, 1977. il. pp. 80-91.

Smithson, Alison. "Review of recent work: Louis Kahn." il., diag. Architectural Design 43 (August 1973): 530.

"Spaces, order and architecture." port. Royal Architectural Institute of Canada. Journal 34 (October 1957): 375-377.

"Span of Kahn." il. Architectural Review 155 (June 1974): 318-320.

Stonorov, Oscar and Louis I. Kahn. Why City Planning Is Your Responsibility. New York: Revere Copper and Brass Inc., 1943. il., plans, port. 14 pp.

_____ . You and Your Neighborhood ... A Primer for Neighborhood Planning. New York: Revere Copper and Brass, Inc., 1944.

"Structure is the giver of light." il. Architecture and Urbanism 3 (January 1973): 32.

Taylor, Ed. "Ed Taylor writes on Louis Kahn." Maltings Free Press 1 (December 1979): 5-6.

Tentori, Francesco. "L'Architetto Louis I. Kahn; ordine e forma nell'opera di Louis Kahn." il., plan, port., sec., elev., diag. Casabella 241 (July 1960): 2-17.

Watanabo, Hiroshi. "Kahn and Japan." il. (pt. col.) (not Kahn's). Progressive Architecture 65 (December 1984): 78-81.

White, Norval. "Kahn, Louis I.," in The Architecture Book. New York: Kroph, 1976. pp. 164-165.

Williams, A. Richard. "Star/nebulae: a personal pantheon." il. Reflections 2 (Fall 1984): 62-69.

Winkelvoss, Wolf. "Zum Tod von Louis I. Kahn: Das Programm ist gar nichts, es ist nur hindernis." il., plans, port. Baumeister 71 (July 1974): 779-784.

Zevi, Bruno. "Incontro con Louis Kahn su sfondo biblico." il. Architettura 13 (March 1968): 702-703.

BOOK REVIEWS

Giurgola, Romaldo. Louis I. Kahn. Boulder, Colo.: Westview, 1975.

    Jordy, William H. [Review]. Society of Architectural Historians. Journal 39 (March 1980): 85-89.

Kahn, Louis I. The Architecture of the Yale Center for British Art. Introduction by Edmund P. Pillsbury, essay by Jules David Prown. New Haven: Yale University, 1977.

    Jordy, William H. [Review]. Society of Architectural Historians. Journal 39 (March 1980): 85-89.

    . Light is the Theme: Louis I. Kahn and the Kimbell Art Museum. Compiled by Nell E. Johnson. Fort Worth: Kimbell Art Foundation, 1975.

    Jordy, William H. [Review]. Society of Architectural Historians, Journal 39 (March 1980): 85-89.

    . Louis I. Kahn: Sketches for the Kimbell Art Museum, organized by David M. Robb; essay by Marshall D. Meyers. Fort Worth: Kimbell Art Foundation, 1978.

    Jordy, William H. [Review]. Society of Architectural Historians. Journal 39 (March 1980): 85-89.

    . The Notebooks and Drawings of Louis I. Kahn, edited and designed by Richard Saul Wurman and Eugene Feldman. Philadelphia: Falcon, 1962 and Cambridge: M.I.T., 1973.

Casson, Hugh. "Drawings by the masters." Architectural Review 133 (June 1963): 386.
Jacobus, John. "Books: The Notebooks and Drawings
of Louis I. Kahn." Society of Architectual Historians. Journal 22 (December 1963): 237-239.
Tentori, Francesco. "Il passato come un amico." il.,
plans, sec., elev. Casabella 275 (May 1963): 26-41.

_____. The Travel Sketches of Louis I. Kahn. An exhi-
bition organized by the Pennsylvania Academy of the Fine
Arts, 1978-1979, designed by Kurt Wiener. Philadelphia:
Pennsylvania Academy of the FIne Arts, 1978.

Jordy, William H. [Review]. Society of Architectural
Historians. Journal 39 (March 1980): 85-89.

Komendant, August E. 18 Years with Architect Louis I. Kahn.
Englewood, N.J.: Aloray, 1975.

Berger, Horst. "18 Years with Architect Louis I.
Kahn." il. Architectural Record 162 (Mid August
1977): 106-107.
Eaton, Leonard K. "Engineer Kahn; 18 Years with
Architect Louis I. Kahn." Progressive Architecture
57 (April 1976): 97-98.
Jordy, William H. [Review]. Society of Architectural
Historians. Journal 39 (March 1980): 85-89.
Lobell, John. "Louis I. Kahn, architect; 18 Years with
Architect Louis I. Kahn." il. American Institute
of Architecture. Journal 65 (July 1976): 176, 178.

Nichols, Frederick D., ed. Papers of the American Association
of Architectural Bibliographers, Vol. XII. Bibliographies
by Jack Perry Brown on Louis Kahn and Arnold L. Marko-
witz on Paul Zucker. New York: Garland, 1978.

Jordy, William H. [Review]. Society of Architectural
Historians. Journal 39 (March 1980): 85-89.

Ronner, Heinz. Louis I. Kahn: Complete Works, 1935-74.
Boulder, Colo.: Westview, 1977.

Brunner, Conrad U. "Louis I. Kahns gesamtwerk 1935-
  1974." il. Werk 64 (June 1977): 69-70, 72.
Jordy, William H. [Review]. Society of Architectural
  Historians. Journal 39 (March 1980): 85-89.
Kenworth, Geoffrey. "The real Kahn." Architect's
  Journal 167 (5 April 1978): 639-640.
Lobell, John. "Kahn viewed as 'artist in an age of
  methodologists.'" il. American Institute of Archi-
  tects. Journal (July 1978): 74, 78.
"Louis I. Kahn; l'Oeuvre Complet 1935-1974." il.
  Architecture D'Aujourd'hui 193 (October 1977):
  xxiii-xxiv.

Scully, Vincent. Louis I. Kahn. New York: Braziller, 1962.

Atkinson, Fello. "Book reviews: the newcomers."
  Architectural Review 134 (August 1963): 81.
McQuade, Walter. "Tallyho, tradition!" Architectural
  Forum 117 (December 1962): 149, 150A.
Pahl, J. [Review of German edition]. il. Deutsche
  Bauzeitung 70 (March 1965): 173-174.
Tentori, Francesco. "Il passato come un amico."
  Casabella 275 (May 1963): 27-28.
Von Eckardt, Wolf. "Makers of contemporary architec-
  ture." American Institute of Architects. Journal
  38 (November 1962): 50.

Stonorov, Oscar and Louis I. Kahn. You and Your Neighborhood; A Primer. New York: Revere Copper and Brass
  Inc., 1944.

"You and your neighborhood ... a primer." il. Architectural Forum 82 (January 1945): 150.

Tyng, Alexandra. Beginnings: Louis I. Kahn's Philosophy
  of Architecture. New York: John Wiley and Sons, 1984.

Hines, Thomas S. "Fortresses for the victims." il.
  Times Litarary Supplement 4258 (9 November 1984):
  1280.
Doordan, Dennis P. "Tyng's Kahn." il. Progressive
  Architecture 66 (April 1985): 125-126.

BIOGRAPHICAL CHRONOLOGY

1901   Born February 20, Island of Saarama, Estonia,
                   Russia.
                   Parents: Leopold and Bertha (Mendelsohn)
                   Kahn
                   Religion: Jewish

1905   Emigrated with family to United States, lived
                   in Philadelphia, PA

1912-1920   Student: Central High School and Pennsylvania
                   Academy of Fine Arts, Philadelphia, PA

1913-1914   Won awards in drawing and painting.   First
                   prize, City Art Contest, sponsored by
                   John Wanamaker

1915   Naturalized citizen

1916-1920   Student: Graphic Sketch Club, Fleisher Mem-
                   orial Art School, Public Industrial Art
                   School for drawing, carving and modeling

1919-1920   Awarded first prize for best drawings in high
                   schools of Philadelphia, sponsored by Penn-
                   sylvania Academy of Fine Arts

1920-1924   Student: University of Pennsylvania, School
                   of Fine Arts.
                   Monumental Entrance, Student competition, 17th
                   Paris Prize of the Beaux-Arts
                   United States Veterans Hospital, Student
                   Competition, Architects Society
                   Shopping Center, Student competition, Beaux-
                   Arts Institute of Design
                   Army Post, Philadelphia, PA, Student competi-
                   tion, Beaux-Arts Institute of Design

July-Sept.   Draftsman: Hoffman and Henon, architects,
1921   Philadelphia

June-Sept.   Draftsman: Hewitt and Ash, architects, Phila-
1922   delphia

1923-1924   Teaching Assistant: University of Pennsylvania

1924   Awarded degree of Bachelor of Architecture

July 1924-   Senior Draftsman: office of John Molitor, City
June 1925   Architect, Philadelphia

July 1925-   Chief of Design: in charge of all drafting and
Oct. 1926   design for all exposition buildings, Ses-
                  quicentennial Exposition, Philadelphia, John
                  Molitor, architect

Nov. 1926-   Worked on city planning studies, municipal
Mar. 1927   buildings, office of John Molitor, City Archi-
                  tect, Philadelphia

April 1927-   Draftsman: office of William H. Lee, architect,
April 1928   Philadelphia

April 1928-   Traveled in Europe
April 1929   Worked on housing studies

1929-1930   Designer: office of Paul P. Cret, Philadelphia
                Worked on designs for Chicago World's Fair
                  of 1933, and on buildings in Washington,
                  D.C. (one being the Folger Library), and
                  France
                Exhibited paintings and drawings made during
                  travels at the Pennsylvania Academy of Fine
                  Arts

1930   August 19, married Esther Virginia Israeli
                Exhibit, Architecture in Government Housing,
                  Museum of Modern Art, New York, NY

Dec. 1930-   Designer: with Zantziner, Borie and Medary,
Feb. 1932   architects, Philadelphia
                Worked on design for Department of Justice
                  Building, Washington, D.C.

Mar. 1932–   Organizer and director: Architectural Research
   Dec. 1933   Group.
                  Thirty unemployed architects and engineers
                     studied Philadelphia housing condition,
                     planned housing projects, made city planning
                     and slum clearance studies, investigated
                     new construction methods, etc.

1933   Exhibited paintings and drawings at the Penn-
                     sylvania Academy of Fine Arts

Dec. 1933–   Squad Head: in charge of Housing Studies,
   Dec. 1935   City Planning Commission, Walter Thomas,
                     architect in charge, under W.P.A.

1934   Registered with the American Institute of Ar-
                     chitects, Pennsylvania and began independent
                     practice

1935–1937   Assistant principle architect, office of Alfred
                     Kastner and Partner, architects, Philadelphia,
                     PA
                  Ahavath Israel Synagogue, North Philadelphia,
                     First building designed and built on his own
                  Jersey Homesteads Cooperative Development,
                     Hightstown, New Jersey, reclamation project
                     for the Resettlement Administration, Washing-
                     ton, D.C. (Assistant principal architect to
                     Alfred Kastner, and co-designer)

June–July   Exhibition of Architecture in Government Hous-
   1936   ing, Museum of Modern Art, N.Y.   Jersey
                     Homesteads Project exhibited

1937   Consultant Architect: Philadelphia Housing
                     Authority

1939   Consultant Architect: U.S. Housing Authority
                  "The Rational City Plan," a part of the Houses
                     and Housing exhibit of the Museum of
                     Modern Art, New York.   This exhibit was
                     also shown at the Pennsylvania Academy of
                     Fine Arts and the Art Alliance, Philadelphia

March 30,   Daughter, Sue Ann, born
   1940

1940   Residence for Jesse Oser, 688 Stetson Road,
                            Melrose Park, PA

April 1941-   Associated in practice with George Howe, Phila-
    Feb. 1942   delphia, PA
                        Pine Ford Acres Housing, Middletown, PA, for
                            the Harrisburg Housing Authority

1942-1943   Associated in practice with George Howe and
                            Oscar Stonorov, Philadelphia, PA
                        Carver Court Housing Development (Stonorov
                            and Kahn, Architects), Coatesville, PA, for
                            the Federal Public Housing Authority

1942   Pennypack Housing, Philadelphia, PA, for the
                            Federal Public Housing Authority
                        Stanton Road Housing Development Project,
                            Alley Dwelling Authority, Washington, D.C.
                            (Project)

1943-1948   Associated in practice with Oscar Stonorov,
                            Philadelphia, PA

1943   Lincoln Road Housing Development Project,
                            Coatesville, PA, for the Federal Public
                            Housing Authority
                        Lily Ponds Housing, Washington, D.C., for
                            the National Capital Housing Authority
                            (Project)
                        Willow Run War Town Development Project,
                            Detroit, MI (Project)
                        New Buildings for 194X: Hotel (Project) De-
                            signed for the Architectural Forum contest,
                            May 1943

1944   Pennypack Store Building, Philadelphia, PA,
                            for the Federal Public Housing Authority
                        Pennypack Administration Building, Philadelphia,
                            PA, for the Federal Public Housing Authority
                        Alterations and additions to Health Clinic,
                            22nd and Locust Streets, Philadelphia, PA
                            (Project)

1944-1946   Philadelphia Psychiatric Hospital, Monument
                            Avenue and Ford Road, Philadelphia, PA
                            (Project)

1945–1949   Residence for Dr. and Mrs. Philip Q. Roche,
               Harts Lane, Miquon, Whitemarsh Township,
               Montgomery County, PA

1946–1952   Consultant Architect: Philadelphia City Planning
               Commission

1946–1954   Triangle Area Reprot for Philadelphia City
               Planning Commission, as consultant
               Mill Creek Redevelopment Area Plan, Philadel-
               phia, PA, submitted as consultant to Phila-
               delphia City Planning Commission (in asso-
               ciation with Kenneth Day, Louis E. McAllister
               and Anne G. Tyng)

1947   Container Corporation of America, Alterations,
               Office Building and Cafeteria, Manayunk,
               PA (Project)

1947–1948   Plan for Midtown–Center City, Philadelphia, PA
               for the Better Philadelphia Exhibition

1947–1949   Residence for Dr. and Mrs. Winslow T. Tomp-
               kins, Apalogen Road and School House Lane,
               Germantown, PA

1947–1952   Chief Critic: Architectural Design at Yale
               University, New Haven, CT

1948   President, T–Square Club, Philadelphia
               Jefferson National Expansion Memorial, St.
               Louis, MO (Competition entry)
               Radbill Oil Company, interior alterations, 1724
               Chestnut Street, Philadelphia, PA

1948–1949   Residence for Mr. and Mrs. Morton Weiss,
               Whitehall Road, East Norton Township,
               Norristown, PA

1949   Coward Shoe Store, Philadelphia, PA
               Residence for Mr. and Mrs. Samuel Genel, NW
               corner Lancaster Avenue and Indian Creek
               Drive, Lower Merion Township, Montgomery
               County, PA

1949-1950	Pincus Therapy Building, addition to the Philadelphia Psychiatric Hospital, Ford and Monument Roads, Philadelphia, PA (Isadore Rosenfield, Hospital Consultant)
1950	Invited by Government of Israel to be Architect Representative to the World Assembly of Engineers and Architects, Friends of Israel, to study Israel's Housing and Planning Report. Trip sponsored by American Technion Society Saint Luke's Hospital, Alterations, Philadelphia, PA Residence for Mr. and Mrs. Jacob Sherman, 414 Sycamore Avenue, Lower Merion Township, Montgomery County, PA
1950-1951	Resident Architect: American Academy in Rome, Italy; travels in Italy, Greece and Egypt
1950-1953	Samuel Radbill Building, Philadelphia Psychiatric Hospital, Ford and Monument Roads (Isadore Rosenfield, Hospital Consultant)
1951	East Poplar Redevelopment Area Plan, Philadelphia, PA (in association with Day, McAllister and Tyng)
1951-1953	Southwest Temple Redevelopment Area Plan, Philadelphia, PA (in association with Day, McAllister and Tyng) Yale University Art Gallery, New Haven, CT (in association with Douglas I. Orr)
1951-1954	Consultant Architect: Philadelphia Redevelopment Authority
1952-1953	Mill Creek Public Housing Project I, 46 Street and Fairmount Avenue, Philadelphia, PA (Kenneth Day and Louis E. McAllister, Associated) Plan for Midtown, Penn Center, Philadelphia, PA for the Philadelphia City Planning Commission

1952–1957   City Tower, Municipal Building, Philadelphia,
              PA for the Philadelphia City Planning
              Commission and the Concrete Institute,
              Sponsored by the Universal Atlas Cement
              Company (in association with Anne G. Tyng)

1953   Made a Fellow, American Institute of Architects.
              Cited for education
              Residence for Mr. and Mrs. Ralph Roberts,
              School House Lane, Germantown, PA

1954   Adath Jeshurun Synagogue, Elkinds Park, PA
              (Project)
              Residence for Dr. and Mrs. Francis Adler,
              Davidson Road, Philadelphia, PA (Project)
              Residence for Mr. Weber de Vore, Montgomery
              Avenue, Springfield Township, Montgomery
              County, PA (Project)

1954–1956   American Federation of Labor Medical Service
              Plan Building, Philadelphia, PA, demolished
              in 1973

1954–1959   Trenton Jewish Community Center, 909 Lower
              Ferry Road, Trenton, NJ

1955   Residence Alteration, house of Dr. and Mrs.
              Francis Adler, Germantown, PA (kitchen al-
              teration)

1955–1956   Bath House, Trenton Jewish Community Center,
              909 Lower Ferry Road, Trenton, NJ Day
              Camp

1955–1957   Martin Research Institute, Research Institution
              for Advanced Study, Glenn L. Martin Com-
              pany, Fort Meade, MD (Project)

Feb.–June   Albert Farwell Bemis Professor at School of
1956   Architecture and Planning, Massachusetts
              Institute of Technology, Cambridge, MA

1956   Washington University, Library, St. Louis, MO
              (Competition entry)

1956-1957   Planning Studies of Penn Center and Midtown
                 Traffic for Philadelphia, PA (Project)
                 Enrico Fermi Memorial Competition, Chicago, IL
                 (Competition entry)

1957-1974   Professor of Architecture, University of Penn-
                 sylvania

1957-1959   Residence of Irving L. and Dorothy E. Shaw,
                 Alterations and additions, 2129 Cypress
                 Street, Philadelphia, PA

1957-1961   Alfred Newton Richards Medical Research
                 Building, 3700 Hamilton Walk, University
                 of Pennsylvania, Philadelphia, PA
                 Residence of Mr. and Mrs. Fred E. Clever,
                 Hunt Tract, Delaware Township, Camden
                 County, NJ

1957-1964   Biology Building, 2800 Hamilton Walk, University
                 of Pennsylvania, Philadelphia, PA

1958   Residence for Mr. Lawrence Morris, Mount
                 Kisco, NY (Project)

1958-1961   Tribune Review Publishing Company Building,
                 Greensburg, PA

1959   Delivered closing remarks, C.I.A.M. Tenth
                 Congress, Otterlo, Holland
                 Residence for Mr. Robert H. Fleisher, Woodland
                 Glen, Elkins Park, PA (Project)
                 Residence for Mr. and Mrs. M. Morton Golden-
                 berg, Hemlock Hedges, Frazer Road, Rydal
                 PA (Project)

1959-1961   Residence of Dr. and Mrs. Bernard Shapiro,
                 Hidden River Road, Penn Valley, Narberth,
                 PA
                 U.S. Consulate Buildings for Angola, Luanda,
                 Portuguese Angola. Chancellery and resi-
                 dence
                 Residence for Mrs. Margaret Esherick, Chestnut
                 Hill, PA

1959-1962   Mill Creek Public Housing Project II, Row
                 Housing and Community Center, 46th and
                 Aspen Streets, Philadelphia, PA

1959-1965   Salk Institute for Biological Studies, La Jolla,
                 CA

1959-1967   First Unitarian Church, Rochester, NY

1959-1974   First Unitarian Church, School Building,
                 Rochester, NY

1960   Awarded Arnold Brunner Prize by National
                 Institute of Arts and Letters
                 Lecturer at Yale and Harvard, University of
                 California, University of Houston, University
                 of North Carolina, Tulane University; fellow
                 at Princeton. Guest speaker for Southern
                 California Chapter, A.I.A., Honor Awards
                 Banquet
                 Invited by Japanese Government to participate
                 in World Design Conference, Tokyo
                 Residence for Dr. and Mrs. Norman Fisher,
                 Mill Road, Hatboro, PA
                 Municipal Building, Mill Creek at Bath Road,
                 Levitown and Bristol Townships, PA

1960-1961   Franklin Delano Roosevelt Memorial Competition,
                 Washington, D.C. (Competition entry)

1960-1965   Bristol Township Municipal Building, Bristol,
                 Levittown PA
                 Erdman Hall Dormitories, Bryn Mawr College,
                 Bryn Mawr, PA

1961   Consultant Architect: Philadelphia City Planning
                 Commission
                 Awarded fellowship by Graham Foundation for
                 Advanced Studies in the Fine Arts to pursue
                 his investigation of larger aspects of civic
                 design.
                 Barge on the Thames, England, for American
                 Wind Symphony, Pittsburgh, PA
                 Carborundum Company, Warehouse and Regional
                 Sales Office, Niagara Falls, NY (Project)

Plymouth Swim Club, Plymouth Township, PA
(Project)
General Motors Exhibition, 1964 World's Fair,
New York, NY (Project)

1961-1962   Market City East Redevelopment Project. Study
made for City of Philadelphia and Graham
Foundation

1961-1964   Levy Neighborhood Playground, Riverside Drive
between West 102nd and West 105th Streets,
New York, NY, with Isamu Noguchi

1961-1965   Fine Arts Building for Fort Wayne Fine Arts
Foundation, Inc. 232½ West Wayne Street,
Fort Wayne, IN

1961-1970   Mikveh Israel Synagogue, Church Walk between
4th and 5th Streets Philadelphia, PA

1961-   Chemistry Building, University of Virginia,
Charlottesville, VA
Shapiro Hall of Pharmacy, Wayne State Univer-
sity, Detroit, MI (Project)

1962   Lectured in Philadelphia, Ontario and Chicago
Fellow, World Academy of Arts and Sciences

March 14,   Delivered Annual Discourse to the Royal In-
1962   stitute of British Architects, London, England

March 28,   Received "1962 Philadelphia Art Alliance Medal
1962   for Achievement"

1962-1974   Shere-e-Banglanagar, Capital of Bangladesh,
Dacca, Bangledesh Institute of Management,
State of Gufarat, with B. V. Doshi and A.
D. Raje, Ahmedabad, India

1963   Single Building Exhibition, Richards Medical
Towers Project, Museum of Modern Art, New
York, NY
President's Estate, Islamabad, Pakistan

1963-1964   Gandhinagar, Master Plan, Capital of Gufarat
State, Gujarat, India (Project)

1964   Member, National Institute of Arts and Letters
               Gold Medal of Achievement, Directors Club of
                    Philadelphia
               Honorary Doctorate, Polytechnic Institute of
                    Milan, Italy
               Honorary Doctorate of Humanities, North
                    Carolina School of Design, University of
                    North Carolina, Raleigh, NC
               Frank P. Brown Medal, Franklin Institute,
                    Philadelphia, PA

1964-1967   College of Art, Philadelphia College of Art,
                    Broad Street between Spruce and Pine
                    Streets, Philadelphia, PA
               Interama, Panamerican Center, Inter-American
                    Center Authority, Miami, FL (Project)

1964-1972   Jewish Martyrs' Memorial, To commemorate six
                    million Jewish martyrs of World War II in
                    Battery Park, New York, NY (Project)

1965   Exhibition, "The Works of Louis I. Kahn," La
                    Jolla Museum of Art, La Jolla, CA
               Medal of Honor, Danish Architectural Association
               Honorary Doctorate of Fine Arts, Yale Univer-
                    sity, New Haven, CT

1965-1968   Dominican Sisters' Convent, Sisters of St.
                    Catherine de Ricci, Media, PA

1965-1974   School of Fine Arts, Fort Wayne Fine Arts
                    Foundation, 232½ West Wayne Street, Fort
                    Wayne, IN
               Theater of Performing Arts, Fort Wayne Fine
                    Arts Foundation, 232½ West Wayne Street,
                    Fort Wayne, IN

1966   Paul Philippe Cret Chair in Architecture, Uni-
                    versity of Pennsylvania, Philadelphia, PA
               Annual Award, Philadelphia Sketch Club,
                    Philadelphia, PA
               Member, Royal Swedish Academy of Fine Arts
               One-man retrospective exhibition, Museum of
                    Modern Art, New York, NY
               St. Andrew's Priory, Valyermo, CA
               Residence for Stern, Washington, DC

1966–1970   Olivetti-Underwood Factory, Harrisburg, PA

1966–1972   Kimbell Art Museum, Will Rogers Road West,
                 with Preston M. Geren and associates, Fort
                 Worth, TX
                 Temple Beth-el Synagogue, Chappaqua, NY

1966–1973   Office Building, Altgar Enterprises, between
                 Baltimore and Main Streets, Kansas City, KS
                 (Project)

1967   Honorary Doctorate of Laws, La Salle College,
                 Philadelphia, PA
                 Honorary Member, College of Architects, Peru

1967–1968   Broadway Church of Christ, office and church,
                 block east of Broadway between 56th and
                 57th Streets, New York, NY

1967–1972   Phillips Exeter Library, Phillips Exeter Academy,
                 Exeter, NH
                 Phillips Exeter Dining Hall, Phillips Exeter
                 Academy, Exeter, NH

1968   Fellow, American Academy of Arts and Sciences,
                 Boston, MA
                 Honorary Doctorate of Fine Arts, Maryland
                 Institute College of Art, Baltimore, MD
                 Faculty Member, City of Philadelphia Art Com-
                 mission, Philadelphia, PA
                 Single Building Exhibition, Palace of Congress
                 Project, Venice, Italy
                 Family Living Mental Therapy, Delaware Valley
                 Mental Health Foundation, New Britain, PA

1968–1973   Hill Central Area Redevelopment, New Haven
                 Public Schools and Housing Board, near
                 Columbus and Washington Avenues, New
                 Haven, CT

1968–1974   Hurva Synagogue, Jewish Community of Jerusa-
                 lem, Jerusalem, Israel
                 Palace of Congress, City of Venice, first project
                 in the Giardini Publici on the site of the
                 Esposizione Internazionale d'Arte, second

project on the site of the Arsenale, Venice,
Italy
Wolfson Center, Mechanical and Transportation
Engineering School, University of Tel-Aviv
Campus, Tel-Aviv, Israel

1969   International Silver Medal for Distinguished
Contribution to the Arts, University of
Connecticut, Storrs, CT
Centennial Gold Medal, Philadelphia Chapter,
American Institute of Architects
February 10-28, exhibition, Louis I. Kahn,
Swiss Federal Institute of Technology, Zurich:
Switzerland: also shown in Delft, Stuttgart,
Venice, Parma, Brussels, Paris, Vienna,
Innsbruck, and Naples

1969-1974   Center for British Art and Studies, Yale University, New Haven, CT

1970   Gold Medal of Honor, New York Chapter,
American Institute of Architects
Fellow, Royal Society of Arts, London, England
Fellow, American Institute of Architects
Honorary Doctorate of Arts, Bard College,
Annandale-on-Hudson, NY
Dual Movie Theater, 2021-2023 Sansom Street,
Philadelphia, PA

1970-1974   Family Planning Center, Royal Government of
Nepal, Khatmandu, Nepal

1971   Philadelphia Bok Award, for outstanding public
services, Philadelphia, PA
Gold Medal, American Institute of Architects
Golden Plate Award, American Academy of
Achievement
Honorary Doctorate of Fine Arts and Paul
Phillippe Cret Professor
Emeritus, University of Pennsylvania, Philadel-
phia, PA
Fellow, Franklin Institute, Philadelphia, PA

1971-1973   Inner Harbor Project, Baltimore, MD

1971-1974   Bicentennial Exposition, 1976 Bicentennial Ex-
                   position, Philadelphia, PA

1972   Creative Arts Medal in Architecture, Brandeis
                   University, Waltham, MA
                   Royal Gold Medal for Architecture, Royal In-
                   stitute of British Architects, London, Eng-
                   land
                   Member, Royal Institute of Architects, Ireland
                   Honorary Doctorate of Laws, Tulane University,
                   New Orleans, LA

1972-1974   Independence Mall Area Redevelopment, Phila-
                   delphia, PA
                   Hotel, Government Hill Development, Jerusalem
                   Israel

1973   Member, American Academy of Arts and Letters

1973-1974   Theological Library, Graduate Theological
                   Union, University of California, Berkeley,
                   CA
                   Franklin Delano Roosevelt Memorial, New York,
                   NY
                   Pocono Arts Center, Luzerne County, PA

1974   Abbasabad Development, Government Complex,
                   Tcheran, Iran
                   Residence for Korman, Whitemarsh Township,
                   PA

March 17,   Died in New York of a heart attack in Penn-
1974   sylvania Railway Station on return from
                   Ahmedabad, India
                   June, Doctor of Human Letters (Posthumous),
                   Columbia University

INDEX TO PAUL RUDOLPH

216   PAUL M. RUDOLPH

INDEX TO LOUIS KAHN